THE OTHER WALLS

THE OTHER WALLS

THE ARAB-ISRAELI PEACE PROCESS
IN A GLOBAL PERSPECTIVE

Harold H. Saunders

REVISED EDITION

WITHDRAWN

PRINCETON UNIVERSITY PRESS   PRINCETON, NEW JERSEY

This book was originally published in 1985 by
the American Enterprise Institute
for Public Policy Research, Washington, D.C.

Published by Princeton University Press, 41 William Street,
Princeton, New Jersey 08540
In the United Kingdom: Princeton University Press, Oxford

Library of Congress Cataloging-in-Publication Data
Saunders, Harold H.
The other walls : the Arab-Israeli peace process in a global
perspective / by Harold H. Saunders. — Rev. ed.
p. cm.
Includes index.
ISBN 0-691-07888-2 — ISBN 0-691-02337-9 (pbk.)
1. Palestine—International status. 2. Israeli-Arab conflicts.
3. Mediation, International. I. Title.
JX4084.I8S28   1991
327.1'6'0956—dc20   90-25783
                                                                              CIP

This book has been composed in Linotron Palatino

Princeton University Press books are printed
on acid-free paper, and meet the guidelines
for permanence and durability of the Committee
on Production Guidelines for Book Longevity
of the Council on Library Resources

Printed in the United States of America
by Princeton University Press, Princeton, New Jersey

1   3   5   7   9   10   8   6   4   2

1   3   5   7   9   10   8   6   4   2
(Pbk.)

*To all those in the peace process
who understand that peacemaking is a way of life—
that peace is never made but is always in the making.*

*To Carol who has happily
joined me in that way of life.*

*And to Cathy, Mark, Robin, and Caryn—
may you and your generation, each in your own way,
learn to seek peace and pursue it.*

Yet, there remains another wall. This wall constitutes a psychological barrier between us, a barrier of suspicion, a barrier of rejection; a barrier of fear, of deception, a barrier of hallucination without any action, deed or decision.

A barrier of distorted and eroded interpretation of every event and statement. It is this psychological barrier which I described in official statements as constituting 70 percent of the whole problem.

Today, through my visit to you, I ask why don't we stretch out our hands with faith and sincerity so that together we might destroy this barrier?

—President Anwar al-Sadat,
Statement before the Israeli Knesset,
Jerusalem, November 29, 1977

Contents

A Shared Land   144
Making Peace Possible on the Other Side   145
A Word to the President on Peacemaking and
Power   145

Preface:
A Personal Statement

This book combines personal essay with analytical study because a deep personal investment has made the Arab-Israeli peace process part of my life. On the following pages I have written personally sometimes as a statement that diplomacy and negotiation too often ignore the human, the psychological, and the political dimensions of conflict and reconciliation. The Arab-Israeli peace process is above all a political—a human—process. It involves a network of interrelated steps aimed at changing the political environment to make new advances toward peace possible. The work of diplomacy is to nourish that political process and to crystallize in agreements the new relationships that it generates.

Such a book cannot be finished. Its end can come only in the fullness of peace among Israelis, Palestinians, and other Arabs; among Arabs and Arabs, Jews and Jews; and among Jews, Muslims, and Christians. Perhaps even the millennium would mark only the beginning of another chapter. Nor is it possible to capture all of the dimensions of the conflict or of peace on a few pages. No book on issues of this sort will be up to the minute on the latest developments.

Such drawbacks do not lessen the importance of the message that we must broaden and deepen our attack on the obstacles to peace in designing approaches to a settlement. This book is bound by neither today's events nor tomorrow's tactics. It discusses neither next steps nor diplomatic issues. It considers ways of razing the nondiplomatic walls that block progress toward peace—the human walls of suspicion, fear, insecurity, mistrust, hatred, and uncertainties about identity. It addresses the political process of peacemaking.

The approach and insights in this book are the product of my intensive involvement in the peace process during months of shuttles and negotiations, countless conversations with the human beings who have suffered in the conflict, and hours spent in study groups as well as from insights born in my own personal loss and pain and simply from living. These insights can never be set firmly and unalterably in type; I hope they will go on changing, because I hope I will go on growing.

I must add a word about personal pain. The Arab-Israeli-Palestinian conflict—like other conflicts—has left few people without their own, individual world of pain. As I flew on the Kissinger shuttles, I saw pain at every turn and in every person, from the president and the prime minister to each diplomat, soldier, lawyer, journalist, teacher, driver, chambermaid, husband, wife, mother, father, son, and daughter. Israelis and Arabs and members of the American Jewish and Arab-American communities became personal friends and shared their sensibilities, their fears, and their pain with me in rich human exchanges.

I was acutely sensitive to suffering during the days immediately following the October 1973 War, when each side's wounds were raw and the trauma was fresh. My wife, Barbara, had died the day before that war had started. Members of my own church, the Lewinsville Presbyterian Church of McLean, Virginia, affirmed my grief and taught me to read in their affirmation their acceptance of me as a person and the beginning of a bridge from myself to other people in pain. The pastors taught me to understand grief and mourning as an extended process through which we human beings can heal ourselves. Only much later did friends in the fields of psychiatry and political psychology explain to me that nations and whole peoples can also go through a mourning process—and that, if they do not, they may find themselves mired in unresolved mourning. While I have been writing this book, I have again dealt with personal pain. A cherished friend, Mary Ann Dubs, struggled with leukemia through twenty-one grueling months, slowly slipped from us, and died on July 23, 1985.

As I reached out on a human level in 1973 to Arabs and Israelis who had suffered in their own ways, I discovered the human bonds that draw together people in pain. I first met Golda Meir after my wife's death on the day when the casualty figures from the 1973 War were announced in Israel. She took my hand and said, "I'm terribly sorry about your loss. I lost a lot of my people. I know how you feel." Moving beyond the pain of individual loss, I realized that many of the highest obstacles to negotiation and peace could be found in the pain of the human beings involved. I discovered that those obstacles could be eroded by acknowledgment on each side of the other's suffering and by open acceptance of a common humanity.

Anwar Sadat subsequently dramatized this truth in his historic visit to Jerusalem. He went to Israel to deliver not a negotiating position but a human message:

> I come to you today on solid ground to shape a new life and to establish peace. . . .
> Any life that is lost in war is a human life, be it that of an Arab

or an Israeli. A wife who becomes a widow is a human being entitled to a happy family life, whether she be an Arab or an Israeli.

Innocent children who are deprived of the care and compassion of their parents are ours. They are ours, be they living on Arab or Israeli land. . . .

You want to live with us, in this part of the world.

In all sincerity I tell you we welcome you among us, with full security and safety. This in itself is a tremendous turning point, one of the landmarks of a decisive historical change. We used to reject you. We had our reasons and our fears, yes. . . .

Yet today I tell you, and I declare it to the whole world, that we accept to live with you in permanent peace based on justice. . . .

What is peace for Israel? It means that Israel lives in the region with her Arab neighbors in security and safety. . . .

Peace is not a mere endorsement of written lines. Rather it is a rewriting of history. . . .

This is Egypt, whose people have entrusted me with their sacred message. A message of security, safety and peace to every man, woman and child in Israel. I say, encourage your leadership to struggle for peace.[1]

The Israelis responded because Sadat demonstrated by his presence that he acknowledged their identity and accepted them as a people. The barriers that he began to dismantle were psychological, human, and political.

A few words about the origins of this essay will help identify some of the special audiences to whom it is addressed.

First, I am writing for everyone still officially engaged in the search for an Arab-Israeli-Palestinian peace. My sense that the peace process is political has roots in my participation in the mediation of five agreements between 1973 and 1979, including the Camp David accords. I deeply believe in that process as politics and diplomacy at their most creative. Although I have left government service, my concern with peacemaking has not diminished. I pray daily for the steady progress of individuals still engaged in the slogging day-to-day work of moving that process forward. In a notebook from 1973 I found I had penned this reflection while sitting in a meeting with Kissinger: "There is all the difference in the world between a man who thinks about what ought to be done, and the man who has to move someone else to do it." I write in humility and defer to the people who must act.

The analytical framework with which I approach the Arab-Israeli peace process originated in a number of talks about negotiation that I gave after leaving the government. The theory of negotiation, I came to feel as I learned more about it, leaves a large void by concentrating on what happens in the negotiating room. My colleagues and I spent much of our time dealing with parties who would not even recognize each other, let alone negotiate with each other. Persuading people to sit down at the table seemed even more difficult than reaching agreement once they were there. My view that we needed to focus more attention on removing the obstacles to negotiation was refined in discussions at the invitation of the Harvard Negotiation Project. It was published in the *Negotiation Journal* in the July 1985 (volume 1, number 3) issue under the title "We Need a Larger Theory of Negotiation: The Importance of Pre-negotiating Phases." I write this book with the negotiation theorist very much in mind. In a sense I am elaborating on the published article, applying its main point to one important international conflict.

My sense of the human dimensions of the conflict has been deeply enriched in the last four years by exchanges with scholars, diplomats, political scientists, social psychologists, and psychiatrists, all of whom have embraced the title of a new academic discipline that they call "political psychology." My experiences with them have included participation in a number of long meetings that brought Israelis, Egyptians, and Palestinians face to face in various configurations and settings. They have all helped me to articulate more systematically the conclusions suggested by my work with human beings struggling in the political arena to make peace.

I have been moved by two documents of the former United Presbyterian Church in the United States of America. One is "The Confession of 1967," which addressed the theme of reconciliation:

> To be reconciled to God is to be sent into the world as his reconciling community. This community, the church universal, is entrusted with God's message of reconciliation and shares his labor of healing the enmities which separate men from God and from each other. . . .
>
> God has created the peoples of the earth to be one universal family. In his reconciling love he overcomes the barriers between brothers. . . .
>
> The church, in its own life, is called to practice the forgiveness of enemies and to commend to the nations as practical politics the search for cooperation and peace. This search requires that the nations pursue fresh and responsible relations across every line of conflict.[2]

The other is a study that was approved by the General Assembly in 1980 and was entitled *Peacemaking: The Believers' Calling*. It includes the statement: "Peace is more than the absence of war, more than a precarious balance of powers. Peace is the intended order of the world with life abundant for all God's children. Peacemaking is the calling of the Christian church."[3]

Although I do not agree with every point made in these documents, they have helped me to see the affirmation of personal pain in a larger theological context. I came to understand that affirmation as a means to reconciliation, as a bridge to other individuals—as I had first learned in practical ways after my wife's death in 1973 and in the course of the grueling professional effort to negotiate peace one difficult agreement at a time. I am keenly aware that other people much my senior also perceived a religious dimension in the assault on the barriers to peace. During their first full day at Camp David, Carter, Sadat, and Begin issued the following statement:

> After four wars, despite vast human efforts, the Holy Land does not yet enjoy the blessings of peace.
>
> Conscious of the grave issues which face us, we place our trust in the God of our fathers, from whom we seek wisdom and guidance.
>
> As we meet here at Camp David we ask people of all faiths to pray with us that peace and justice may result from these deliberations.[4]

I have decided not to use names in thanking the people who have contributed to my understanding. So many individuals in the United States, the Middle East, and Europe have participated with me over the years in the search for peace and in recent months have specifically labored to suggest refinements in these pages that it would be impossible for me to mention them all. Some might even be uncomfortable if they were named. You all know how in so many different ways we have thought and worked together in the cause of peace. I am grateful to each one of you.

In addition to this broader expression of gratitude, I owe special and warm thanks to a number of individuals at the American Enterprise Institute.

To William J. Baroody, Jr., president, and to the trustees of the American Enterprise Institute I am grateful for the time given me for study and research after my twenty-five years of intensive involvement in government and in the conduct of international relationships. I left the

State Department in February 1981, having resigned as assistant secretary in Algiers while working on the agreement for release of our hostages in Tehran. The four years that have passed since then have enabled me to place that experience in larger analytical contexts—to develop conceptual frameworks and to test them against experience but also to understand the experience more fully by walking away from the trees to see the shape of the forest. I learned to speak more freely, knowing that my government would no longer be held accountable for my words. Institutions such as the American Enterprise Institue provide a unique meeting ground near the policy makers where the realities of experience can encounter the insights of analysis. The people who lead and support such institutions perform a special service to our nation.

Resident fellow Judith Kipper, my colleague, has brought to the Institute a steady stream of political leaders, scholars, and analysts from the Middle East to engage in dialogue with American policy makers and leaders of public opinion. I have benefited from that program along with many others, as well as from the continuous sharing of insights from our separate perspectives.

To Vice President Tait Trussell and members of his committee on publications, my appreciation for their concerted help in planning early publication and broad distribution.

Joan Rambo has been an essential and supportive partner in producing this book. Just as important as her patient and intelligent performance of that task have been our personal dialogue and her sensitive day-to-day management of the complex network of meetings, travel, teaching and speaking appointments, and writing assignments that nourished my thoughts. Above all, I am grateful to her for caring that the words I write here reflect part of me.

I am grateful to Diana Richman for assembling the photos for the cover and for her help in proofreading.

In order to avoid distracting and cumbersome phrases, I have used the word "he" throughout this essay in referring to leaders. Please understand the pronoun to mean "he or she." I have the highest respect for my female colleagues. I recall in particular the special privilege of working with Golda Meir, the outstanding woman whom Israel called to be its prime minister. Second, I also have the highest respect for men and women who lead their peoples and would in any public situation refer to them by their titles—Presidents Carter and Reagan, Prime Ministers Begin, Shamir, and Peres, King Hussein, President Assad, Presidents Sadat and Mubarak, Chairman Arafat. For the sake of reading economy, I have often resorted to using only their last names.

Professional experience has taught me that any statement on the subject of Arab-Israeli peacemaking will offend or anger someone. Sentences are read for their omissions as well as for their content. Any statement that does not incorporate all sides of an argument will be cited as evidence of bias. To my readers, I can say only that I write with malice toward no one, in recognition of the personal pain that binds us as human beings and from an awareness of our common yearning for peace as the intended order of God's world. In that spirit, I invite you to join me in approaching the "other walls."

HAROLD H. SAUNDERS
July 26, 1985
Washington, D.C.

Notes

1. *The Search for Peace in the Middle East: Documents and Statements, 1967–1979*, Report prepared for the Subcommittee on Europe and the Middle East of the Committee on Foreign Affairs, U.S. House of Representatives, by the Foreign Affairs and National Defense Division, Congressional Research Service, Library of Congress, Committee Print CP-957 (Washington, D.C.: U.S. Government Printing Office, 1979), pp. 224–27. The full text of President Sadat's speech appears in appendix VI.

2. *The Book of Confessions* (New York: United Presbyterian Church, Office of the General Assembly, 1967), paras. 9.31, 9.44, 9.45.

3. *Peacemaking: The Believers' Calling* (New York: United Presbyterian Church, Office of the General Assembly, 1980), p. 5.

4. "Joint Statement Issued by President Carter, President Anwar al-Sadat of Egypt, and Prime Minister Menachem Begin of Israel," September 6, 1978, in *Weekly Compilation of Presidential Documents*, September 11, vol. 14, no. 36 (1978), p. 1501.

1991 Acknowledgments

Since the first edition of this book in late 1985, two changes have taken place in my work that require special mention:

First, at the beginning of 1987, I became a visiting fellow at The Brookings Institution in Washington, D.C. I am grateful to President Bruce MacLaury, to John Steinbruner, Director of the Foreign Policy Studies Program, and to William Quandt, who was Acting Director when the arrangements for my move were made. Brookings has provided a warm and supportive environment for which I am grateful.

Second, as my new Introduction and Epilogue indicate, I have broadened the scope of my work to emphasize the conduct of international relationships more widely. In doing so, I have continued to work in close collaboration with colleagues at the Charles F. Kettering Foundation in Dayton, Ohio, and am grateful to President David Mathews for the intellectual stimulation and support in providing an opportunity to reflect on political processes both within and among nations. It is in this context that I have engaged in extensive nonofficial dialogue with Soviet and, more recently, Chinese colleagues on the nature of the relationships between our nations and especially on how our interactions in the Third World intersect, reveal, and affect our overall relationships.

In addition, while this edition was being prepared for printing, Iraq invaded Kuwait on August 2, 1990. I am grateful to Margaret Case, Lauren Oppenheim, and their colleagues at Princeton University Press not only for their sensitive handling of this project from beginning to end but particularly for enabling me to add a brief section to the 1991 Introduction to relate the concept of the peace process to the Gulf crisis and to the aftermath of the war that began on January 16, 1991.

As footnotes to the new Epilogue indicate more precisely, I have written in a variety of contexts to develop my concept of relationships among nations and to apply the concept to particular situations. This has resulted in almost simultaneous separate publications in which analysis starts from my observations on our changing world and introduction of the concept of relationship. I am grateful to the publishers (see Introduction, note 17; and Epilogue, note 3 for citations) for agreeing to this practice.

Since early 1987, I have been generously supported in this work by the Miriam and Ira D. Wallach Foundation, the John D. and Catherine T. MacArthur Foundation, the Ford Foundation, the Carnegie Corporation of New York, and the United States Institute of Peace. While expressing my thanks to colleagues at Brookings and at each of these institutions for their support, I hasten to add that none is responsible for the views I express.

Finally, I am grateful to Louise Skillings both for putting this new work into presentable form and for helping similarly with all of the other writing that provided the building blocks.

H.H.S.
February 27, 1991

1991 Introduction: Negotiation Embedded in a Political Process

A Process of Changing Relationships

The Arab-Israeli peace process was, when it produced five agreements between 1974 and 1979, a series of negotiations embedded in a larger political process. This book was finished in mid-1985—a year of opportunity in the peace process. This introduction to the new edition was finished in mid-1990—a moment of more questionable but still potential opportunity. But this is not a book about moments or negotiations. It is about the political process of changing relationships among Israelis, Palestinians, and other Arabs. That process, not the headlines of any moment, remains its focus.

Although this is a book about the Arab-Israeli-Palestinian peace process, by extension it offers insight into how nations and peoples might build more cooperative relationships in today's world. It applies to both making peace and preserving peace. It applies not only to Arabs and Israelis but also to Americans, Chinese, and Soviets, or to Germans East and West in a larger European community. It applies to Central America, many parts of Africa, northern Ireland, Afghanistan, and Cambodia.

We are on the bridge between two paradigms in trying to understand and act in a rapidly changing world on the eve of the twenty-first century. For four hundred–plus years we in Western civilization have focused on the nation-state as the organizing unit in the interaction of peoples. States will continue to dominate the world stage so far as we can see. At the same time, we are experiencing a slow, uneven, incomplete but steady diffusion of power—both to new states that do not have the traditional attributes of power and to groupings of people who seem to have no raw power at all. As we speak of a shift from a bipolar to a multipolar world, we are now thinking not only of more states with increasing influence but also of other coalitions of peoples within and across state borders. We recognize interdependence and interaction built around interests ranging from "common security" to the "global commons."

As we stand on that bridge, we find that some of our familiar concepts are not defined in ways large enough to explain today's world accurately and that customary instruments of statecraft do not reliably produce the results we expect of them. That experience commands us to reach for a more complete and realistic conceptual framework for studying, teaching, and conducting international relationships. For the first time, all of us, scholars and practitioners together, have an opportunity for fundamental rethinking that can include all peoples—east, west, south, and north.

This rethinking must be rooted in the full range of human experience, not only in compartmentalized theories. This book is not the place for integrating new insights, but in-depth reflection on changing Arab-Israeli-Palestinian relationships can be a place for generating insight that may have larger implications. Visiting Hungary shortly after it cut down its part of the Iron Curtain and watching the Berlin wall crumble emphasized vividly that physical walls sometimes shield us from deeper problems—the "other walls." When the physical barriers come down, not seeing and facing those other obstacles and threats to peace can leave seeds of the next conflict in place to germinate. Bringing those obstacles into sharper focus and addressing them in our actions could help lay broader and sounder foundations for building and keeping the peace. I hope you will join me now in probing the "other walls" in that wider perspective.

Two Views of the Peace Process, 1985–1990

The purpose in sketching developments since 1985 is not to provide a detailed narrative but to see them through the lenses offered in this book. How policymakers bring a situation into focus begins to define how they will act. The aim of this book is to suggest looking at the Arab-Israeli-Palestinian conflict through lenses that reflect what we learned about the peace process as a political process when it produced results.[1]

On February 11, 1985, news flashes announced that King Hussein of Jordan and Palestine Liberation Organization (PLO) Chairman Yasser Arafat had signed an agreement laying the foundations for a Jordanian-Palestinian confederation (or federation) in the context of an Israeli-Jordanian-Palestinian peace agreement.[2] From the perspective of this book, that agreement presented the U.S. with an

opportunity to begin speaking of negotiations for the purpose of arranging an act of Palestinian "self-determination in association with
Jordan." Such an association had been a condition of both the Carter
and the Reagan administrations, as well as of Labor Party members
of the Israeli government, to avoid creation of an independent Palestinian state.

The word "self-determination" is for the Palestinians a symbol
of recognition of their identity as a people with claim to a state in
their homeland—Palestine. The U.S. had for a decade shied away
from the word because Israelis adamantly refuse to contemplate creation of a Palestinian state. In the minds of Americans at Camp David
in September 1978 from President Jimmy Carter down, "A Framework for Peace in the Middle East Agreed at Camp David"[3] had described an act of self-determination within a negotiated framework—
election of a Palestinian self-governing authority, participation of its
representatives with Egyptians, Israelis, and Jordanians in negotiations on the final status of the West Bank and Gaza, submission of
the results of the negotiation to a vote by the elected representatives
of the West Bank and Gaza. But we had only written that the Palestinians "will participate in the determination of their own future."
They perceived that artful phrase as avoidance of accepting them as
full-fledged parties to the peace. Now the Hussein-Arafat agreement
offered an opportunity to arrange expression of Palestinian identity
in a relationship with Jordan.

In May 1985 during a visit to Washington, King Hussein proposed to President Ronald Reagan and Secretary of State George
Shultz a four-stage political process. It would begin with an informal
meeting between U.S. Assistant Secretary of State Richard Murphy
and a group of Jordanians and "nondeclared PLO Palestinians" and
lead to PLO acceptance of UN Security Council Resolution 242,[4] including Israel's right to exist, to a U.S. meeting with a Jordanian-PLO
delegation, and then to an international conference on a comprehensive peace. It was assumed that the conference would include direct
negotiations between Israelis and such a delegation. The Preface to
the original edition of this book was written in that environment of
apparent opportunity.

For a variety of reasons that opportunity expired, and on February 19, 1986, King Hussein declared it ended. The U.S. never came
to closure on the initial meeting and eased away from the whole scenario by the end of the summer in 1985. King Hussein included strik-
ing language on direct negotiations in a speech at the UN that fall.
The U.S. reneged on a presidential commitment to provide new
weapons for Jordan's U.S.-equipped armed forces.

The purpose here is not to assess blame. As usual, there was enough responsibility for all involved. From the perspective presented in this book, the U.S. spent the fall of 1986 trying to determine how negotiation in a possible international conference might be organized; it paid little attention to the politics of nurturing a clear-cut Palestinian commitment to make peace with Israel and an Israeli sense of need to test that commitment in negotiation. While some good work was done in trying to design an acceptable conference, the U.S. left Jordan to produce a more explicit statement of Palestinian readiness to make peace with Israel. The Palestinians understood that Israel might not be able to recognize their nationhood until a negotiating process had begun, but they valued U.S. recognition and might have found enough reassurance in serious U.S. attention to their concerns.

On December 9, 1987, frustrations among Palestinians in the West Bank and Gaza exploded into a sustained uprising—the *intifada*—against the constraints and indignities of life under Israeli military occupation. Their frustration reflected not only the conditions of life but also the failure of their own expatriate leadership—the PLO—to develop a political program for changing their status through negotiation. The Israelis responded militarily rather than politically.

After seven months of continuing Palestinian demonstrations, King Hussein declared on July 31, 1988 that Jordan would discontinue its legal and administrative links with the West Bank in order to make clear that the future of those Palestinian territories now rested fully in Palestinian hands.[5] The king acted not from lack of concern for developments there or for the Palestinian cause; they intimately affect Jordan's own future. He had apparently decided to press Palestinian leaders to take responsibility by depriving them of what has been called a "Jordanian crutch." This may have been the forcing act—against the background of the intifada—that precipitated the significant steps by the PLO that followed.

On November 15, 1988, the Palestine National Council (PNC) in Algiers adopted (1) a declaration of independence for a Palestinian state, rooting its international legitimacy in United Nations General Assembly Resolution 181, which in 1947 approved partition of Palestine into a Jewish and an Arab state; and (2) a political statement calling for an international conference on the Middle East "on the basis of Security Council Resolutions 242 and 338 and the guaranteeing of the legitimate national rights of the Palestinian people, foremost being the right of self-determination." The statement spoke of Palestinian self-determination being achieved "in a manner that will ensure security and peace arrangements for all countries in the region" and reiterated "its rejection of terrorism in all its forms."[6]

At a session of the United Nations General Assembly in Geneva on December 13 and in a press conference there the following day, Chairman Arafat reiterated the PLO's acceptance of Resolutions 242 and 338 as the basis for negotiating with Israel "peace for both the Palestinians and Israelis" and stated explicitly that "the existence of the Palestinians . . . does not destroy the existence of the Israelis." He also repeated, "We totally and categorically reject all forms of terrorism." The words used eventually in the follow-up press conference met the requirements of a U.S. formula laid down in September 1975,[7] and U.S. Secretary of State George Shultz immediately announced that the U.S. would fulfill its promise to begin a dialogue with the PLO.[8]

On January 20, 1989, George Bush became President of the United States and James A. Baker, III became the new Secretary of State. At the time of the inauguration, experts in Washington divided into two schools of thought on how the new administration should proceed in the peace process.[9]

The more constricted approach stated that the conflict was not "ripe" for settlement and that the president should keep his distance because he could win little from it in U.S. politics. The administration should content itself with some efforts at changing the political climate while making only a limited active effort to move the process forward. One facet of this argument was that Syria was building its military forces to achieve parity with Israel and that the administration should spend its early months assuring that the military balance would not tip against Israel.

The second approach held that the Arab-Israeli conflict is rarely ripe for resolution unless someone works to ripen it. This approach had guided three administrations between 1974 and 1979. It did not urge the president to present a U.S. "peace plan." It argued rather that the U.S. should actively encourage Palestinian efforts to build on the recent declarations of their position by making concrete their vision of a peaceful and nonthreatening Israeli-Palestinian relationship. Providing a specific picture of the relationship might help bring the debate in Israel down to practical questions and focus Israeli consideration of the new Palestinian position. Serious Israeli deliberation might lead to specific steps on both sides that could begin changing the political environment and open the door for discussions of how to move toward a new relationship. This approach acknowledged that the situation is forbidding but argued a U.S. obligation to help ripen it by working imaginatively behind the scenes to help the parties develop an active political scenario for breaking the impasse.

When President Bush went beyond the more limited approach at least to the extent of meeting and hearing out Middle Eastern leaders during their visits to Washington in early April 1989, he faced a practical choice between these two ways of looking at the peace process. That choice brings us back to the essence of the peace process presented in this book—and to refinements in that characterization through my further thinking since the book's first appearance.

One possible approach for the president and secretary was to consider their main task to be starting an Israeli-Palestinian negotiation. In April 1989, the vehicle for such an effort was a proposal that Israeli Prime Minister Yitzhak Shamir brought to President Bush for arranging elections in the West Bank and Gaza to choose Palestinians to negotiate with Israel. Many observers—including many Israelis—felt this proposal was a delaying action because Shamir still rejected Israel's withdrawing from "one inch" of territory, opposed dealing with the PLO, and agreed at most to allow some Palestinian administration under continuing Israeli control.

The argument for developing the Israeli proposal and making it the basis of discussion with the PLO was that it offered a vehicle for engaging the Israeli government in negotiation. The argument against working exclusively with that proposal was that the Palestinians felt—with reason—that the Israelis did not perceive elections as a step toward serious negotiations about a new, long-term relationship. Under those circumstances, PLO leaders would be unlikely to engage without assurance, at least from the U.S. and perhaps from the Soviet Union, that the negotiations would lead to a serious second round on the longer-term relationship. It was clear that Israelis who did not want such a negotiation would tie up the diplomatic process in details to prevent progress.

A second approach—but not a mutually exclusive alternative—was to see the primary task not as beginning negotiation but as "changing the Israeli-Palestinian relationship." Since both bodies politic seemed to have moved about as far as they could in the present climate, this approach focused on a series of political acts designed with two purposes in mind. The first would be to refocus the debate in each body politic by providing realistic alternatives to the present course of action. The second would be to change perceptions and increase confidence that ultimately a peaceful relationship is possible.

In this context, the first task would be focusing dialogue between the Israeli and Palestinian bodies politic (1) on their visions of a peaceful relationship and (2) on a scenario of interacting steps for moving toward that vision. The Palestinians had changed their position but were still sending unclear signals. Some Israelis argued passionately for testing the Palestinian position to rid themselves of the "demographic time bomb" that would result from taking a potential Arab majority into the Jewish state, while others turned off their hearing aids to the new Palestinian position. Private talks were proliferating, but with little precision, continuity, or follow-through. Exchanges by video cassettes and television interviews and discussions were possible but few. Governments could focus debate on whether to negotiate and about what, but authorities seemed unlikely to talk directly or reflectively and openly about the common destiny of the two peoples in their common homeland. Such steps could be complementary, recognizing what officials and nonofficial parties can and cannot do. Working out terms of reference for negotiation addresses issues in technical and legalistic terms while often sweeping gut feelings and fundamental values underneath mechanistic formulas. At this stage, only citizens may be able to discuss real obstacles to peace—the "other walls."

This book lays the foundation for thinking about this second approach. It argues that decisions on whether to negotiate at all and for what purpose are made in the political arena—not in the antechambers of the negotiating room. Negotiation is unlikely to begin without a supportive political environment. Negotiation will be rudderless unless (1) those involved share some vision of the ultimate Israeli-Palestinian relationship and (2) the parties develop complementary steps outside the negotiating room for moving from a present stalemate toward an envisioned relationship. Agreements will not be creatively implemented without an understanding body politic. If negotiations fail, alternatives are likely to take shape first in the political arena. The purpose of this Introduction is to revisit the analysis of the "other walls" presented in the first edition and to see the shape of those walls as the 1990s begin. As walls in Europe crumble, what is the state of those between Arabs and Israelis?

The "Other Walls" in a 1990 Perspective

In the half-decade since this book was first published, how have the feelings and perceptions of the participants in the peace process changed? How have the politics in the process changed? How does one identify the underlying obstacles—the "other walls"—to movement toward peace now? Is the situation more "ripe" for movement toward peace, or less so? Is there more or less to work with in helping it ripen?

The common answer is that Arab-Israeli relations during this period have been largely "dismal and unhopeful," to use the words of one scholar. Certainly there is reason for painting a bleak picture. At the same time, relationships may be in the process of profound change—even though the odds may remain against constructive change if the parties are left to their own initiatives. The global setting is also changing profoundly.

How one answers depends in part on one's vantage point. Scholars or analysts may accurately state with every effort at objectivity that the situation *is* not ripe—or *is* even less ripe—for change. A few policymakers struggle with a different analytical question: How might the situation *become* ripe? If the consequences of a straight-line projection of the present situation seem dangerously destructive to the interests of many involved, the policymaker may ask: "Understanding the resistance to change as fully as possible and the formidable odds, can I do anything prudently to help ripen the situation?" Those involved in the peace process in the 1970s used to say: "The odds of success are small. But our job is to start with a five or ten percent chance of success, move it up to fifteen or twenty, and then press for a break or to beat the odds."

Whatever conclusion for action is drawn from the analysis, the starting point is defined by answers to the questions around which the chapters in this book are organized: How might we describe where each party stands in relation to the conflict? How does each party define the situation, weigh the impact on its interests, and envision alternatives and the obstacles to achieving them? Where does each stand in moving toward commitment to resolving the conflict? What instruments is each inclined to use in moving from where it is to where it would prefer to be?

To focus this discussion, it may be fair to set developments in the ten-plus years since Camp David in this perspective: The first half of the 1980s saw a series of efforts to deal with the Israeli-Palestinian problem in the context of the "Jordan option"—crafting a solution that would permit expression of the Palestinian identity "in association with Jordan." Developments since this book was first published in 1985 have increasingly focused attention on the Israeli-Palestinian conflict itself.

The Jordan option may not have been realistic even in the early 1980s, but it visibly though slowly passed away after 1985. By 1985 some Israelis were already warning that Israel's tightening grip on the West Bank and Gaza had internalized the conflict, transforming it from a conflict between Israel and an external enemy into an internal intercommunal conflict.[10] The practical consequences of that analysis had become clear by 1990.

In U.S. minds, implementation of the Egyptian-Israeli peace treaty—by design in the Camp David accords—had cleared the way to put the Israeli-Jordanian-Palestinian relationship at the top of the agenda in the peace process. The Carter administration had bequeathed to the Reagan team an ongoing negotiation on setting up under the Camp David Framework a self-governing authority for the Palestinians in the West Bank and Gaza. The Reagan administration had put those negotiations on the back burner in 1981. In some ways, the Hussein-Arafat agreement of February 1985 was an Arab effort to put that issue back on the agenda again—though under terms of reference quite different from those written at Camp David.

When the 1985 initiative lost momentum, developments—in hindsight—began to move toward more intense Israeli-Palestinian conflict, dialogue, perhaps negotiation, and potentially ultimate peaceful resolution. These reflections on this period are written in that perspective.

In 1985, a majority of *Palestinians* seemed tentatively ready to take the first pragmatic steps toward peace with Israel, but significant fault lines dividing the Palestinian community as a whole paralyzed any thought of taking the initiative. By the decade's end many of those fault lines remained, but the balance of initiative within the Palestinian movement, between the Palestinians and the rest of the Arab world, and perhaps in the peace process itself had shifted importantly. Two precipitating acts helped to crystallize the steady fundamental shift in the substantive and operational stance of the Palestinian movement.

First was the outbreak of the intifada. Following the end of the Hussein-Arafat dialogue in February 1986, Palestinians saw Jordan focus attention on relationships with other Arab countries and concentrate on other problems, such as the Iran-Iraq war. They saw key elements in Israel opposed to changing the Israeli-Jordanian-Palestinian relationship—despite the efforts of the Labor Party—and a U.S. administration unwilling to work imaginatively toward including Palestinians in the peace process. We cannot be sure why frustration in the West Bank and Gaza boiled over in December 1987 and not earlier or later, but as local leadership formed to coordinate sustained resistance, initiative in the Palestinian movement passed to those living under occupation. Yet they needed support from leaders representing the whole Palestinian community—exiles as well as those living in Palestine. Pressure mounted on the PLO for a political program to complement the sacrifice of those engaged in active resistance.[11]

Second was a decisive change in the ties of *Jordan* with the West Bank. As resistance stretched into its seventh and eighth months— unlike previous outbreaks that had lasted only days or weeks—the king concluded that the time had come to try to precipitate a clear-cut Palestinian initiative and political program. He had long recognized that the health of the Hashemite Kingdom depended on a Jordanian-Palestinian relationship in which the Palestinians found fulfillment in defining and expressing their identity in political forms of their own choosing. He had made serious efforts over two decades to define that relationship under Jordanian sovereignty. In July of 1988 he seems to have decided that—while Jordan still had a strong interest in a close relationship with Palestinians in the West Bank and Gaza—the only path to that goal lay in putting Palestinian destiny in Palestinian hands. He continued to trust that the Palestinians once independent—if fairly treated by Jordan—would then feel able as equals to work out at least the practical relationship with Jordan that both sides would see as reflecting the interdependence of their interests.

The king seems to have judged that the Palestinian uprising provided a change in the chemistry of the Jordanian-Palestinian relationship and, potentially, even the Israeli-Palestinian relationship, which produced a moment ripe for a forcing political act. As the resistance maintained momentum, PLO leaders considered with increasing urgency how to fashion a political program to take advantage of the moment the uprising had created. It may not be overstating the point to say that, in the king's judgment, the uprising provided an opportunity for the same restoration of self-esteem that Sadat had built from Arab performance in the 1973 War. Against that background and with responsibility placed entirely in his hands, Arafat had little choice but may also have felt justified in taking greater political risk to establish a Palestinian presence in the peace process.

Believing he still could not expect a serious Israeli response to a Palestinian initiative, Arafat set his sights on the U.S. The change in the Palestinian position in November and December 1988 seemed aimed at starting a working relationship with the U.S. that might initially justify the Palestinian initiative and then produce stepping stones toward full PLO participation in the peace process. More than a year after that formal dialogue began, the Palestinians remain deeply disappointed in mid-1990 at the painful U.S. reluctance to engage in direct, in-depth, and prolonged substantive discussion of how the peace process might move forward with Palestinian participation. The Palestinians saw the U.S. as still not willing to treat them as equal partners in deciding how Israeli and Palestinian lives in their common homeland can be arranged with safety, dignity, and self-determination for both. The irony is that the Palestinians—for all their remaining internal differences and indecisiveness in projecting an unequivocal position—may be more ready psychologically and more able politically to move slowly into peace with Israel than at any previous time.

The response of *Israel* to the Palestinian initiative through much of the population was barely to hear it or to dismiss it as not representing a real change in the PLO position. In any case, the PLO remained for many Israelis—perhaps a slowly decreasing number—an unacceptable negotiating partner. Underlying its response was Israel's continued struggle for peace within itself—a deep-rooted struggle to define the appropriate political and social expression of the Jewish experience in a modern state. If anything, that struggle has intensified since 1985. It seems to have moved in two contradictory directions, but the apparent contradictions may lie in the fact that they are moving on different time lines.

Most obviously, the center of gravity in Israeli politics seems to have moved to the right, ostensibly favoring the Likud. From the fall of 1986 until the breakup of the national unity government in early 1990, a Likud prime minister has headed that government, and Labor Party leaders were unable to increase support in the 1988 elections enough to assert even a rotational claim on the prime minister's office. The Palestinian uprising seemed at first to reinforce those who argued that Israel must maintain firm military control in Palestinian areas to protect Israeli security. By early 1990, a marked increase in Jewish emigration from the Soviet Union to Israel—perhaps motivated mainly by President Mikhail Gorbachev's effort to improve his human rights performance in the eyes of the U.S. body politic—gave the "annexationists" in Israel hope that Israelis could still win the battle of the birthrates with the Palestinians. In any case, those who are committed to retaining Israeli control—even asserting formal sovereignty—over all the land west of the Jordan River continued to play a significant role in the government.

Moving at a slower pace in shaping tangible consequences were the gradual and still not sharply defined shifts in perception resulting from the intifada. While many Israelis still succeeded in preserving a wall that permitted them not to acknowledge the Palestinians as human beings, many others serving with the military occupation in the West Bank and Gaza came literally and intimately face-to-face with the Palestinians. "He pointed his gun at me," said one Palestinian fourteen-year-old of his encounter with a young Israeli soldier. "I looked him in the eye for a long time." What is the impact on that young Israeli? What is the impact on the Israeli parent who sees her or his son ordered to beat Palestinians with sticks or stones or to kill? Israelis are for the most part a people of conscience. What bloody incident might bring these Israelis into the streets as some four hundred thousand demonstrated after the massacre in the Sabra and Shatilla refugee camps during the 1982 Israeli invasion of Lebanon?

Increasing fragmentation has continued to characterize Israeli political, social, and religious life; votes for political parties reflect far more fault lines than simply different views on the ultimate Israeli-Palestinian relationship.[12] Divisiveness and uncertainty paralyze thought of an Israeli initiative. The point made in 1985 still seems apt: "the search for an Arab-Israeli-Palestinian peace is part of the Jews' own struggle for peace within themselves, which they call *shalom*. One of the agonies of Israel today is that Jews have lost touch with each other about the Jewish experience in modern Israel as it should be. Any political effort to achieve peace must provide an opportunity for Jews to discuss among themselves how the yearning for greater peace can be fulfilled." It is not at all clear that the government crisis in mid-1990 will pave the way for answering that central question.[13]

Recognizing that the new Bush administration might begin pressing for negotiation, Prime Minister Shamir brought to Washington in March 1989 his proposal for negotiations on holding elections in the West Bank and Gaza. Pondering this proposal along with stiff Israeli resistance to dealing with the larger Palestinian community and the PLO, many analysts—and certainly the Palestinians—have read it as an instrument for responding to American insistence on negotiation while protecting Israel's capacity to string out any real progress either toward or in negotiation.

The question is where the primary focus in the peace process should fall. The willingness of the U.S. to work with the Israeli proposal reflects at a minimum an understandable tactic of engaging Israel on whatever terms it proposes. The U.S. seemed intent on trying honestly to turn Israel's proposal into genuine progress or, failing that, to demonstrate Israel's unwillingness to negotiate seriously and to pave the way for a different approach. Whatever the tactic, a viable strategy for the peace process seemed to require a larger perspective if it were to address the deep-rooted obstacles to peace.

As this book states, the Palestinians believe they are asked to give up land they consider rightfully theirs in order to make room for a people persecuted in other civilizations. That being the case, "the challenge in bringing the Palestinians to the table is how to enable them to accept the loss of part of Palestine." In some ways, the vehicle for letting go of physical losses that cannot be recovered may lie in enabling them to find in their place full acceptance of their identity. In my view, that statement is just as accurate and central in 1990 as it was when I first wrote it in 1985.[14]

As this book also states, Israel's security needs—in addition to the essential ability to defend itself—include fulfillment of a deep craving for acceptance as a people whose unique history lies at the core of their identity. Whatever the words of official Palestinian declarations, Israelis do not yet feel in Palestinian actions the acceptance for which they yearn. Beyond that, Israelis, too, face yet another potential loss. The generation of Israelis now in its young maturity has grown up knowing only an Israel controlling all the land west of the Jordan River. For them, a one-state solution in Palestine is a physical possibility—indeed, almost a de facto reality. To use the original language, "Whereas their parents saw a Jewish state in a partitioned Palestine as a historic triumph, this generation would see a partitioned Palestine as a profound loss."[15]

In that context, the task in the peace process at the beginning of the 1990s is not just to arrange a negotiation, whatever the subject and as important as that might be to crystallize change begun in the political arena. The overall task is to lay out a scenario of interacting political steps to begin changing the Israeli-Palestinian relationship—including engaging both peoples in actions that make it possible for each to accept the additional losses they face in the context of gaining new fulfillment and security. As I wrote in 1985, "The kind of full peace Israel seeks . . . can come only when Israel is prepared to accept the Palestinians to the extent that it wants to be accepted by them." The same is reciprocally true of the Palestinians.

Diplomacy remains essential to defining politically, socially, and economically workable relationships that are viable and secure. But one lesson of the 1970s was that the diplomats and negotiators are unlikely to succeed until leaders have put the politics right. Putting the politics right requires a peace process that is not just a negotiation but a political process for changing the relationships between peoples.

This picture—as the perspective offered at the outset suggests—focuses on the Israeli-Palestinian dimension of the conflict. *Egypt* has remained committed to its obligations under the Egyptian-Israeli peace treaty and the approach in the Camp David accords of moving next to deal with the Israeli-Palestinian conflict. Egypt has played an active role in trying to launch a formal Israeli-Palestinian dialogue. *Syria* continues to spend most of its external energies in Lebanon but retains a closely related interest both in influencing the outcome of an Israeli-Palestinian settlement and in its own territorial settlement with Israel. It seems as difficult as ever to find ways to engage Syria in the kind of peace process most of the other parties envision.

Reconstituting the Peace Process

Chapter 9 lays out what it means operationally to see the peace process[16] as a political process of interacting steps to change the political environment so as to make possible movement toward an agreed resolution of conflict and a new relationship. Most of the acts suggested there remain relevant to the present situation, but points on generating a political scenario need to be highlighted in the conditions created by the historic restatements of the Palestinian position in November and December 1988.

Reformulation of the Palestinian position with precision of wording on PLO acceptance of Resolutions 242 and 338, PLO readiness to accept and make peace with Israel, and PLO renunciation of terrorism were necessary additions to the diplomatic and legal framework for resolution of the conflict. The predictable Israeli resistance to taking them seriously demonstrates that diplomatic and legal formulations are not enough by themselves to change the Israeli-Palestinian relationship.

Part of the problem is that many Israelis do not believe—some do not want to believe—that the new words reflect a genuine change of Palestinian heart and intention. In that context, one problem is that PLO leaders did not immediately recognize the need to surround their words with credible, compelling, flesh-and-blood evidence that they envision a relationship between Israelis and Palestinians in which neither would feel threatened.

As Palestinian officials listen to persisting Israeli concerns, many respond with positions they believe do not threaten Israeli identity or security when translated into practical measures. To Israelis' concern that the PLO just wants a state as a base for destroying Israel, they say they once thought that way but they have concluded Israel is here to stay and they need to concentrate on developing their own state or they will end up with nothing. They also say they could not challenge Israel without inviting their own destruction. On security, they borrow vocabulary from Europe and speak of a "mutual security" agreement to prevent violence from either side and say that a Palestinian state will need no more military force than necessary to fulfill its obligations under the agreement. On the Palestinian "right of return" that causes Israelis to fear inundation by Palestinians who left their homes in 1948, PLO officials say either that the right will apply only to the Palestinian state once established or that practicalities of implementation will protect Israeli identity.

These points may not satisfy Israelis. The operational question is whether hearing those points face to face consistently in varied settings would make them more credible. Would it make them more human and lead to a different view of the Palestinians than that produced by present demonizing mythology and dehumanization? Could the Palestinians present their views in such a way as to cause some significant part of the Israeli body politic to feel that Israel could be making a costly mistake not to probe the Palestinian position to determine whether it offers a possible starting point for dialogue, negotiation, and potentially a changed relationship?

It is tempting in this situation to look to Sadat's visit to Israel in 1977 as a model for a precipitating act that changed Israeli perceptions and the shape of Israeli debate, but we do not see a repetition of such an act. The question is whether other steps could be taken in this different part of the conflict that would have some of the same consequences. All the technology of satellite television and of audio, video, and facsimile communication are available and are slowly coming into use.

Against the background of those reflections, a political scenario for beginning to change the Israeli-Palestinian relationship could begin by working with the Palestinians to develop a series of steps to make their position credible and compelling to the Israelis. In beginning this work, there are roles for Americans, Soviets, and Europeans, both official and nonofficial. The task is to put together a sustained series of interviews, discussions, "fireside chats," panels involving leading Palestinians—live, in print, on audio and video tape—for delivery to Israeli audiences week after week. As opportunities arise, more and more Israelis could be woven into the exchanges. The purpose would be to say enough in enough places over a long enough time to invade and pervade the internal Israeli debate.

From the beginning, building the scenario would equally require involving Israelis interested in a wider hearing and consideration of the Palestinians' ideas within the Israeli body politic. That dialogue might need to be focused initially through intermediaries, but it could quickly become a direct exchange through the many existing Israeli-Palestinian channels. Israelis could help focus the effort in three ways: (1) they could sharpen the substance of Palestinian comments by assuring a precise picture of current Israeli concerns and arguments; (2) they could enlarge the range of opportunities for reaching Israeli audiences repetitively; and (3) they could help reshape Israeli debate and response in such a way as to build, in essence, a dialogue between Israelis and Palestinians.

At some point as this dialogue without a table matures, the time would come to consider some precipitating act to crystallize debate in both the Israeli and the Palestinian bodies politic around a decision to take a concrete step to move the dialogue to a practical plane. Just for purpose of illustration, one approach might include three elements:

The first would develop around a Palestinian proposal for talks. In a publicized speech on Jordanian television, Arafat might (1) describe his detailed vision of a peaceful Israeli-Palestinian relationship and (2) invite Israel to name eight or so individuals—official or non-official—to sit down at a set date and place for several weeks to discuss a two-part agenda. During their first days together, they would talk in detail about the relationship they envision; then they would turn to the kinds of steps that would be necessary on both sides for getting from here to there.

The second element would develop around the Israeli response. If such a speech were part of an evolving scenario discussed in the early planning stages with those in Israel interested in such a next step, those Israelis would steadily lay the groundwork for serious Israeli discussion of how to respond. The debate would cut across the full spectrum of feelings in Israel, but at bottom the issue would be whether Israel could afford not to explore an opportunity to probe the Palestinian position.

Third would be the role of the international community. In addition to involvement in the first stage of the scenario, at this point the work of the larger powers individually or together, in or out of the UN, would be to offer support for a proposed dialogue. It would even be possible for Soviet and U.S. authorities to communicate quietly to decision-makers that they "would not understand" refusal to engage seriously in dialogue or to send individuals who could participate with open minds and spirits.

As such a scenario unfolded, opportunities would arise for those in authority—in Israel, in the intifada, in the PLO—to take steps on the ground to convey a greater sense of readiness to talk. Changes in practice in violent confrontations or in the administrative rules of the military occupation governing a wide range of daily Palestinian life could provide evidence of increased readiness to consider changes in the relationship. Changes in the tactics of those conducting the uprising could provide evidence of readiness to talk.

The point is not the details of a scenario; they would emerge in the process of dialogue about a scenario. The point is the need to think in terms of steps to change the political environment—not just to prepare a negotiation—and the need for those involved in the relationship to think and act together.

The Soviet–U.S. Relationship and the Peace Process

Chapter 8 concludes with the thought that the roles of the Soviet Union and the U.S. will depend partly on the state of the overall relationship between those two nations. The period since 1985 has almost directly coincided with Gorbachev's assumption and consolidation of leadership in the Soviet Union and a historic change in the relationship. Two points may be particularly important to develop my thinking in this book about the potential role of these two parties as mediators.

First, the "new political thinking" stimulated by Gorbachev on how nations relate, among many other subjects, seems to perceive relations among nations as political process. Before 1985, and especially at the height of the peace process in the 1970s, the U.S. had happily left the Soviets on the sidelines. Admittedly, much of the reasoning behind that U.S. approach reflected fundamental distrust and strategic reluctance to "legitimize" the Soviet presence in this sensitive area. But it had also included the judgment that the process as conducted by the U.S. in the 1970s was not an approach for which we felt the Soviets, with their heavy institutional and diplomatic approach, were suited. In the early 1990s, it may not be inaccurate to say that Gorbachev has on occasion led the way as an imaginative practitioner in the politics of change both within and among nations.

Second, the substance of the Soviet and the U.S. visions of what an Arab-Israeli-Palestinian peace might look like is closer than ever. One could argue that the distance between the Soviet and U.S. positions was never very great—that what governed the distance was fear that a position would somehow give advantage to the other, perhaps by giving advantage to the other's ally. Two changes seem to have taken place. One is that the two powers may be slowly—the point cannot be conclusively stated in early 1990—reducing their use of regional conflicts as major arenas for their own competition. Another is that the Soviet Union has since 1985 actively developed a working relationship with Israel, while the U.S. opened its door, with Soviet help, to dialogue with the PLO. With those changes in relationships, the two powers have shown more flexibility in stating their positions on aspects of a peace agreement. There has also been a slight shift from rigid adherence to the positions of regional friends to somewhat more readiness to accept what the process produces.

Underlying these points are the longer-range questions of whether the evolution of a constructive problem-solving Soviet-U.S. relationship can be politically sustained and whether dramatic changes among peoples elsewhere in the world will somehow influence Arab-Israeli-Palestinian relationships. Neither can be answered with confidence yet.

In 1990, Soviet-U.S. cooperation in the peace process seems possible substantively. In the U.S., it is still an open question whether the U.S. body politic would give its leaders political permission to cooperate unreservedly with the U.S.S.R. on matters vital to the future of the Jewish state. Many Americans do not forget the painful experience with Russian anti-Semitism that made them refugees and brought them to the U.S. Seeing the PLO through Israeli eyes and still harboring a deep-seated fear of Jewish annihilation, they are not ready to set aside their image of a radical Palestinian state bent on Israel's destruction with a Soviet Union in the background at a minimum unconcerned about the fate of Jewish life anywhere. These words may not reflect prevailing American feelings, but they reflect views backed by enough political strength to make them a factor—at least in shaping Congressional opinion—in any president's policymaking. As attitudes toward the permanence of change in the Soviet Union shift, this factor may also change.

It is more difficult to write of the politics of Soviet policymaking toward the Arab-Israeli peace process, but Soviet and American citizens in nonofficial discussions do talk about this subject now. Two conflicting tendencies seem to be potential factors in the Soviet body politic, although neither seems yet in 1990 to exercise the same kind of influence that U.S. leaders have faced for some years. One is an underlying continuing thread of anti-Semitic feelings. The other is a range of pro-Arab feelings rooted in a number of contacts and cultural affinities in some of the southern and Central Asian Soviet republics. Perhaps it seems premature even to mention such factors while the Soviet Union—for all of its remarkable changes—still seems far from that time when a developed and politically articulated public judgment will have a formative impact on policymaking. But since it is possible to think and talk about this subject in 1990, as it was not in 1985, it seems appropriate to focus attention on it.

The Persian Gulf Crisis of 1990–1991

Iraq's invasion of Kuwait on August 2, 1990 focused attention on three questions in the Middle East: Is it possible in a world where war is becoming too devastating to fight anywhere to think more creatively about a process of political settlement as an effective and just alternative to war? Does experience in the Arab-Israeli-Palestinian peace process offer insight into generating a truly regional Middle East peace process? Does thinking about a regional peace process in turn enlarge our understanding of the Arab-Israeli peace process itself? The new Epilogue places these questions in a global perspective.

A more general concept of political settlement would include two components, not unlike those in the Arab-Israeli peace process. One would be the substantive agenda—the issues that would have to be addressed in building constructive relationships for a more stable Middle East. The other would be the scenario for addressing that agenda—the political process that might provide a coherent overall context for changing relationships in the region.

Following the invasion, Iraqi President Saddam Hussein tried to build a broad political constituency in the Arab world by exploiting a range of issues on a large Middle East agenda. Although the United States—rightly, in my view—rejected formal linkage between ending Iraq's occupation of Kuwait and other issues on the agenda, that agenda remained to be addressed, whether before war or after.

The issues on that agenda could be grouped under five principles:

[1] respect for the territorial integrity and national identity of each state in the region and the right of citizens to choose their own form of government;

[2] protection of each state's right to live in peace and security free from the threat or use of force (including UN or regional peacekeeping forces, limitations on arms buildings, and international regimes to curb weapons of mass destruction);

[3] a commitment as it is possible to move toward resolution of conflicts to hear thoughtfully and responsively the underlying grievances, fears, and concerns as well as the concrete claims of each party (including, for instance, Iraq's expressed resentment at other Arab nations whom it felt it had shielded from Iranian aggression);

[4] settlements of all legitimate claims and debts by peaceful means in accordance with the UN Charter and the principle that all serious grievances must be heard (including Iraq's earlier debts to Arab countries, Kuwait's claim for reparations, and the ultimate lifting of the embargo on Iraq's exports and imports);

[5] development of new contexts for resolving regional conflicts (including not only reconstitution of the Arab-Israeli-Palestinian

peace process but evolution of a larger political process to encompass other conflicts and issues on the larger Middle East agenda).

It is not enough in the context of the Gulf crisis to print the agenda for a political settlement any more than it is sufficient in the Arab-Israeli context to stop with a vision of a peaceful relationship. It is equally important to develop the political process in which that agenda can steadily be addressed. Before the war, it was possible to pose a process of political settlement of the crisis as an alternative to war. After the war, it is necessary to develop a process of political settlement of building a more stable and peaceful Middle East.

Before the war, a possible scenario started from setting a larger time frame for international pressure, economic sanctions, and defensive military deployments coupled with third-party efforts to try to bring about a peaceful winding down of the crisis. This approach would have required avoiding creating an atmosphere of personal confrontation, showdown, and deadline in order to create a climate in which aggression was firmly opposed but peaceful resolution of the conflict might be possible. In the fall of 1990, a number of significant individuals attempted mediation and failed. It may well be that any such efforts were premature before a prolonged quarantine of Iraq had taken its full toll. It may also be that the combative atmosphere created locked both of the principal adversaries into a confrontation from which neither could back down, whatever the stature of the mediators. There was no guarantee that such efforts would ever have succeeded, but it is conceivable that one could have constructed a political scenario built around addressing some of the issues on the political agenda that would gradually have triggered a series of interactive steps leading to disengagement and ultimate Iraqi withdrawal from Kuwait.

Those who worked from memories of Hitler's rise and World War II argued that any such attempt would have led to unjustifiable compromises with a dictator and aggressor. They also argued that such aggression should in no way be rewarded.

The response to those arguments was agreement that aggression should not be rewarded but argument that pressing for unconditional surrender also had its costs. In the not-distant future, those costs may well include military confrontation with an aggressor who can deliver chemical, biological, or nuclear weapons. At that point the choice will be the one the Soviet Union and the United States tested during the Cold War—how to make clear the costs of aggression without subjecting aggressor and victim alike to the horrors of such warfare.

In the war's aftermath, the political agenda remained very much the same as the prewar agenda, albeit in changed circumstances. The question after the war is whether leaders will conclude that they have solved such problems as the proliferation of weapons of mass destruction or the conflict between Iraq and its neighbors by defeating Iraq militarily or whether they will still see the need to address the larger Middle East agenda imaginatively. If they are prepared to devote at least as much energy to building the peace as they did to prosecuting the war, they will need to think in terms of a larger political process—a Middle East peace process.

Beginning before the war, some thoughtful public figures proposed a larger international conference such as the Congress of Vienna after the Napoleonic wars to address the whole range of Middle Eastern issues. Others suggested looking to the European experience in the Helsinki process—the Conference on Security and Cooperation in Europe (CSCE)—as a way of addressing a disparate collection of issues under a larger inclusive political umbrella. The point raised by this book is whether we should not look to the Arab-Israeli peace process as the model for a larger Middle East peace process.

In the aftermath of the 1973 War, the larger political process in which the shuttle negotiations were embedded dealt with a range of issues well beyond the Arab-Israeli conflict. An oil embargo was lifted. U.S. diplomatic relations were gradually restored with six Arab countries. Joint commissions on economic cooperation were established between the United States and four Middle Eastern countries. Disengagement agreements contained provisions for preventing future conflict through limited armaments zones, international inspection, improved communications, and confidence-building measures. The political agenda was broad and was partly made possible by progress on the negotiating agenda, just as in turn progress on the political agenda made negotiation possible.

The European experience is instructive not primarily because of the Helsinki process but because of the vision of those after World War II who decided that repeated wars were not the way to deal with Europe's problems, and began building economic and political interactions in Europe that led, four decades later, to the evolution of a political and economic community. That evolution was made possible not only by the acts of governments but by political acts of reconciliation among members of the bodies politic involved. Such an experience has already begun through extensive private efforts in the Arab-Israeli arena. The question now is whether the vision of a larger Middle East process could extend those efforts to include a larger

xli

number of regional parties and begin generating a vision of a larger Middle East peace.

Those who argue that the world needs to pay more attention to the political processes of political settlement—to the peace process— face a difficult struggle following the Gulf war. It is particularly difficult in the wake of a war that succeeded in turning back aggression and defeating the aggressor. Some Americans would add that it was a war with remarkably few casualties. They will omit notice of extensive damage within Iraq and large human losses—victims of the actions of their leader as well as of the munitions that hurt and killed them. They will also omit notice of the costs of the war, particularly the costs to programs not funded for the improvement of human life in many nations.

The issue is no longer only that humanitarian issue or even the argument over whether a war was just. Important as those arguments remain, a compelling new argument has placed itself at the top of the agenda. Even during the Cold War, Soviet and U.S. leaders concluded that nuclear weapons made war too costly as an instrument of policy. The United States did not oppose militarily the Soviet repression in Hungary in 1956 or in Czechoslovakia in 1968 because it did not want to risk nuclear war. The war against Iraq may be the last significant situation in which the world has the luxury of attacking even a Third World aggressor who is unable to unleash weapons of mass destruction.

The opportunity in the autumn of 1990 was to use the Gulf crisis to develop and to hone political instruments for blocking and turning back aggression. In the end, that opportunity was set aside. The war that was fought may be the last (one hopes) twentieth-century war— not a war to lay the foundations of the "new world order" of which leaders spoke. The challenge remains—to demonstrate that aggression can be turned back politically in a world where war would impose intolerable costs even on those acting against aggression. One way to meet that challenge remains the subject of this book.[17]

A Global Perspective

I cannot conclude this Introduction without recording a point that is increasingly on the lips of those immersed in the peace process. As they have watched a brief period of remarkable change from the Soviet Union to South Africa and from Beijing to Berlin, they have wondered quietly how long it might be until Israelis, Palestinians, and other Arabs might crowd into the streets and squares shouting, "Enough!"—and stay there until political authorities listen.

Whatever the timetable of such change might be, if any, it remains my view that opportunity in the 1990s—as in 1985—can only be seized through a broader approach to the peace process than that followed in the 1980s. In 1985, when this book was first published, I made that case mainly in terms of experience in the Arab-Israeli arena. Now, in 1991, I am making a broader argument. Now, the case for that view is based not just on analysis of the deep-rooted obstacles to peace in the Arab-Israeli arena presented in this book—the "other walls." The case is, day by day, compellingly grounded in thinking on a global scale about how nations and peoples relate in today's world. Setting that global perspective is intended to be one of the new contributions of this volume; it is the focus of the new Epilogue.

Notes

1. My analysis in this perspective covering the entire decade after the Camp David accords in 1978 appears as "Reconstituting the Arab-Israeli Peace Process" in William B. Quandt, ed., *The Middle East: Ten Years After Camp David* (Washington, D.C.: The Brookings Institution, 1988), Part IV.

2. The text of this agreement is in appendix X.

3. The text is in appendix VII.

4. The text of Resolution 242 is in appendix I.

5. The text of King Hussein's speech appears in appendix XI.

6. The texts of the PNC documents are in appendixes XII and XIII. Resolutions 242 and 338 are in appendixes I and IV, respectively.

7. "The United States will continue to adhere to its present policy with respect to the Palestine Liberation Organization, whereby it will not recognize or negotiate with the Palestine Liberation Organization so long as the Palestine Liberation Organization does not recognize Israel's right to exist and does not accept Security Council Resolutions 242 and 338." "Memorandum of Agreement Between the Governments of Israel and the United States on the Geneva Peace Conference," September 1, 1975, in *The Search for Peace in the Middle East: Documents and Statements, 1967–79,* Report by the Foreign Affairs and National Defense Division, Congressional Research Service, Library of Congress (Washington, D.C.: U.S. Government Printing Office, 1979), p. 15.

8. Arafat's speech is in appendix XIV, and his press conference statement in appendix XV. The U.S. response to the Arafat statements is in Appendix XVI.

9. These two schools of thought were captured by two election-year study groups assembled by two private Washington research institutions. The first was the essence of *Building for Peace: An American Strategy for the Middle East: The Washington Institute's Presidential Study Group,* published by the Washington Institute for Near East Policy, an institution close to the pro-

Israel lobby. The second was reflected in *Toward Arab-Israeli Peace: Report of a Study Group*, published by The Brookings Institution. Each had proponents in the team around President Bush and Secretary Baker. The two approaches were also reflected in sharply different memos prepared for a project co-chaired by Gerald R. Ford and Jimmy Carter, *American Agenda: Report to the Forty-First President of the United States of America*. The differences were diluted or ignored and a cautious approach presented in an overall memo on foreign policy by Warren Christopher and Lawrence S. Eagleburger on p. 7 of the *American Agenda*.

10. Please see, for example, Meron Benvenisti, *The West Bank Data Project: A Survey of Israel's Policies* (Washington, D.C.: American Enterprise Institute, 1984), p. 64: "The data on the West Bank and Gaza compiled in our project strongly suggest that the processes set in motion in 1967 and accelerated in recent years have created social, economic, and political interactions between Israel and the territories that have assumed quasi permanence. . . . The significance of that ultimate achievement of Zionist aspirations, more than territorial, is that the Palestinian problem has now been internalized."

11. For fuller discussion of the Palestinian experience in this period, please see two chapters in William Quandt, *Ten Years after Camp David*: Rashid Khalidi, "The Palestine Liberation Organization," pp. 261–78; Emile Sahliyeh, "Jordan and the Palestinians," pp. 279–318.

12. Please see Naomi Chazan, "Domestic Developments in Israel," in William Quandt, *Ten Years after Camp David*, pp. 150–86.

13. Please see Chapter 3.

14. Please see Chapter 4.

15. Please see Chapter 3.

16. "Reconstituting the Arab-Israeli Peace Process" is the title of my chapter in William Quandt, *Ten Years after Camp David*, pp. 413–41. The same approach is also developed in "The Arab-Israeli Conflict in a Global Perspective," my chapter in John D. Steinbruner, ed., *Restructuring American Foreign Policy* (Washington, D.C.: The Brookings Institution, 1988), Chapter 8, pp. 221–51. I have used the title again here because I believe the peace process cannot simply be restarted after a decade of fits and starts; it needs to be rebuilt from the foundations up.

17. For a fuller discussion of these issues, please see my article, "Political Settlement and the Gulf Crisis," in *Mediterranean Quarterly*, vol. 2 (Spring, 1991), and my chapter, "A Broader Peace Process for the Middle East," in Judith Kipper and Harold H. Saunders, eds., *The Middle East in Global Perspective* (Boulder, Colo.: Westview Press, 1991), Chapter 15. Because these were written almost simultaneously, some of the same ideas and formulations appear in more than one place. Each publisher has accepted this practice.

1

The Arab-Israeli Peace Process

Breaking Down the Barriers to Peace

On November 19, 1977, American television screens showed the Egyptian airliner as it drew to a stop on the tarmac of Ben Gurion Airport in Israel. For the first time in modern history, an Arab leader on a mission of state under the eyes of a captivated world stepped onto Israeli soil. Egyptian President Anwar Sadat walked slowly along a line of waiting leaders of the Jewish state, shaking hands with each in turn. These were the modern stewards of four thousand years of Jewish history. They were men and women diverse in political orientation, personality, and views regarding the future of their state—but they were one in yearning for peace and acceptance. Sadat came offering peace and acceptance, that "sacred message . . . of security, safety and peace to every man, woman and child in Israel."[1]

Three weeks later, a colleague and I rode in a car with an Israeli friend of long standing, a highly respected diplomat. We were driving from the airport to Jerusalem. Over the years this friend had been resolutely skeptical that an Egyptian leader could sincerely want and negotiate peace with Israel. As we traveled back and forth between Egypt and Israel, we had repeatedly told him that Sadat was ready to make peace—that a new spirit characterized the leadership of Egypt. He remained doubtful. That day as our motorcade gathered speed heading from the airport toward the Judean hills and the City of Peace, he turned and said, with the seriousness and awe of personal discovery, "He really wants peace." Most of the men and women of Israel had shared in this discovery.

Progress toward an Arab-Israeli peace depends first on convincing human beings—individually and then collectively—that peace is possible. The political leader's ability to change the political environment is a prerequisite. Only after political change has occurred do the diplomat, the mediator, and the negotiator stand a chance. The obstacles to peace lie in human minds and hearts. They are psychological, human, and political. Peace will remain unattainable until we have a political strategy for breaking down the "other walls" that block our path.

When President Sadat spoke on November 20 in Jerusalem before the parliament of the Israeli people and to a watching world, he presented a negotiating position about which the Israelis did not want to hear—withdrawal to 1967 borders, a Palestinian state, an Arab role in east Jerusalem. At the same time he carried another, more basic message to the people of Israel and delivered it to them face to face at the seat of their government: Egypt accepts Israel and is ready to make peace with Israel. This second message the Israelis did hear—and wanted to hear. Sadat's visit became the act of a statesman changing the political environment and was not mainly the act of a negotiator.

Sadat set forth his own diagnosis of the obstacles to peace:

> Yet, there remains another wall. This wall constitutes a psychological barrier between us, a barrier of suspicion, a barrier of rejection; a barrier of fear, of deception, a barrier of hallucination without any action, deed or decision.
>
> A barrier of distorted and eroded interpretation of every event and statement. It is this psychological barrier which I described in official statements as constituting 70 percent of the whole problem.
>
> Today, through my visit to you, I ask why don't we stretch out our hands with faith and sincerity so that together we might destroy this barrier?[2]

In May 1985 King Hussein of Jordan in Washington spoke of the same barriers using other words:

> The Lebanese tragedy has caused both Israelis and Palestinians to reassess the validity of their previous policies. Both are now considering, simultaneously, the need for a negotiated peace. Each is skeptical. The Palestinians need hope. The Israelis need trust. It is important for all of us to provide the hope and trust they need. If we fail to do so, hope will surely turn to deeper despair and trust to invincible suspicion. The dangers for all of us, including them, will be much worse than before.[3]

Lyndon Johnson also made the point on June 19, 1967: "We are not here to judge whose fears are right or whose are wrong. Right or wrong, fear is the first obstacle to any peacemaking."[4]

This book argues that progress toward an Arab-Israeli settlement depends not just on negotiating agreements but also—indeed first—on building the human and political environment necessary for sustained negotiation. Progress toward peace depends on breaking down the barriers to negotiation and reconciliation—the other walls. If we ignore the politics of breaking down these barriers, the mediator and negotiator may never have a chance.

I do not say that progress in the peace process requires us to sweep away all hatred and misunderstanding. To make such a statement would be like stepping in quicksand. Sadat himself noted on numerous occasions that peace in the sense of normal relations would have to wait "for the next generation." That did not stop Sadat from trying to change attitudes enough so that a carefully negotiated agreement could capture the change, and consolidate a new political environment as the framework for another step. The diplomats and negotiators too often go to the other extreme, trying to negotiate without attacking the barriers—without preparing the political foundations.

What Is the Peace Process?

The subject of my book is what in the 1970s we began to call the Arab-Israeli "peace process." With U.S. help, parties to the Arab-Israeli conflict concluded the Egyptian-Israeli disengagement agreement of January 1974, the Israeli-Syrian disengagement agreement of May 1974, a second Egyptian-Israeli interim agreement in September 1975, the Camp David accords between Egypt and Israel in 1978, and the Egyptian-Israeli peace treaty in 1979. The president and secretary of state were extensively involved; Secretary Kissinger shuttled back and forth, and President Carter hosted unprecedented negotiations at Camp David and concluded them in his March 1979 trip to Egypt and Israel.

More specifically, the subject of this book is the *politics* of the peace process—the part of the process that takes place outside the negotiating room in the political arena. The peace process is more than conventional diplomacy and negotiation. It encompasses a full range of political, psychological, economic, diplomatic, and military actions woven together into a comprehensive effort to establish peace between Israel and its neighbors.

The phrase "peace process" probably has no definition in the literature of political science or international relations. We coined it in 1974–1975—using it perhaps imprecisely at first—because we needed a shorthand expression. Kissinger's shuttles and the mediated agreements held the headlines and public attention, but the negotiations were not all that was happening during those trips.

We did indeed mediate three Arab-Israeli agreements in 1974–1975, but even more important than the negotiations were the profound political reorientations that changed the political environment so that it would support those negotiations. President Sadat tried through peace to free resources to improve life in Egypt. He turned from Soviet arms and centrally planned economic development to U.S. diplomacy and an open door to Western economies. In February 1974, by promising to try to mediate an Israeli-Syrian disengagement, Kissinger elicited Saudi agreement to lift the oil embargo. Cooperative relationships between finance ministers in the key oil-producing states and Washington helped stabilize the impact on the global economy of rapidly accumulating oil revenues. Arab leaders began increasingly to accept Israel as a permanent presence and began to talk about peace. In those days, we probably hung too much on the commonplace statement that "the pursuit of an Arab-Israeli settlement is the centerpiece of American strategy in the Middle East."

As time passed, we started to use the phrase less broadly. We referred less to our own regional strategy and more pointedly mentioned the politics and diplomacy involved in bringing the parties in the conflict to the peace table and to agreement once they had begun negotiating. The more the political situation settled down after the 1973 War and the oil embargo, the more we concentrated on ways of bringing about the next step in negotiation. During his first year in office, President Carter focused on arranging for resumption of the Middle East Peace Conference in Geneva to negotiate a comprehensive peace. In his second year he focused on ways of translating Sadat's visit to Jerusalem into concrete agreements and practical progress toward peace. That year witnessed the unique negotiations at Camp David and the beginning of negotiations on the Egyptian-Israeli peace treaty. The third year saw ratification of the peace treaty and the beginning of negotiations on autonomy for the Palestinian inhabitants of the West Bank and Gaza. We understandably came to see the peace process in terms of the negotiations and the agreements they produced.

The more sharply we examine the process as it occurred back in the 1970s, however, the more acutely we become aware of the political character of the tools used to move that process forward. From our perspective in the mid-1980s, we can again sense the frustration we felt during those long periods when it seemed impossible to get negotiations started. We remember that the 1973 War and President Sadat's visit to Jerusalem—both political acts—largely created the environment for negotiation. We also recall that even the breakthroughs in negotiation resulted from political acts, that is, from Carter's unprecedented invitations to Camp David in 1978 and from his sudden trip to Egypt and Israel in 1979. These events set the stage for the diplomatic formulations that, in a supportive political environment, could break negotiating stalemates.

Any negotiating process encompasses two large periods—one that precedes actual negotiation and one that starts when negotiators are gathered around the table. The theorists and the diplomats normally concentrate on identifying the formulas and techniques that are useful in the negotiating room. They have historically paid less attention to ways

4

of persuading people to enter that room. I make this distinction to under-score the heavily political character of the job that must be done before negotiations can begin. Techniques that may prove effective when the parties are sitting at the table may not be adequate in the earlier period, when the main task is to create a positive political environment. It remains important to build political support even during negotiation, but we neglect the politics of getting to negotiation.

The first period is sometimes a long and complicated stage, when parties are deciding whether or not to commit themselves to a peaceful settlement—or at least they are deciding that they will seriously explore the possibility of negotiating and will try to define what a negotiation would look like. Some leaders may explore out of conviction. Others may do so because they feel under pressure. In either case, one purpose will be to determine whether negotiation might produce a politically defensible agreement. The first period is mainly a time when political foundations for negotiation are built.

The second period chiefly involves active negotiation. What goes on around the negotiating table has its own character and intricacy. Even at this point, sustaining serious negotiation and eventually winning support for its results may depend heavily on the political foundations laid earlier and on their reinforcement during the negotiation and afterward. The necessary foundations will be built outside the negotiating room.

By placing present diplomatic situations in such an analytical framework, we may be better able to identify the real obstacles to a negotiated peace and to concentrate our efforts on breaking them down. Revival of the peace process in the mid-1980s will require the United States to pay much more attention to laying the political foundations for negotiation than it has paid at any time in the past. The first years of the 1980s were a period of stagnation. After the Egyptian-Israeli treaty had been signed in March 1979, attention shifted to Israel's eastern frontiers with Jordan, to the Palestinians, and to Syria. On those frontiers the foundations for negotiation had not been laid. Large political obstacles remained. The tools for overcoming them are more likely to involve building confidence than drafting the right formulas and texts. The other walls that block the way to peace are often barriers in human perception and feeling that are all too infrequently addressed by the diplomatic options papers.

A Word about Politics and Diplomacy

I do not intend to distinguish between politics and diplomacy rigidly or artificially, but it is critical to reflect on differences in focus. The diplomacy practiced by a statesman can be a political art; politics are the object of the diplomat's analysis and reporting. Nevertheless, there is a sharp distinction in the world of government between the diplomats and those who wield political power. Apart from natural differences in background and abilities, anyone who has served, as I have, on the National Security Council staff, bridging the gap between presidents and career officials, has felt the deep-seated mutual suspicion. I mention the distinction here solely to draw attention to the politics of the peace process.

The words "politics" and "diplomacy" in their dictionary definitions carry different connotations. Politics normally prompts us to think of relationships within a political community that are ordered so as to provide organization, direction, protection, control, and regulation for individual members. Diplomacy is normally regarded as meaning the art of conducting relations and negotiations between nations to settle differences between them and to maintain a relationship based on common interests.

More important is the difference that stands out in stark terms for the diplomats, elected officials, and political appointees in governments. The distinction between the people who lead governments and those who staff them is keenly felt within those governments. In the United States, career Foreign Service officers are prohibited by law from participating in our national politics except to cast their own votes. (I recall a note in which President Nixon warned the National Security Council staff not to mention domestic politics in memos to him.) Career officers are frequently banned from meetings at the higher political levels. Such professionals are associated with an analytical community outside government in which academic specialists in international relations study regional cultures or try to refine concepts such as interests and models of negotiation. In short, career officers are encouraged to think analytically and not in terms of political maneuver and influence.

In the American system, political maneuver and influence wielding are most often left to the president and his advisers at the political levels of government. There politicians work in a world where success depends on the ability to control and rally other human beings. In this world human emotion controls as much as reason—emotion in the form of ambition and insecurity, hope and defensiveness against assaults on identity, inspiration and challenges from political opposition, addiction to power, and uncertainty.

The difference came home to me one morning as I sat at the large table in the conference room next to the Jerusalem office of the Israeli prime minister. My colleagues and I had spent most of the night working on papers for the next day's talks and negotiations. As we sat on one side of the table beside our president, facing the Israeli prime minister and his team on the other, I thought, "We spent most of the night writing what the president should persuade the prime minister to accept. Now the president actually has to persuade that man across the table to do what the president wants him to do. How different the jobs of the politician and the diplomat!"

Close cooperation between the political and the career levels of government has been a principal American achievement at the high points in the peace process. Kissinger during the shuttles was obliged to operate at some distance from the White House, but he reported to the president scrupulously and in detail to insure close coordination and full, continuing support. Nightly we drafted a telegram explaining the issues of the day and each side's positions. President Carter at Camp David used his professional diplomatic team well, and it equipped political leaders to reach agreements that could win the support of their peoples. As we sat together on the helicopter lifting off from Camp David, national security adviser Zbigniew Brzezinski said, with some surprise as well as satisfaction, "The White House and the State Department worked well together." Such moments of cooperation are not necessarily the rule. At less distinguished moments the national security adviser and the secretary of state have feuded.

Politics and diplomacy would be inseparable in an ideal world, but in the real world we must recognize that their practitioners may naturally have different perspectives on a problem. Each may ignore some important aspects. If the Arab-Israeli peace process is seen as a highly political process and not only as a negotiating process, politicians as well as diplomats will need to be heavily and continuously involved, because their abilities and influence will be indispensable. Diplomats will have to think harder about how to support the politicians in their efforts.

A Conflict between Two Peoples

A first step in focusing political efforts to achieve peace involves defining the conflict that the peace process must be designed to resolve. In the case of the Arabs and the Israelis, the definition has itself been the subject of heated controversy.

The Arab-Israeli conflict has pitted two peoples—Jews and Palestinian Arabs—against each other within the larger conflict between Israel and neighboring Arab states. Over the years, perceptions of the strife have changed. Neither the people-to-people conflict nor the state-to-state conflict can be ignored. I underscore the human center of the conflict because the most deeply rooted barriers to peace lie there. States will not resolve their conflict until the two peoples with claims to the same land resolve theirs. The Arab states cannot accept Israel until the Israeli-Palestinian dimension of the conflict has been justly and compassionately addressed.

The effort to achieve peace between Jews and Arabs in Palestine dates back more than half a century. In the beginning, the conflict engaged two peoples, each believing that it belonged in the same land. The conflict between the two peoples—between the two national movements—continues. To it was added in 1948 a conflict among states. The existing Arab states rejected the partition of Palestine between Jews and Arabs and refused to recognize or accept the newly independent State of Israel. When Israel had declared its independence in May 1948, the recurring violence between the two peoples became all-out war as Arab armies attacked the new state. After more than a year of fighting, armistice agreements were signed between states in 1949. The conflict that had lasted for more than two decades between two peoples, Jews and Palestinian Arabs—between two national movements—became the Arab-Israeli state-to-state conflict. Until the early 1970s the Arab states played the Arab role in Palestine. The Palestinians lived as refugees or as ethnically distinct groups in others' states.

The feelings of the two peoples, although momentarily submerged in the politics of states, were no less acute. During a visit to the Middle East just before the 1967 War, I was taken by my Israeli host to Yad Vashem, the memorial in Jerusalem to the victims of the Nazi Holocaust. "Until you understand this, you cannot understand the people of modern Israel," he said. A few days later, one of the managers of a Palestinian refugee camp near Jericho told me that he could walk to the hills of east Jerusalem and see his former home across the armistice line. "We want the world and especially you Americans to recognize that we have suffered injustice," he added. The Jews had their state, but their pain governed their actions. The Palestinians were a dispersed and—except in Jordan—a stateless people, but their consciousness as a people slowly took political form. In 1964 the Palestine Liberation Organization (PLO) was established.

The Six Day War, June 5-10, 1967, changed the character of the conflict more than most of us recognized at the time. At the end of that war, Israel controlled all the land west of the Jordan River—all the land of Palestine that had been partitioned by the armistice lines of 1949. For the first time one-party control of the entire area for a prolonged period became a physical possibility. This stark fact rekindled the full range of intense Israeli and Palestinian nationalist feelings and hopes. A new generation of Israelis grew to adulthood picturing their state as including all the land west of the Jordan. People who were determined to make control of that territory permanent became a powerful political force within Israel. The Palestinians began to see that their chances of expressing their identity as a people by establishing their own homeland in Palestine were fading.

8

Partly reacting to this threat to their identity, the Palestine Liberation Organization in the early 1970s achieved widespread recognition as the organization of the Palestinian movement. In 1974 the Arab states formally declared the PLO the "sole legitimate representative of the Palestinian people."[5] The Arab governments stepped back to let the Palestinian people speak and negotiate for themselves. Partly because the land on which they want to establish their homeland lies between Israel and Jordan, reconciliation of the Israeli and Palestinian peoples seems integral to any resolution of the state-to-state conflict.

The notion that a conflict between two peoples lies at the heart of the conflict between states has been controversial. In November 1975, the Middle East Subcommittee of the House Foreign Affairs Committee invited the Ford administration to send a witness to hearings on the Palestinian problem. As the lowest ranking of four people who could have been sent, from Kissinger down, I was delegated. I was chosen so that the testimony would seem more analytical than political or policy related in character. In a prepared statement cleared well in advance with Kissinger, I expressed the views of the officials then engaged in the peace process:

> We have also repeatedly stated that the legitimate interests of the Palestinian Arabs must be taken into account in the negotiation of an Arab-Israeli peace. In many ways, the Palestinian dimension of the Arab-Israeli conflict is the heart of that conflict. Final resolution of the problems arising from the partition of Palestine, the establishment of the State of Israel, and Arab onposition to those events will not be possible until agreement is reached defining a just and permanent status for the Arab peoples who consider themselves Palestinians.[6]

The Israeli government and the Israeli lobby condemned this statement—which was the first comprehensive one made by the United States on the subject—and thereby gave it wide currency in the Arab world. The Israelis declared that the heart of the conflict was not the Palestinian problem but Arab refusal to accept Israel. In 1978 at Camp David, and in the Knesset's subsequent endorsement, Israel itself agreed to "negotiations on the resolution of the Palestinian problem in all its aspects."[7] Today, in the mid-1980s, the solutions of the two conflicts are much more widely regarded as interdependent.

At the height of reaction to the statement, Kissinger dismissed reporters' questions, asking them whether they expected him to pay attention to every statement by a deputy assistant secretary. When I walked into his office at one point, he said with an unusually benign smile, "You caused quite a fuss. But I cleared it." There was no question in American

9

minds that resolving the conflict between the two peoples was the key to acceptance of Israel by Arab governments.

Peace Efforts, 1967–1973

The substantive and procedural elements of the peace process were laid out and tested in the years between the 1967 and 1973 Wars, but the barriers to peace were not removed. The question is whether those barriers could have been removed by peaceful means or whether only another war could shake them.

Before the larger consequences of the Six Day War had been fully understood, political leaders in the United States agreed that new efforts should be made to resolve the conflict once and for all. This time, they said, Israeli troops will stay put until there is peace. Like many other basic choices with regard to the direction of policy, this one was made instinctively—not by formal decision. No one ever sat down and examined the consequences of the position that had been taken.

On November 22, 1967, the Security Council of the United Nations nevertheless enshrined the objective in Resolution 242—a painstakingly balanced formula for an Arab-Israeli peace settlement that had one notable omission—political participation by the Palestinians, whom Resolution 242 mentioned only as refugees although Arab governments had been actively involved in negotiating its wording.[8] While any paraphrase of so delicately balanced a resolution risks distortion, it seems fair to say that Resolution 242 called for a "just and lasting peace," recognition, and security for all states in the region, including Israel, in return for Israel's withdrawal from territories occupied in the war. Resolution 242 pursued the position toward the Palestinian question that the United States had taken since the mid-1940s—that Palestine should be partitioned and shared by Jews and Palestinian Arabs. In the American view, the parties could evolve the terms of peace only in negotiations. "Clearly the parties to the conflict must be the parties to the peace," said Lyndon Johnson on June 19, 1967.[9]

Under the Johnson administration, responsibility for negotiating a settlement within the framework of Resolution 242 passed to Ambassador Gunnar Jarring, a representative of the United Nations secretary general. Although the United States provided active diplomatic support for the Jarring Mission, the president in 1967 and 1968 felt that the U.S. government was too heavily engaged in Vietnam to play a central role as mediator.

When the Nixon administration came to office in January 1969, with Henry Kissinger as national security adviser, the administration gave higher priority to dealing with the Arab-Israeli conflict but still did not put forward a U.S. mediation effort until a war of attrition across the Suez Canal had intensified in early 1970 and the Jarring Mission seemed to have lost momentum in early 1971. The Nixon administration's early effort instead attempted to establish a larger international political environment—particularly through a new relationship with the Soviet Union —in which the Arab-Israeli impasse might be surmounted.

During the first years after the 1967 War and the passage of Resolution 242, the aim in working toward a peaceful settlement was to negotiate a comprehensive settlement, which we called a "package deal." All outstanding issues had to be addressed in a settlement before real peace could exist. In other words, all outstanding issues between Israel and each of its neighbors had to be resolved, and there had to be understanding on various critical issues, including the status of Jerusalem, a refugee settlement, and freedom of passage through international waterways such as the Strait of Tiran.

In early 1971, focus began to shift to taking partial steps toward peace. The United States played a central role during the summer of 1970 in mediating a ceasefire and standstill agreement to end Egyptian-Israeli fighting. It was coupled with an agreement to attempt a diplomatic settlement. When Ambassador Jarring was unable to arrange a full-scale negotiation, President Sadat in early 1971, with tacit U.S. and Israeli encouragement, suggested trying to negotiate an agreement for partial withdrawal around the Suez Canal, so that the canal could reopen to world shipping. The effort eventually foundered, but the stage was set for a series of steps and interim agreements that would gradually advance toward comprehensive settlement.

Like the 1967 War, the full implications of Anwar Sadat's inauguration as president of Egypt after the death of Gamal Abdel Nasser in September 1970 were not at first fully understood. Unlike his predecessor, Sadat was determined to relieve the human problems of Egypt. To achieve that goal he needed to end the Arab-Israeli conflict, which had drained Egypt's resources, energies, imagination, and manpower for almost three decades.

In the early summer of 1973, having explored a half dozen other methods, Sadat determined that he had no alternative but to go to war. It was a war not to recapture all of Egypt's lost territory but to change the political environment. The limited purposes of that war were (1) to restore Arab honor by erasing the humiliation of the 1967 defeat so that Egypt could negotiate with Israel from a position of dignity and (2) to bring the superpowers more actively into the negotiating process with concern for a fair settlement. He succeeded on both counts.

The 1973 War set the stage for the peace process of the mid-1970s. The war ended with passage of Resolution 338 in the United Nations

Security Council.[10] That resolution called for immediately beginning negotiations within the framework of Resolution 242. In addition to agreeing on the wording of Resolution 338, the foreign ministers of the United States and the Soviet Union agreed to convene the Middle East Peace Conference in Geneva in December 1973 as cochairmen under the auspices of the secretary general of the United Nations. This step paved the way for the beginning of the intense diplomatic and political effort that came to be called the Arab-Israeli peace process.

When Kissinger flew into Cairo for the first time in early November, he and Sadat seemed almost immediately to be speaking the same political language. Apart from an end to the conflict with Israel, Sadat told the secretary of state, the economic progress of Egypt depended on reorienting the focus of Egypt's prime international relationships from the East to the West, where the resources, creative impetus, and technology for development could be found. Kissinger could not resist the opportunity to shift the map of strategic allegiances in the Middle East. In Sadat, however, Kissinger found a man prepared to engage in political maneuver that might at least enable him to test how much the war had shaken the barriers to Egyptian-Israeli negotiation.

In January 1974, at the height of the first shuttle, I spoke with an Egyptian colleague in the garden of Sadat's house at the Barrages, where the Nile delta begins. He, too, had lost his wife a short time before, so our conversation was warmly personal. As our talk shifted back to the negotiations, he lamented that the United States had not more actively supported peace efforts between 1967 and 1973. "We're surely involved now," I replied. "Yes," he said quietly but poignantly. "But it took a war to get you here."

Kissinger argues that only an event with the impact of war could have created the political environment for negotiation. I continue to wonder whether the war would have been necessary if the United States had marshaled the same intense political effort in 1971 or early 1973 that it did in the first half of 1974, after the oil embargo and the tragic waste of the war. Whatever answer history may provide, the peace process of the 1970s was influenced by the experience of 1967–1973.

Why Should a President Care?

Why should the human being who is president of the United States be interested, spend his time and energy, and invest his political capital in trying to promote Arab-Israeli peace? The role that powerful nations outside the Middle East—particularly the Soviet Union and the United States—will play in changing the political environment is a critical question. During the 1970s, President Sadat called the United States a "full

12

partner"—not just a mailman or a mediator but a partner, introducing its own views and ideas to produce a fair solution. During the 1970s, we learned that progress was possible but that it required intense involvement at the highest political levels of our government. I shall address the role of third parties—mainly the superpowers—in a later chapter. The issue for Americans is how much of its energy and resources the United States should invest in the peace process. More specifically, in our system of government the question is: Why should a president care?

Although some of the parties to the Arab-Israeli-Palestinian conflict may have different views, I suggest that (1) steady pressure toward an Arab-Israeli-Palestinian peace serves the interests of the United States; (2) peace is possible, and substantial progress has been made; (3) once political foundations have been laid, a settlement can be achieved only through some carefully prepared process of negotiation.

First: Steady pressure to move toward a just and secure peace settlement serves the interests of the United States.

To sustain its position as a world leader, the United States must be able to use its power effectively in good times and in bad. The issue is not only whether active U.S. involvement in the peace process will produce visible progress in the near future but also whether global stakes and interest in maintaining a strong U.S. position in the Middle East justify effectual involvement appropriate to the situation. The issue is whether the United States will be seen as a world power effective in recognizing early enough how change will affect its interests and in asserting its influence to shape events as much as any outsider can. I do not prescribe a mindless interventionism; I maintain, rather, that the United States must be seen to have a clear purpose both when it acts and when it does not act.

Most observers view the Middle East as being in transition from one political era to the next. Few Americans have recognized the full meaning of the changes that are taking place. In the 1970s there seemed to be an opportunity to realize the just and secure Arab-Israeli-Palestinian peace settlement that the United States had envisioned for almost thirty years. That opportunity seems to be disappearing. If it continues to do so, a long-term alternative will perhaps be a shift in the strategic and political map of the Middle East. Syrian military forces are becoming steadily stronger, with significant Soviet help. The Syrians are already the dominant power in Lebanon. When the Iran-Iraq war winds down, the armed forces of Iraq—still a treaty partner of the Soviet Union despite its resumption of relations with the United States in 1984—will be battle tested and well equipped. Jordan, long a quiescent buffer on Israel's longest border, has a population that is two-thirds Palestinian. It will be subjected to unique pressure to become more Palestinian and to become a base from which pressure can be exerted on Israel to create a Palestinian state. Islamic fundamentalism could turn a negotiable conflict between states into a religious conflict that has no peaceful solution in the near term. If it does, the United States will lose the opportunity—at least until after the next war—to help negotiate peace between Israel and its neighbors in a way that will enhance the long-term future of Israel and that of responsible Arab governments as well as the stature and position of the United States.

The approach taken to the Arab-Israeli-Palestinian conflict will shape the future. Experience from 1974 through 1979—apart from the civil war in Lebanon—seemed to demonstrate that an active political process moving toward a settlement provides a constructive alternative to war and radical political programs and engages the United States in productive relationships with the key countries in the Near East. If the situation is allowed to drift, leaders who would risk a negotiated settlement will forfeit a politically defensible alternative to policies that aim for radical solutions. Drift increases the vulnerability of governments that we regard as moderate.

Not every American will agree with me. Some will advise the president that, because the Arab-Israeli conflict is intractable, he should not invest his energies or prestige in a no-win situation. The scene in the Middle East, they will argue, has changed since the Egyptian-Israeli peace treaty was signed in 1979. An unprecedented coalition of opposing parties governs Israel; the last election showed Israel to be deeply and broadly divided. The Palestine Liberation Organization is also fragmented, and it is difficult to know what its leadership could do if precise decisions on peace were required. No progress has been made since 1980 in continuing the negotiation of the Israeli-Palestinian settlement designed at Camp David. Although President Sadat's successor is committed to the peace treaty, failure to advance toward an Israeli-Palestinian settlement, together with the Israeli invasion of Lebanon, has strained Egyptian-Israeli relations. More broadly, Islamic fundamentalism remains strong, and governments across the Middle East face a rising generation that might sweep them away. Until the parties in the Middle East pull themselves together, some American advisers may argue, the United States should stand back.

I take a different view. The influence of a great nation may be measured more by its approach to intractable problems than by its approach to those that are susceptible to early solution. Leaders sometimes establish their influence most significantly in the most difficult moments, as they begin struggling to change a situation that threatens to become desperate. To be sure, there are moments when it is wise for the United States to stand back and let pressure work on the parties to a conflict to assess their own interests and the actions they are prepared to take in pursuing them. Even then, a quiet American role—played with confidence and purpose—can help shape options and can strengthen leaders who want to move toward peace but need encouragement and help. On other occasions, after careful and usually private preparation, visible American involvement can crystallize agreements that create a new political environment. Whatever the particular moment, a great power must decide the precise nature and timing of its own involvement after considering its situation, where it wants to go, and how it envisions getting there.

In the 1970s, political forces supporting a negotiated peace were turned loose by the 1973 War, by President Sadat's visit to Jerusalem, by President Carter's unprecedented intervention at Camp David, and by Prime Minister Begin's decisions in making peace with Egypt. When those forces had been set in motion, mediators had a chance of working out agreements. In the first half of the 1980s, the forces became depleted and fragmented. Any new effort to revive the peace process now must begin not with negotiating formulations but with a new focus on ways of releasing and positioning fresh political forces to demand peace. The question is whether the United States can creatively and effectually help shape that process. Americans can be proud of themselves when they help others effectively move toward peace. We work for peace because it is right, and it eases human suffering. Moreover, any president should want to make the United States a country that knows where it is going and how to get there.

Second: Progress toward peace has been achieved and remains possible. There is common ground for negotiation where little existed before 1973.

Despite the remaining obstacles to negotiation and settlement, we cannot disregard the positive changes of the past decade. People who do not want to negotiate stress the negative viewpoint. In reality, the glass is partly full—not completely empty.

To begin with, the historic peace treaty between Egypt and Israel passed its sixth anniversary in March 1985 despite the strains to which it has been subjected. It survived the fading of the post–Camp David talks on autonomy for the inhabitants of the West Bank and Gaza. It was severely tested by the 1982 Israeli invasion of Lebanon. Erosion has unquestionably taken place. Egypt expressed its intense disapproval in the normal diplomatic way, by recalling its ambassador to Israel—a measure that was, as President Mubarak said, "the least I could do." Beneath the diplomatic reaction, Egypt suffered deep political disillusionment regarding Israel's use of force in Lebanon and the bombing of the Iraqi nuclear reactor. Israel in its turn became disillusioned at Egypt's reluctance to proceed with normalization. As was stated repeatedly during negotiation of the treaty, the quality of the normalization of relations continues to depend on the quality of the continuing peace process as it addresses the relationship between Israel and the Palestinians and also that between Israel and its other eastern neighbors. Yet Egypt remains committed to the peace process for its own reasons. As Egypt slowly resumes normal relations with the Arab states while maintaining its relationship with Israel, Arab-Israeli relationships could subtly change if the political environment is constructive.

In a longer perspective, the declaration of Arab leaders from their summit meeting in Fez in September 1982, with Palestinian leaders participating, contrasts sharply with the "three nos" of the 1967 Khartoum summit declaration—no recognition of Israel, no negotiation with Israel, no peace with Israel.[11] Egypt, Jordan, Syria, and Lebanon have all met and negotiated with Israel, stating their intent to negotiate an eventual peace. The Fez Declaration mentions Israeli withdrawal to pre-1967 lines and the establishment of an independent Palestinian state and calls for protecting the security of *all* states in the area. Arab leaders have unequivocally stated both privately and publicly that the phrase "all states" includes Israel.

Whatever mental reservations may be revealed by the Arabs' failure to mention Israel by name, these statements do differ from those made in 1967. Syrians, for instance, have said quite straightforwardly that they will explicitly name Israel when Israel has put its negotiating map on the table, as the Arabs have done. The Arab position has changed; Arabs now recognize that Israel is established and must be dealt with. I do not mean that Arabs fully accept Israel's presence or that Arabs would acknowledge Israel's "right" to part of Palestine. I mean rather that the Arab world no longer insists on a one-state solution in Palestine but instead accepts a two-state solution.

As a result, Israel today has a choice that it did not have a decade or more ago. It can test the Arabs' statements that they are ready to make peace with Israel provided that Israel shares the land west of the Jordan River with the Palestinians, recognizing the Palestinians as a people with equal rights. Today, and not in the earlier periods when Israel negotiated with Jordan and Egypt, Israel can consider that an Arab party negotiating after the Fez Declaration has the backdrop of an Arab summit decision that accepts the security of all states in the region. Alternatively, Israel can leave the Arab statements untested and perpetuate its control over territories it occupied in 1967 to bring 1.3 million more Arabs within the State of Israel.

Clearly, areas of wide disagreement still exist, but individuals who want to explore the possibilities for developing a basis for negotiation must identify points on which agreement is emerging. Some are evident from a reading of Resolutions 242 and 338, the Camp David accords, President Reagan's speech of September 1, 1982, the Fez Declaration from the Arab summit in 1982, and the Hussein-Arafat agreement of February 1985.[12] Even more important, people in the Middle East show a readiness to reach a settlement with Israel that did not exist in the early 1970s. Common points, stated in different ways from different premises and with different objectives in mind, exist in the following areas:

- The objective of Middle East diplomacy should be to achieve a just peace in the Middle East.
- A just peace requires international guarantees for peace among *all* states of the region. The Fez Declaration does not mention Israel by name, but Arab leaders have stated on the record that the Fez Declaration envisions peace with Israel. Israel does not include a Palestinian state in its conceptualization, but many Israelis acknowledge that a Palestinian identity must find political expression in Palestine apart from Israel.
- Peace among all states of the region will require Israeli withdrawal from territories occupied in 1967. The Arabs say withdrawal from "all" those territories and include east Jerusalem. Camp David allows for negotiation of the "secure and recognized boundaries" mentioned in Resolution 242, but Camp David also envisions Israeli withdrawal. Not all Israelis agree that withdrawal entails Arab sovereignty in the areas from which Israeli troops would withdraw, but they seem to recognize that military occupation is an abnormal condition and should not continue.
- If Israel is to withdraw from territories occupied in 1967, there must be a transitional period under an interim authority during which the political life and the security of the areas from which Israel has withdrawn can be organized. The Camp David accords call for a five-year transitional period; the Fez Declaration calls for a few months. The Camp David accords call for an elected Palestinian self-governing body as the transitional authority; the Fez Declaration calls for supervision by the United Nations. The concept of transitional arrangements, however, has found expression in authoritative statements made on both sides.
- Freedom of worship and religious rights for all faiths concerned with the holy shrines of Jerusalem and the West Bank must be guaranteed.

I mention these points not because their utterance by both sides indicates wide agreement on the details of a settlement but to underscore the contrast between the situation today and that in the period before 1973. The reservations that attend statements of Arab positions today differ from those of 1967 in significant ways that cannot be overlooked.

I do not mean, furthermore, that the parties are united internally around these common points; they are not. Yet although neither side is monolithic, on each side the number of people who would find common ground for negotiation is increasing.

Let me state the point I am making carefully: There is more common ground for negotiation than there was in 1973. A significant number of Arabs are ready for peace with Israel if Israel will share Palestine with the Palestinians. A significant number of Israelis believe that a just peace requires that Palestinian identity find political expression. As yet there is no common view of the precise nature of the settlement.

One purpose in moving toward negotiation would be to test the accuracy of the statement in the preceding paragraph. People who do not press the test cannot be serious about negotiating a settlement.

Third: Once political foundations have been laid, a peace settlement can be achieved only through a carefully prepared process of negotiation.

Only in the give and take of negotiation can the essential interests of each party be determined and the achievable solutions defined. The parties must consider the alternative solutions before they can decide realistically which ones are politically sustainable. Politically sustainable agreements alone will stand the test of time and will continue to be observed by each party. Only a negotiated agreement can define trade-offs and safeguards precisely enough so that governments' decisions will be lasting. Perhaps most important, only in preparing for negotiation can leaders test the other side's determination to reach agreement and decide whether the political risks involved in negotiating are worth taking.

The remainder of this book focuses on the obstacles to negotiation on Israel's eastern borders and on how those obstacles might steadily be dismantled. One key to breaking an impasse is to understand why parties will *not* talk.

We may legitimately debate the steps toward negotiation that are possible at any given time, but a serious discussion requires an understanding of the prerequisites for negotiation. A serious peace effort is an essential and constructive part of American policy in the Middle East even if it moves very slowly. Whether or not everyone agrees with this statement, the analytical community has an obligation to describe the options that would be open to the policy makers if they wanted to revive the negotiating process. The purpose of this book is to analyze where we are in the Middle East peace process and what could be done to move negotiations forward.

The Essence of This Book

This book is less concerned than the Brookings report of 1975 or the Seven Springs report of 1981 with describing a possible settlement.[13] Like the agreement at Camp David, it seeks to define a way of looking at

18

the problem and a process that will lead us toward a settlement. Specifically, we need to know how to shape a political environment in which negotiation can take place and agreements can be fashioned and implemented. My aim is more to refocus perspectives and discussion than to define specific steps or solutions.

The analytical framework that I present in the next chapter, "A Fresh Look at the Peace Process," is essential for an understanding of my approach to the peace process and my emphasis on building political foundations. The first and closing sections of chapters 3 through 7 on Israel, the Palestinians, Jordan, Syria, and Eygpt, can be read independently of the full chapters. Chapter 9 suggests political steps that leaders can take to build the political foundations for negotiation; the concluding section, "Making Negotiation Happen," provides a menu of such steps. Chapter 10 describes the peace process as I hope a leader might conceptualize it.

In turning to more detailed analysis, we should remember the challenge that confronts the leaders of nations. The peace process of the mid-1970s was triggered by the 1973 War. The Lebanon War in 1982 showed that there is no military solution to the Israeli-Palestinian conflict. Will yet another war or a bloodbath in the West Bank be needed to bring the process to life again? Have the politics of impasse so paralyzed leaders that no peaceful alternatives remain? Can statesmen perhaps skillfully turn the politics of impasse into the politics of progress?

Notes

1. *The Search for Peace in the Middle East: Documents and Statements, 1967–1979,* Report prepared for the Subcommittee on Europe and the Middle East of the Committee on Foreign Affairs, U.S. House of Representatives, by the Foreign Affairs and National Defense Division, Congressional Research Service, Library of Congress, Committee Print CP-957 (Washington, D.C.: U.S. Government Printing Office, 1979), p. 227.

2. Ibid., p. 226.

3. His Majesty King Hussein, Address delivered at the American Enterprise Institute for Public Policy Research, Washington, D.C., May 1985, p. 11. (Text available from the Jordan Information Bureau, 1701 K Street, N.W., Washington, D.C. 20006.)

4. *The Search for Peace in the Middle East,* p. 289.

5. Ibid., p. 273. The text of the communiqué from the Arab League summit conference at Rabat in October 1974 appears in appendix V.

6. Ibid., p. 305.

7. Ibid., p. 21. The text of "A Framework for Peace in the Middle East Agreed at Camp David" appears in appendix VII.

8. Ibid., p. 93. The text of Resolution 242 appears in appendix I.

9. Ibid., p. 288.

10. Ibid., p. 97. The text of Resolution 338 appears in appendix IV.

11. The text of the Fez Declaration, originally published in the *New York Times*, September 10, 1982, p. A8, appears in appendix IX. The text of the Arab League summit conference communiqué from Khartoum, found in *The Search for Peace in the Middle East*, p. 269, appears in appendix II.

12. The text of President Reagan's speech, in *Weekly Compilation of Presidential Documents* September 6, vol. 18, no. 35 (1982), pp. 1081–85, appears in appendix VIII. The text of the Hussein-Arafat agreement, published in Foreign Broadcast Information Service, *Daily Report: Middle East and Africa*, February 25, 1985, appears in appendix X.

13. *Toward Peace in the Middle East: Report of a Study Group* (Washington, D.C.: The Brookings Institution, 1975). Joseph N. Greene, Jr., Philip M. Klutznick, Harold H. Saunders, and Merle Thorpe, Jr., *The Path to Peace: Arab-Israeli Peace and the United States, Report of a Study Mission to the Middle East* (Mount Kisco, N.Y.: Seven Springs Center, 1981).

2

A Fresh Look at the Peace Process

Finding the Right Focus

In 1977 the United States was trying to revive the Middle East peace negotiations using tools that were not likely to break down the real obstacles to peace. We were energetically using the tools of the lawyer and the diplomat—working papers and carefully drafted diplomatic formulas—yet as President Sadat saw, large human and political obstacles still blocked the path to peace. When President Carter wrote, asking for Sadat's support, Sadat saw the U.S. approach running out of steam and Carter unable to give it the political push it needed. He went to Jerusalem.

By the end of the 1970s, Americans had come to think of the Arab-Israeli negotiations in terms of the familiar pictures of Egyptians and Israelis sitting across the table from each other, with lawyers exchanging texts, military men swapping maps and timetables, and political leaders meeting to sign agreements. Most Americans let slip from mind the nearly thirty years of bitterness and hatred, the terrorist and retaliatory attacks, and the five armed conflicts that preceded those around-the-table negotiations. Memory faded of those years when one side would not even speak of peace with the other, when face-to-face negotiations were impossible. In the 1980s the peace process slowed almost to a stop. It then became critical to step back and refocus our picture of that process.

When the new American presidential term began in January 1985, sustained Arab-Israeli peace negotiations had been suspended for more than four years. The Israel-Syria disengagement of 1974, "A Framework for Peace in the Middle East Agreed at Camp David" in 1978, the Egypt-Israel peace treaty of 1979, the Fahd Plan of 1981, President Reagan's speech of September 1, 1982, the Fez Declaration of 1982, the Israel-Lebanon agreement of May 1983—all were on the record. Shortly after President Reagan's second inauguration, on February 11, 1985, a new initiative was launched, beginning with an agreement between King Hussein of Jordan and Yasser Arafat, chairman of the Palestine Liberation Organization. Each of the documents played a role in recording and consolidating changing perceptions. Yet despite the shift in the political environment, negotiations did not start again. Something was lacking.

The key to getting negotiations started lies in understanding why people fear coming to the table. That is why I have chosen to focus on the political and psychological blockages in the period before negotiations begin and on specific political strategies for reducing those obstacles. Let us start, then, by analyzing how the peace process works and then consider the positions of each of the main parties to the conflict in the perspective of that framework. Careful analysis should help us understand more vividly where the peace process stands, why parties hesitate to negotiate, and what might be done to create a political environment more favorable to negotiation. It is not enough to write another paper on "next steps in the Middle East." My aim is to suggest a different focus—a political focus—in approaching the barriers to peace.

The Peace Process: An Analytical Framework

My experience in the Middle East peace process during the 1970s suggests that that process has five parts. I do not feel rigidly bound to the list below, but the overall analytic approach seems to me conceptually useful in identifying what needs to happen at different points along the path to negotiation and beyond.

Although I might equally well speak of these "parts" as "stages" or "phases" of the process, I do *not* view them as a succession of discrete stages, each of which is complete before the next begins. Experience has a chronological element, but in human terms, important issues are rarely completely resolved. Later changes in course are seldom impossible, and an early decision is often refined as later decisions are made in new contexts. For our purposes here it is important to give special thought to the particular questions, decisions, and activities that predominate in each of the five stages.

Psychiatrists who follow the progress of an individual mourning a personal loss observe a similar progression of stages marked by partial retracing of steps. They identify a chronological unfolding of changes in perception—changes that reflect continuous reshaping rather than a progression of discrete stages. They also explain that, before a person's basic perceptions can be changed in any context, the person must often give up some important part of his picture of the world. As people's pictures of reality change, they must often be helped to find ways of mourning what they have given up. When Israel took the final steps in withdrawing from the Sinai in April 1982, for instance, the government bulldozed Yamit— Israel's last settlement there. It did so to prevent the settlers from returning in secret. The government probably did not intend by its action to demonstrate the finality of the loss, but its action served the purpose of allowing an outburst of anger over the loss and paved the way for eventual acceptance.

Defining the Problem. Early in the negotiating process, each party will define its feelings, objectives, and aspirations in relation to a situation, interpreting the situation by itself and in relation to the larger world view and objectives of policy makers. It may seem academic to say that the negotiating process begins with a definition of the problem, but in policy making, how one defines a problem begins to determine what one will do about it. Bear in mind that Israel, the Palestinians, the Arab states, and the United States are all deeply divided internally on the issue of the Arab-Israeli conflict. Heated national debate can focus on the definition of a problem because people with a stake in the direction policy will take know that how the problem is defined will shape policy decisions. Disagreements lead factions that hold different views to kill each other. Palestinians are assassinated for envisioning a negotiated settlement with Israel. For the first time, Israelis are talking about Israelis killing Israelis who hold different visions of the future of the Jewish state.

Since negotiation is shared decision making on a shared problem, we must understand (1) how nearly unified or divided each party is internally in defining its objectives and (2) how the parties differ from each other in their definitions of a problem. In the real world, we cannot expect unanimity before negotiations begin, but by comparing definitions to see where they diverge we take an essential analytical step in identifying the barriers.

A critical moment in the preparation for negotiations comes when each party through its own political processes attempts to form an internal political base of operations. In doing so, the party must try to narrow or eliminate differences between constituents who view their objectives differently or must at least try to establish a framework within which progress can be made toward reconciliation. The political steps that leaders must take for that political purpose become part of the larger political process that surrounds a negotiation.

Where parties differ, it is important to consider how their basic pictures of the problem can be brought closer or at least how differences can be seen as complementary rather than conflicting. Both Israelis and Palestinians show acute distress when people on one side define the problem without acknowledging the existence of the other side. Each side buttresses its own position by ignoring the other or by treating people on the other side as nonpersons. It is easier to ignore the rights, the claims, or the pain of other people when we treat them as an abstraction rather than as individual human beings.

An early condition for negotiation is that each side must define the problem as being at least partly shared with another party. Each side's definition must somehow acknowledge the hopes and pain of the other side. Only when each side sees the other side's problems as part of the problem will the two definitions together suggest that a jointly attempted solution is worth considering. In the mid-1980s, Israel and its eastern neighbors still define the problem in sharply differing ways and do not give sufficient weight to the legitimate concerns of the other side.

A first task in trying to break down the barriers to negotiation, then, is to understand what might change a party's picture of the problem. Part of the purpose is to strengthen individuals on all sides who are ready to move toward a common or complementary definition of the problem as a basis for negotiation.

Developing a Commitment to Negotiate. The most critical period in the peace process comes when leaders are deciding whether to commit themselves to a negotiated settlement. If policy makers are uncomfortable with the direction that the present situation seems to be taking, they begin looking for alternatives. Particularly if they believe themselves unable to achieve what they want by unilateral action, they begin thinking that negotiation—a bilateral approach—may be necessary, possible, and worth exploring. Although negotiation itself is the central element in the negotiating process, the time when a commitment to a negotiated settlement crystallizes in policy makers' minds is the moment of truth, the real heart of that process. Without that commitment, negotiation cannot start. Most of the years of the Arab-Israeli-Palestinian conflict have been spent in this precommitment phase, and hence real negotiation has not been possible.

In many cases, developing the commitment to negotiate is the most complex part of the peace process because it involves a series of interrelated judgments. Before leaders will negotiate, they have to judge (1) whether a negotiated solution would be better or no better than continuing the present situation, (2) whether a fair settlement could be fashioned that would be politically manageable, (3) whether leaders on the other side could accept the settlement and survive politically, and (4) whether the balance of forces would permit agreement on such a settlement. In more colloquial language, leaders ask themselves: How much longer can this present situation go on? Is there another way, and could I live with it politically? Could my adversary live with it? Are the cards stacked against me, or could I get a fair settlement from a negotiation?

Before a new direction can be taken in this early period of the peace process, the political environment must be rearranged. Judgments of the highest political and human order—about how much damage or pain a party can suffer—are required. Also required are the courage and fore-

24

sight to say, "This can't go on any longer," and judgments about where a course of action will lead over the long term. Astute political judgments must be made about when a constituency is ready to move to a new position, and skill is needed to create the catalyst. Understanding of the other side's human and political needs is necessary to help its leaders reach the decision to negotiate. Decisions must be made on peace and war. This early period is a time for political moves and not yet a time when the parties are ready for the negotiators, although they may participate in defining alternatives. The diplomats' main job at this stage is to help presidents, kings, prime ministers, and chairmen see their choices clearly and change the political environment. The barriers to peace will crumble only when the heads of government commit themselves and persuade their constituencies to join them.

Let us consider each of the four judgments involved, remembering that decisions in one area will affect decisions in another, so that conclusions must constantly be reviewed and revised.

First is a *judgment that the present situation no longer serves a party's interests.*

Before negotiation can begin, leaders on each side must conclude that the present situation no longer serves the interests of that side. Furthermore, not negotiating must seem less likely to serve each side's interests than a negotiated settlement would. Finally, delaying negotiation and allowing time to pass must seem, in each side's judgment, not likely to create a more attractive situation and possibly even likely to harm the party's interests. Each side may even conclude, "This can't go on much longer."

Otherwise stated, in analyzing why a party refuses to negotiate, we must determine why that party believes that perpetuating the present situation serves its interests. We must understand what those interests are and why one side may regard the possible outcomes of negotiation as less attractive than the alternatives to negotiation. Our analysis might help us understand how to change that assessment.

As they affect national policy, interests must be understood on two levels.

First, they may be defined analytically as an objective set of concerns important to a nation's security and economic well-being. Analysts may disagree about the exact nature of an interest—for example, exactly what energy requirements will be in the future—but they can make some kind of rational statement defining interests. In this form, a list of fundamental interests can remain much the same over time.

Second, political leaders will shape their own understanding of their nation's interests in the political arena. In assessing the concerns of the people at a given time, leaders will assign different priorities to those interests, and it is normally in that shape that interests begin to have operational consequences. I acknowledge that I have gone beyond the normal definition of interests, but for operational purposes it is necessary to consider how a political leader uses the concept of interests when he attempts to achieve political objectives.

Then, too, once we have agreed that interests as they influence policy are defined in the political arena, we must go beyond the classic definition of an interest. Interests sometimes need to be seen in psychological terms as well as in economic or in strategic terms. Sometimes, for instance, people have an interest in not giving up their pain; they find emotional nourishment in remaining victims. A politician must deal in the political arena with the fact that such psychological needs may shape popular judgments. Political leaders who are moving toward negotiation recognize that the resistance to negotiation—the "other walls" that bar the way to negotiation—may be more psychological than substantive.

Second is a *judgment that the substance of a fair settlement is available*.

Before parties will commit themselves to negotiate, leaders must be able to see that they could live politically with the shape of a settlement that might emerge from negotiation. If they believe that time is running out, they must be able to answer the question "What else can I do?" They need to be able to see that a settlement could include the elements they have defined as key. This judgment adds a comparative dimension to the first. It enables a leader to decide whether allowing the present situation to continue will harm his interests more or less than any foreseeable negotiated settlement.

What do we mean when we speak of the "shape of a settlement"? Most basically, we are referring to such concrete aspects of a settlement as how borders will be drawn and how security measures will be arranged. We may also have in mind the nature of the relationship that will exist between the parties to the negotiation. People want to visualize what it would be like to live with the new relationship. The effort to visualize fills out a picture of a settlement because it requires people to view their present enemies less as abstractions and more as persons. This shift in attitude is critical in answering the leader's question: "Can I build political support for a settlement like this?"

When the Palestine problem came to a head in the mid-1940s, for instance, two possible geographical and political solutions were envisioned—a single state or a partition. One approach involved the creation of a binational state in Palestine in which Jews and Arabs would live with individual political, civil, and religious rights under the same sovereign roof. Given the tension between the two peoples, much of the world at the time judged that they would not be able to live together, sharing sovereignty. The second option, therefore, was to divide the land between them. The United Nations General Assembly supported this second option in November 1947. The concept of partition also formed the basis for Resolution 242 after the 1967 War and the Camp David accords in 1978. After the 1967 War, the United States envisioned that Israel would return to something like its pre-1967 borders in return for peace, recognition, and security. That has remained the U.S. position.

The debate over the shape of a settlement still begins with the question of whether one party will control all of Palestine or whether the land will be shared in some way that allows each party's identity to find political expression there. Most Israelis believe that demands for a binational state aim to end the Jewish state. Palestinians view some Israelis' desire to annex all the land west of the Jordan River as seeking to prevent the Palestinian identity from finding political expression. In preparing for negotiation it is of fundamental importance for each people to envision a settlement that reflects the craving of both peoples for separate political expression of their identities.

For some individuals the shape of a settlement is defined primarily from longstanding philosophical conviction, but for a majority judgments about what is possible with the other human beings involved are also important. Many Israelis believe that the land must be shared by the two peoples, but to refine their picture of a settlement they must next determine how the two parties would coexist in that land. The key questions are not only borders, including arrangements in Jerusalem, mutual security, and the character of the political regime in any territory from which Israel withdraws, but also the nature of the relationship that would exist between the two peoples under a peace settlement. Consideration of the relationship, in other words, involves consideration of the rights of individuals to live, work, and engage in commerce across borders; the economic and security cooperation between the two jurisdictions; and the likelihood of a lasting peace in view of the nature of the political relationship.

It is difficult to picture the coexistence of Israelis and Palestinians without having a dialogue about coexistence. In the past, the Arabs have foreseen a three-step process: (1) Israel will withdraw, leaving the territories from which it withdraws to be supervised by a United Nations transitional authority; (2) the Palestinian state will be created; and (3) the new Palestinian state will then negotiate its relationships with its neighbors. Israel's dilemma has been that this scenario does not permit people to envision the shape of the settlement on key issues such as security and political, human, and economic relationships before withdrawal takes place. It does not permit people to determine borders in relation to cooperation on maintaining security in the new relationship, nor does it provide an opportunity for the two peoples to make the necessary psychological adjustments. The main equation in Resolution 242 is that Israel should withdraw in return for peace, recognition, and security, but Israel is surely unlikely to withdraw without knowing whether its neighbor will recognize and live at peace with Israel or whether the Israelis can adjust to different borders and relationships.

The shape of a settlement, it seems, can become clear only in the details of coexistence as defined through dialogue or negotiation, yet the dialogue does not begin partly because neither side can see the shape of a settlement it could live with. The Camp David accords provided for two stages of negotiation and a five-year transitional period during which Palestinians in the occupied territories would first be elected to a self-governing body and then would take part in negotiations on the final status of the West Bank and Gaza and on its relations with the neighboring states, Jordan and Israel. The Arabs rejected that design for negotiation partly because they thought that it aimed to split the Palestinian people into two groups—those in the occupied territories and those outside—and that it did not recognize the right of the whole people to self-determination.

Thinking about how to add a clearer picture of the shape of a settlement to the negotiating process leads quickly to the particular problem of describing a Palestinian political entity. The Arabs will be quick to say that they do not know what Israel they are being asked to negotiate with. But it is almost inherent in the dilemmas of a liberation movement—especially a deeply divided movement—that potential negotiating partners will not see the shape of a final government. In addition to the fact that Israel refuses to negotiate with the PLO, Israelis also believe that Palestinian independence would be followed almost immediately by a bloodier than normal power struggle, making it doubly difficult to know who Israel's neighbor in vacated territory would be. The neighbor's probable identity is one of the most difficult missing pieces to fit into the overall picture.

Third is a *judgment that leaders on the other side will be willing and politically able to negotiate such a settlement.*

One side may be ready to negotiate but may refuse to do so because it does not want the humiliation of offering to negotiate and finding that the adversary will not negotiate seriously. A related consideration is whether the two sides could overcome suspicion and mistrust enough to work together. Leaders may manipulate strong feelings to avoid facing central substantive issues. Whatever the case may be, substantive issues are unlikely to be addressed seriously until the psychological barriers have been identified and dealt with.

Even if some common view about the shape of the settlement began to form, each side would still speculate as to whether the other side would accept such a settlement. The judgments involved would require some understanding of what the other side really needs and wants, of leaders' strategy for achieving their aims, and of leaders' ability to develop political support for a settlement. Such judgments would also involve firmly held suppositions about the other side's position: "The Israelis will never withdraw," or "The Palestinians want a state so they can move in a second stage to destroy Israel." Each side must be able to believe that any concessions it makes can be reciprocated.

At this point, most Israelis claim to believe that the Palestinians' basic objective is the destruction of the Jewish state. These Israelis will hear no evidence to the contrary, and they will cite the charter of the Palestine Liberation Organization, which called for a binational state in Palestine, thus ending the existence of the Jewish state. Those Israelis do not hear the resolutions of the Palestine National Council that have passed since 1974, which in a sense supersede the charter by saying that the Palestinians seek a state of their own in land from which Israel would withdraw. Similarly, the Israelis do not entertain the possibility that some Palestinians have concluded—as some Zionists did in 1947-1948—that half a loaf is better than none; much less do they feel that these Palestinians should be encouraged. Whether because they fear negotiation with the Palestinians, because they seek permanent control in the West Bank, or because they are understandably extra cautious in protecting their security, many Israelis do not believe that leaders in the Palestinian movement may be trying to build political support to negotiate with Israel. A small but appreciable minority of Israelis do not agree with these views, but politicians in both of the main blocs cater to the opinions of the majority.

The Palestinians, on the other hand, believe that neither of the other important actors—Israel and the United States—would support a settlement that would give them a genuine opportunity for self-determination and would allow them to organize themselves politically in their own way in any part of Palestine. They believe that the United States is thoroughly committed to objectives, however they may be defined by particular Israeli leadership, or is unwilling or unable to sway or to disagree with Israel. Even many of the Palestinians who would seriously consider negotiating do not know what they would have to say and do to help Israeli leaders who seek ways of convincing Israelis that peace and secure coexistence are possible with Palestinians who are governing themselves.

In addition, there are questions about whether policy makers on either side can negotiate with the certainty of finding political support for any agreement they negotiate. Both Israelis and Palestinians have problems of this kind. Chairman Arafat has not been supported by all mem-

29

bers of his own organization in developing a common negotiating position with King Hussein. Palestinian leaders in the territories occupied by Israel who could be invited to join negotiations to set up a Palestinian self-governing authority in the West Bank and Gaza see no way of giving themselves a mandate to speak for the Palestinians in such negotiations. Both Jordanians and Palestinians understand that the Syrians will oppose any negotiation from which they are excluded. Although Israel has a well-tested system for choosing leaders and giving them a mandate, the deep divisions within Israel, including different viewpoints on dealing with the Palestinians, impose constraints on any government, whatever its view. Any government led by one of the major parties knows that some kinds of settlement could meet with strong and possibly violent opposition. A broad coalition government would have to sort out deep internal disagreements before it could negotiate.

Whatever views may be held regarding the shape of a settlement, progress toward negotiation requires an understanding and willingness to work with the politics of decision making on each side. Serious negotiations will be possible only when leaders on each side begin to be concerned with presenting their positions so that the other side can see how its needs will be met.

Fourth, a commitment to a negotiated settlement will require a *judgment that the balance of forces will permit a fair settlement.*

A party may believe that the balance of power so favors his adversary that the adversary will not negotiate seriously. Before committing himself to negotiation, he will begin looking for ways to restructure the balance of forces so as to increase the chances that negotiation will be fair.

Leaders on both sides must believe that there is a realistic possibility of achieving important objectives before they will commit themselves to a negotiation. The act of commitment will in itself be highly controversial within their political constituencies. Moreover, some cultures tend to view proposing negotiation as a sign of weakness, so some constituents would see a commitment to negotiate as weakening their position at the negotiating table and as simultaneously fueling internal opposition.

The Palestinians consider the Israeli leaders so powerful militarily and so firmly in control in the occupied territories as to feel no pressure to negotiate. The Palestinians recognize that the Israeli government's openly stated policy is not to withdraw from all the territories and that the Arab side at this time does not have the means to force withdrawal. They also feel that the United States stands behind Israel by default, if not by will. Palestinian leaders see no reason to commit themselves to negotiation—an act that they regard as implying recognition of Israel—when that commitment would in their analysis lay them open to criticism for beginning a negotiation and coming away empty-handed.

Palestinians do not believe that the United States can ensure fair negotiation of all outstanding issues. Israel's policy of expropriating land in the West Bank and Gaza for settlement and security purposes is regarded by Palestinians as especially strong evidence that Israel is resolving the key issue of control over the land unilaterally outside negotiation.

The situation in Israel is complex. The Begin government, supported by the Knesset, committed itself formally to negotiations with Jordan and to two stages of negotiation on the West Bank and Gaza after Camp David. No outcome was precluded, and some of Begin's right-wing critics immediately broke with him, charging that he had opened the door to a Palestinian state. Some leaders in his own party who did not support that commitment in the Knesset, such as Yitzhak Shamir, subsequently in their governmental capacities recognized the Camp David accords as a commitment on the part of the State of Israel. As Israeli officials, they seemed bound to honor that commitment; as human beings, they seemed committed to what the experts call "surface negotiation"—that is, to going through the motions without really wanting an agreement. As human beings they viewed de facto Israeli control as preferable to any conceivable outcome from negotiation. These Israelis identify on the horizon no force capable of making them negotiate seriously. Then, in 1984, formation of a national unity government brought the Labor party back into the government alongside Shamir and his colleagues. Labor leaders believe that Israel must withdraw from some of the West Bank.

It is important to take into account the role of powers from outside the region, especially the United States and the Soviet Union. When the peace process was at its height in the 1970s, the United States took a stand in favor of fair negotiation. It did not try to impose a settlement, but it did try to assure a reasonable outcome that would reflect interests on both sides. Arab parties in the 1980s increasingly view the United States as unable or unwilling to ensure that all outstanding issues will be fairly negotiated despite Israeli resistance. The Soviet Union was established after the 1973 War as cochairman of the Geneva Middle East Peace Conference, which met in December 1973, but the Soviets were moved to the sidelines during most of the later 1970s when the United States was the primary mediator. The Soviet Union is handicapped in the negotiations because it lacks a normal relationship with Israel. In the mid-1980s, most of the Arabs—even those who are friendly to the United States, such as King Hussein—demanded that the Soviet Union be included in the negotiating process to balance the Americans, whom they regard as pro-Israeli.

One way of breaking the impasse is for Palestinian leaders to understand, as Israelis do, that, if there is no negotiation, the United States will back Israel through inertia, but if there is a negotiation, the United States will move toward the center to press for a fair solution. Arabs have every right to question the truth of this statement, but experience suggests that it is more often true than not.

Arranging a Negotiation. The third part of the peace process consists of making arrangements once the parties have decided to try to negotiate. At some point when leaders begin seriously considering the possibility, it will become important to think about how a negotiation might be arranged. Four kinds of issues will have to be dealt with: (1) What will be the overall strategy and character of the negotiations? (2) What will be the mechanics of the negotiations? (3) How will the parties be represented, particularly the Palestinians? (4) What will be the substantive starting point—the terms of reference—for the negotiation?

Determination of the larger *strategy and character of the negotiations* will necessitate dealing with various outstanding issues.

• Will the negotiations aim at a series of bilateral discussions or at a comprehensive negotiation bringing all the parties to the Arab-Israeli-Palestinian conflict together? In 1977, when the Carter administration attempted to resume the Middle East Peace Conference at Geneva, a central issue was whether the negotiations would proceed through meetings of country delegations—Egypt-Israel, Israel-Jordan, and Israel-Syria—or whether they would bring together representatives of all of the governments involved in a discussion of functional issues such as boundaries, security, refugees, passage through waterways, and diplomatic relations. The United States, Egypt, and Israel judged that, practically speaking, negotiations could not be restricted to the least-common-denominator Arab position, and Syria resisted being left to negotiate alone with Israel. The issue in the mid-1980s remains whether Jordan and Syria must come together with the Palestinians in a negotiation or whether negotiations could be conducted on each individual front under a common umbrella.

• Will the negotiations aim for further interim steps or for a final settlement now? Even though the agreement at Camp David outlined a final peace agreement between Egypt and Israel, in turning to the Palestinian and Jordanian fronts the Camp David accords outlined an interim step for establishing a Palestinian self-governing authority before a second round of negotiations addressed the final status of the West Bank and Gaza. In late 1982 when King Hussein discussed the Reagan initiative with the president, he urged that the negotiations proceed directly to a discussion of the final status of those territories and their relationship to

Israel and to Jordan. When it appeared impossible to cover so much ground in one jump, the king argued for compressing into a few months the period between the interim move to a self-governing authority and the negotiations on the final status of the territories.

• How much should be attempted in secret negotiations before the negotiations become public? Even in the highly visible Kissinger shuttles of 1974-1975, much of a possible agreement was outlined in general discussion before there was any recourse to text or to maps. The farther the secret dialogue can proceed, the more likely the negotiating parties are to describe the potential for agreement in ways that political constituencies will find attractive.

• What opportunities exist for moving toward negotiation through third parties rather than reaching early understandings through secret meetings between principal figures or between high-level representatives of each side?

In other words, leaders must grasp both the shape of a possible settlement and the shape of the negotiating process before they will commit themselves. The amount of ground that each stage of negotiation attempts to cover will affect the ability of leaders to justify the negotiation to their publics.

A second issue will be to consider *the mechanics of the negotiation*. In 1977, the Carter administration's initial objective was to resume the Middle East Peace Conference at Geneva. Had the parties succeeded in that objective, they would eventually have found themselves with a negotiating format that was relatively easy to visualize in advance.

In the mid-1980s, it is difficult to foresee what a suitable location and format for negotiation might be. The option of a comprehensive negotiation remains. The Soviet Union has called for an international conference, and Jordanians, Syrians, Palestinians, and even Egyptians have nominally supported the proposal. This option will continue to meet resistance in Israel and in the United States, however, particularly because it is cumbersome and because it implies involvement on the part of the Soviet Union, which has no present relationship with Israel. Even the Soviets recognize, however, that much preparatory work would be needed before a conference could meet. Most Arabs—except the Syrians—would quickly forgo a conference for any other format that promised results.

In the absence of a comprehensive negotiation, discussions are likely to proceed in two stages: (1) A period of secret exchanges seems likely at the outset. These could take place either in the Middle East—perhaps in a small boat in the Gulf of Aqaba or at meetings in the West Bank or Gaza—or in European capitals or on the fringes of the United Nations. (2) When negotiations become more detailed, it may be necessary to find

33

some more permanent site. At this point, it seems likely that the parties would prefer some semiofficial place such as a chateau in Europe to the more formal facilities of the United Nations in Geneva or New York.

A third question to be answered is: *Who represents the Palestinians?* Even if the PLO publicly and directly accepts Resolutions 242 and 338, acknowledging Israel's permanence, some Israelis insist that they will not negotiate with the PLO. If Israeli resistance is not overcome by a Palestinian statement of readiness to negotiate a peace settlement, the question is whether Palestinian groups other than the PLO might form in order to serve as acceptable negotiators. A Palestinian committee might form with the authority of the Palestine National Council for this purpose, or a committee of West Bankers might form with a mandate from the Palestine National Council. Alternatively Palestinian representatives might be incorporated into the delegation of an established Arab state such as Jordan. This possibility was discussed in 1977, was agreed to at Camp David, and was incorporated in the Hussein-Arafat agreement in 1985.

In 1977 some progress was made toward persuading Israel to accept the inclusion of Palestinian representatives in the delegation of an Arab state. Given the continued difficulty on both sides of finding an acceptable compromise, the solution in the Camp David accords was to allow the inhabitants of the West Bank and Gaza to elect a self-governing authority, which would represent those Palestinians in negotiations. The Camp David approach was rejected by the Palestinian movement on grounds that it represented an effort by Israel and the United States to divide the Palestinian movement and to exclude the PLO. This problem could be resolved through a variety of informal arrangements whereby West Bank negotiators would work from a PLO mandate, but various decisions would be necessary that may not be possible.

Finally, some *terms of reference* for the negotiation must be developed. The purpose of establishing terms of reference is to ascertain at the outset that the parties have the same overall objective in the negotiation and that similar principles will guide decisions on the elements of a settlement.

When parties are as far apart as the Arabs and the Israelis, it can be difficult to find terms of reference, and most of the documents written for this purpose over the years have contained ambiguities that conceal important differences. Resolution 242 provided peace in exchange for territory but was vague about the amount of territory that Israel should give up and about whether the point would be negotiated. The Camp David accords established a process of negotiation to deal with the West Bank and Gaza but could not precisely address the question of Palestinian political self-expression in those territories. The final declaration adopted by the twelfth Arab summit at Fez in Morocco on September 6-9, 1982, called for United Nations Security Council guarantees of "peace among all states of the region including the independent Palestinian state" but did not mention Israel by name. During a visit to President Reagan at the end of May 1985, King Hussein stated publicly that he was authorized to say that the "Palestinians are willing to accept Resolutions 242 and 338, and the principles they contain, as the basis for a settlement,"[1] but it was not clear how much of the PLO would agree.

Despite the negative impact of the ambiguities, the three documents reveal common elements in the position of Arabs and Israelis. These common elements are evident within the context of differing overall perspectives and should not be interpreted as a sign of overall agreement. Nevertheless, they reflect positions that have changed significantly in the past decade, and they should therefore not be dismissed out of hand. One of the persistent difficulties in communication between the two sides in the Middle East is that each side reacts to the negative elements in the other side's position without noticing elements that might form the basis for eventual agreements. Such is the case here.

Negotiation: Trying to Reach Agreement. It is apparent that, in many ways, negotiation has already begun in the earlier stages of the process, especially during the 1970s when an American "full partner" in the process moved back and forth, communicating one party's views to another—or at least communicating American views informed by the ideas of each party. A central feature of the Kissinger shuttles and his many exploratory conversations was his concern with talking the parties toward a common view of the shape of a settlement. Sustained American involvement itself helped create a political environment more favorable to negotiation, and the subtle introduction of American ideas about bridging gaps brought pictures of the shape of a possible settlement closer. The exploratory exchanges before negotiation gradually became almost indistinguishable in substance from the eventual negotiation, but they could either cease or continue indefinitely, as some negotiations do.

In terms of the larger political process, however, there is a moment when leaders visibly shift gears and parties begin trying to reach agreement. The process can begin secretly, and the moment may come while the negotiation is being arranged. Still, at some point in political life a leader must make public the decision to try to negotiate an agreement, must begin building political support for the shape of the agreement he hopes to reach, and must position himself to deal with the risks of failure. Although I recognize that analysts may find other ways of defining the start of negotiation, in my experience the negotiating process takes on a different character when the participants decide that they will try to

35

reduce what they have talked about to a written agreement, which will elicit commitments by each side, changing the relationship between the parties and itself becoming subject to the judgment of bodies politic on both sides.

If we take this perspective, a crucial purpose of the preparatory thinking and discussion is to accumulate the evidence that the risk of negotiation is justified—that negotiation can succeed, that the outcome could improve the situation, and that failure would be manageable. Simply discussing the elements of a settlement is different from trying to write them down in a potentially binding document that will be submitted to decisive public political judgment. It is true that one party may enter negotiation for some political purpose without intending to work toward agreement, but a leader who takes such initiative runs the risk that the act of negotiating will create a momentum of its own and will generate pressure for agreement.

The period of actual negotiation—the fourth stage in the peace process—is complex in itself, involving intricate relationships and solutions to problems, but I will not examine it in detail here. It has been more extensively discussed than the period on which I focus in this book. We Americans are more comfortable with the negotiating part of the process, and we have much recent experience with it. Before returning to the analysis of the intensely political period that precedes negotiation, however, let us briefly consider implementation.

Implementation and the Peace Process. The fifth part of the peace process is the period when agreements that have been reached are implemented. Implementation is an important part of the negotiating process and not only because the purpose of negotiation is to produce an agreement that the parties have a stake in implementing. In diplomacy, as in some other areas, careful implementation of one agreement may be the starting point for the next negotiation. Even a signed and ratified peace treaty only begins a new stage in a relationship. On the human level, too, we must remember that changes in perception and attitude often occur in small, incremental, scarcely noticeable steps.

In the 1970s, the American strategy came to be called "step-by-step diplomacy." Kissinger showed Arabs and Israelis how they could break the problem down into negotiable pieces, evolving agreements that would build confidence and would change the political environment and counting on implementation to provide the new starting point for next steps. Step-by-step agreement, we argued, can make possible negotiation tomorrow of points that could not have been negotiated yesterday. The implementation of one agreement becomes an important prelude to negotiation of another. For this reason and others, we coined the phrase "the peace process."

In addition we argued that peace is never made but is always in the making. Like other human relationships, peace must be constantly tended, nurtured, and developed. In 1977 and 1978 in the Egyptian-Israeli negotiations we came to define peace as including not just the end of belligerence but also the normalization of relations. We repeatedly asserted that the quality of normalization would depend on the quality of the next round of negotiations that would deal with Israeli-Palestinian problems, as agreed at Camp David. President Sadat had stated that peace as the normalization of relations is "for the next generation." He believed that no one could decree such peace; relations would become normal when peoples felt normal in the relationship. The fact that the negotiations stalled after Camp David—in combination with the Israeli invasion of Lebanon—has slowed building an Egyptian-Israeli peace as well as the negotiation of an Israeli-Palestinian-Jordanian peace.

If any cultural gap divided Americans and many of our Arab colleagues—excluding the Egyptians—in the search for peace before 1985, it was American failure to communicate convincingly that peacemaking is a process, not a precisely defined achievement. The Arabs wanted to see the destination; we argued that the destination would be defined in the process. As one Jordanian told me in October 1978: "We are a desert people. When we leave an oasis, we need to know where the next oasis is. That's why there is no place in our vocabulary or our culture for the American concept of a negotiating process." In the years since, Jordanians and Palestinians became more pragmatic and focused more on the steps for getting from here to there. It may be that people have more understanding in the mid-1980s of the "peace process" and of the importance of implementation in changing the political environment preparatory to the next negotiation.

The inherent weakness of any step-by-step process remains that which the Arabs have identified: Any party can drop out when it has gained what it wants. When a party drops out, however, it must recognize that it disrupts, perhaps for a long time to come, the larger process on which ultimate peace and security depend.

Where We Are in the Peace Process

In terms of this analytical framework, since attention turned in 1979 to Israel's eastern frontiers we have clearly been in the first two stages of the peace process. The issue has been not how to draft an agreement acceptable to the parties but how to remove the obstacles to negotiation. As we have seen, there is a need for political maneuver on the highest plane more than for diplomatic drafting. Political steps are just as much a part of the peace process as negotiation itself.

We need a new and different starting point for the peace process.

37

The first issue is not whether parties are willing to negotiate on the basis of the Camp David accords, the Reagan initiative, the Fez Declaration, or the Hussein-Arafat understanding, but whether (and how) the concerns that block negotiation can be addressed so that specific terms of reference can be considered.

In the following sections I will analyze more precisely the obstacles that prevent each party from committing itself to a negotiated settlement between Israel and its eastern neighbors. Each chapter proceeds from a capsule of the party's position to examine the party's views on the definition of the problem, the effect of the passage of time on the party's interests, the shape of a possible settlement, the ways in which that party thinks the other side might react to such a settlement, and whether the balance of forces would permit negotiation of such a settlement. Finally, in each case I have ventured some thoughts about ways of approaching the party so as to address its psychological, political, and human needs.

Note

1. His Majesty King Hussein, Address delivered at the American Enterprise Institute for Public Policy Research, Washington, D.C., May 1985, p. 6.

3
Israel: Struggling to Define Itself

Peace, Security, and Acceptance

Israel is a nation struggling for peace within itself and with its neighbors. The struggle for peace is a struggle to define itself. Any effort to negotiate peace between Israel and its neighbors must begin with an understanding of how that effort will affect the internal political and social processes by which Israelis are struggling to shape modern Israel.

For a people who have suffered centuries of persecution and the incomprehensible horrors of the Nazi Holocaust, security is the overriding objective, but Israelis are divided over the exact location of borders that would provide it. Many Arabs acknowledge Israel's need to affirm its security but ask for Israeli recognition that both sides of a border must be secure if confidence in a peaceful relationship is to be ensured. A problem in Israel is that it has become all but impossible to separate what security on Israel's eastern border requires from strong emotional, historical, philosophical, and religious attachment to the lands of the biblical kingdoms. The compulsion to establish borders that would provide modern expression of the biblical kingdoms commonly confuses discussion of the combination of political relationships, high-technology surveillance, demilitarization and arms limitation, security stations, troop deployments, and borders that are the elements of common security in today's world.

The need for security reflects a deep human craving for acceptance. That craving is a normal part of human development. We reach out with trust and learn mistrust; we reach out for acceptance and learn rejection. Because Jewish experience has included rejection and traumatic persecution, the yearning for acceptance is especially strong in Israel. The Israeli attitude also reflects the weariness of war and isolation and the view that long-term security will depend on developing some reciprocal political relationship with neighbors. The Israeli people search every Arab statement and move for implied acceptance or rejection of the Jewish state.

"I want them to recognize my feelings—my feeling that I belong in this land too," one Jewish philosopher said with passion. "I want them to recognize that Israel is not the creation of the Holocaust or the last plantation of Western imperialism." That philosopher then described acceptance at its fullest as a mutual act: "I don't claim exclusive right to this land. The Third Jewish Commonwealth cannot be built on the obliteration of the rights of another people. I want the Arabs to speak to me as if they are acknowledging that God gave this land to Abraham and both of his sons, Isaac and Ishmael—that there are two peoples who belong here. And I want to understand their pain. I want to get inside their agony."

Not all Israelis would make the second part of that statement. They are deeply divided over the future shape of their state, and many cannot accept other people who also claim to belong in that land. Many Israelis claim a dominant right to the land. Those who would share Palestine to make peace would be receptive to an Arab approach made in the spirit of sharing the land. People who think that fulfillment of the Zionist dream requires lasting Israeli control of all the land west of the Jordan River do not believe—or want to believe—that any Arab can ultimately accept Israel within any borders. Many of them try not to see the Arabs as human beings; otherwise they could not dull their own consciences in suppressing any Arab grievances over lost homes and lands.

In some ways, the search for an Arab-Israeli-Palestinian peace is part of the Jews' own struggle for peace within themselves, which they call *shalom*. One of the agonies of Israel today is that Jews have lost touch with each other about the Jewish experience in modern Israel as it should be. Any political effort to achieve peace must provide an opportunity for Jews to discuss among themselves how the yearning for a greater peace can be fulfilled.

Defining the Problem Is Defining Israel

In Israeli eyes, the overriding problem is to secure the future of Israel and the Jewish people. The political dimension of insecurity is that Arab states, with a few recent exceptions, have not openly and unequivocally shown themselves ready to accept and to make peace with Israel as a state in the Middle East. As I noted earlier, most Israelis would define the political problem as establishing state-to-state relationships that would be normal between states at peace rather than as the need to make peace between the Israeli and Palestinian peoples. Israelis shift the focus away from the conflict between the two peoples, saying that Arab states' acceptance of Israel is the heart of the problem because Arab states have fought Israel. Arab governments, on the other hand, see no way of resolving the conflict until the Israelis accept the Palestinians as a people with rights to political self-expression.

Beyond their common concern with the recognition and security of their state, Israelis are deeply divided over the future character of Israel. One Israeli leader described the two camps as "annexationists" and "partitionists."

One camp is represented by the policies of the governments of Prime Ministers Begin and Shamir from 1977 to 1984. In their eyes, the problem is how to establish permanent Israeli control over all the land west of the Jordan River, what they call "Eretz Israel," the "Land of Israel." This view, rooted in the revisionist school of Zionist thought, expresses itself in one of two positions toward the Palestinian Arabs. (1) The Palestinians are not a separate people entitled to the right of self-determination; they are "Arabs" and can live anywhere in the Arab world as an ethnic minority. (2) If the Palestinians want a state of their own, they can turn the Hashemite Kingdom of Jordan into the Palestinian state; two-thirds of Jordan's people are already Palestinian. Jordan was part of the British Palestine Mandate until 1922 and was in the area to which the Balfour Declaration applied. According to this second view, those Palestinians who choose to remain in the West Bank and Gaza, which these Israelis believe Israel should control perpetually, may be granted a form of autonomy to administer their own affairs under close Israeli supervision.

A second camp in Israel holds views generally reflected in the position of the Labor party of Shimon Peres, who became prime minister in the late summer of 1984. This camp embraces a wide spectrum of views. Small numbers talk with PLO members and would accept an independent Palestinian state. Most of the Israelis in this camp still see a "Jordanian option" for returning part of the West Bank to Jordanian control. Although they do not recognize the Palestinians' right to "secede" from a Jordanian-Palestinian relationship and form an independent state, these Israelis would allow Jordan and the Palestinians to define the terms of their relationship.

Philosophically, many Israelis have begun to see the Palestinians as a people and as individual human beings with dignity and aspirations of their own. These Israelis are mostly on the left of the political spectrum but have also included Moshe Dayan, when he was alive, and Ezer Weizman on the right. They are concerned about the corrosion of their own values when Israelis, maintaining a military occupation, consistently deny the rights and often the humanity of those under occupation.

Practically speaking, they judge that Israel cannot incorporate the 1.3 million Palestinians in the West Bank and Gaza together with the 0.7 million in pre-1967 Israel without diluting the Jewish character of Israel. If Israel incorporates that Arab population, Arabs will constitute a minority of almost 40 percent. If they are given the vote, they will eventually turn Israel into a secular, binational state. If they are not given the vote, they will be repressed or expelled by methods that will violate Judaic values. This group of Israelis fears that the Palestinian problem can be internalized only at the price of destroying Israel. In the eyes of this camp, the only solution is to divide the land somehow between Israelis and Palestinians.

Debate becomes difficult when people who favor some withdrawals fail to differentiate among the central issues. If the real issues that concern *all* Israelis are security and acceptance—and not reestablishing the shifting borders of biblical Israel—then by identifying the issues that are distinctly related to security it should be possible to reserve the debate about the future shape of the Jewish state for a separate forum.

The Israeli camps differ in the degree to which individual Israelis can continue to ignore the Palestinians as individuals. As long as Palestinians can be regarded as only "terrorists" or "Arabs," the Israelis will find it relatively easy to ignore, repress, expel, or even kill them. Those Israelis who have met Palestinians as individuals and have learned to know them as human beings have begun to question their own ability to maintain human values while ignoring the values of the Palestinians.

I shall discuss the shape of possible solutions in either camp's eyes in a later section. Here I am concerned with ways of introducing thoughtful reflection into the debate within Israel. Attention in Israel needs to focus on whether Israelis can realistically choose between (1) aiming to control all the land to the Jordan River *and* to reach peace with their neighbors *and* to preserve the Jewish state and (2) allowing Israel to withdraw from territory occupied in 1967 *and* preserving the security of the state.

One Palestinian asked whether the strong moral reaction in Israel against the Israeli war in Lebanon could somehow be transferred to the Palestinian problem. Some Israelis are deeply concerned that most Israelis do not know what goes on in the areas under military occupation. Some Israelis have watched the corruption of the individual Israeli soldier who is encouraged by some of his immediate superiors to view the people under occupation not as individual human beings but as a subhuman group—as "cockroaches in a bottle," to use the words of one former top-ranking Israeli commander, now in the Knesset. Some Israelis have also seen money pass to military and civilian administrators in return for permits and other actions necessary to Palestinian daily life.

One former Stern gang member who has described his assassination assignments in the 1940s found himself unable to sit face to face with a Palestinian doctor and to remain unmoved while the doctor spoke of personal and professional indignities suffered at the hands of the Israeli occupation; the Israeli said the experience changed his views about Israeli-Palestinian relations. Some Israelis believe that Israel would view the problem differently if more Israelis came face to face with the individual human beings they hold under military rule.

Israelis stress that a clear-cut Arab offer to negotiate a secure and lasting peace would have immense impact in focusing debate in Israel. I asked Israelis in early 1985 how the Israeli body politic would respond if the Israeli government were invited by King Hussein and representative Palestinians to negotiate without preconditions. The answer quickly came that the major parties are committed to negotiation without preconditions. I then asked what would happen when the negotiations turned to the issue of Israeli withdrawal from the West Bank. In this case the response was complex and uncertain. Israelis who hold the Labor party view and are committed to territorial compromise would negotiate. Some who are committed to perpetuating Israeli control in all the land west of the Jordan River might refuse to negotiate about land, because the only possible outcome would be withdrawal to some extent. Others who would like to control all the land, however, might reason as follows: Israel cannot both control all the land and make peace; some compromises will have to be made; it would be better to participate in shaping those compromises than to walk out. In short, the act of negotiation itself will be critical in focusing Israeli debate.

Finally, in the event of negotiation the whole body politic would wrestle with the outcome. A prime minister who wants to gather political support for a peaceful settlement will want as complete a package as possible before he enters the political arena. He will also need to have a political record of success in other important areas; such a list in early 1985 included restoring the economy, dealing with Lebanon, normalizing relations with Egypt, and coping with other important domestic issues.

Israel's choice is complicated by the ironic fact that the nation in the mid-1980s is deeply—and more or less evenly—divided in the absence of an Arab offer to make peace on the eastern front. A generation of Israelis has reached maturity having known nothing but Israeli control of all the land west of the Jordan River. A one-state solution has become a reality for these people. Whereas their parents saw a Jewish state in a partitioned Palestine as a historic triumph, this generation would see a partitioned Palestine as a profound loss.

In addition to Israelis' internal disagreements over the shape of Israel's final borders, Israel's security, settlement, and administrative practices in the West Bank and Gaza have by design established a presence that will be difficult to withdraw or modify. Apart from the debate as to whether these facts on the ground are reversible, a neat surgical partition along 1967 lines with minor rectifications would be much more difficult in the mid-1980s, if it remains possible at all, than it would have been right after the 1967 War.

Israel's national unity coalition government formed after the 1984 elections may prove so tenuous that decisions on important issues determining the future of the state will be impossible to make without bringing down the government. On the other hand, it may prove that the only way Israel can deal with issues of profound importance is within a broadly representative small leadership group such as a national unity cabinet. This notion may reflect wishful thinking, but it should not be lightly dismissed. Israel is in transition—economically, demographically, spiritually, and politically. Perhaps issues of great magnitude cannot be resolved through elections, which can only polarize the country. Perhaps leaders could be encouraged to conduct a political experiment to the advantage of state rather than party.

In short, Israel will define the problem for negotiation as part of Israel's definition of itself. For this reason it is important to consider how new steps in the peace process will be treated within the Israeli political process.

How Much Longer Can This Situation Go On?

Israelis have generally preferred not to think about the longer-term consequences of present actions and situations. I have asked many Israelis and American Jewish friends how I should interpret their short view of the future, in view of their deep sense of history. "When you live as we have," they reply, "you feel lucky to live through each new year—let alone try to look decades into the future." Nevertheless, the two main parties in Israel instinctively divide in their sense of how the passage of time affects their interests.

The Israeli government from 1977 to 1984, under the leadership of Prime Ministers Begin and Shamir, did not wish to be put in a negotiating situation where the only reasonable outcome would be some agreement that Israel would leave a substantial part of the West Bank and Gaza. These governments openly sought to use time to tighten Israel's control over the territories. Begin viewed the Palestinian autonomy agreed to at Camp David as a final settlement—not as the transitional arrangement envisioned by American and Egyptian participants at Camp David. Any alternative to negotiation of a final settlement that left Israel in de facto control of the territories occupied in 1967 seemed preferable to a negotiation in which the very terms of reference—for instance, United Nations Security Council Resolution 242 or the Camp David accords—would call for some Israeli withdrawal.

44

Israelis are not unanimous in their view of how passing time affects Israel's interests. The Labor party leadership and possibly even a slim majority of the people recognize that, the more time passes, and the more Israel becomes entrenched in the West Bank and Gaza, the more difficult it will be politically to arrange an Israeli withdrawal. For this portion of the Israeli population, negotiation seems necessary, but in appealing to these people, leadership faces the challenge of dramatizing the urgency of an early agreement. Even the Israelis who might agree philosophically and practically that it would be dangerous to try to absorb an Arab minority of 40 percent are comfortable enough for the moment to wonder whether they really must move now.

The most compelling argument would be that a realistic offer to negotiate peace has been made and must be dealt with now. A second argument would be supported by a rising public sense of the ugliness of occupation. This argument could be dramatized in a variety of ways—for example, through increased press attention, demonstrations by concerned Israelis, publications or television presentations that lay out the facts of occupation practices, civil disobedience by West Bankers and Gazans, and, most dangerous of all, bloody riots in the West Bank. The Israelis who are in touch with Palestinians in the occupied territories hear people talk with increasing alarm about attitudes among the young people. Even those who are economically well off and hold decent jobs say they will wait a little longer for movement toward a fair settlement but then "will fight." Also indicative of the radicalization of youth was the episode in late 1984 in which campus elections at one West Bank university produced a complete sweep for Islamic fundamentalists. In short, changes in population composition and attitudes such as those that occurred in Iran in the late 1970s may be making a showdown increasingly likely, though without incidents like the ones in Iran it will be difficult to warn the Israeli citizenry that it is imminent.

In early 1985, Prime Minister Peres and his Labor party colleagues faced a deadline of a quite different kind. In connection with their coalition agreement with the Likud, Peres agreed that Yitzhak Shamir of the Likud would take over as prime minister in the fall of 1986. If Peres is to remain prime minister, he will have to produce results by fall 1986 that will strengthen his political position so that he can either reform the governing coalition or call new elections with a chance of increasing his party's representation in the parliament.

One perplexing question has been why some Israelis who are committed to establishing the Third Jewish Commonwealth in wide historic borders do not worry about incorporating within those borders a 40 percent Arab minority. More specifically with respect to the impact of passing time, it is perplexing that responsible government leaders are willing to use the tactic of allowing their government to drift into a decision that they may have made personally but have not tested openly with the electorate. To American analysts, such a step would seem to change the Jewish character of the state so dramatically as to make that course dangerous. Since many Israelis apparently do not share the feeling, the question is why people who fear the present drift have failed to dramatize its apparent dangers.

Perhaps Israeli leaders have feared that forcing public debate on the issue would cause too much division, especially in the absence of a clearly available Arab negotiating partner. Perhaps, alternatively, Israelis have for the most part not wanted to learn that their military government, however good its intentions may be, degrades the people living under it and those conducting it. Israelis who understand what is happening as more and more time passes believe that the methods of perpetuating Israeli control produce a form of corrosion eating at the soul of the Third Jewish Commonwealth.

The Shapes of a Settlement

Even within the two schools of thought defining the future of the Jewish state, there is no consensus about the exact shape of a settlement. Where the specifics of a settlement are concerned, each bloc encompasses different views.

People who want perpetual Israeli control over all the land west of the Jordan River have not resolved among themselves how they would deal with the 1.3 million Arabs in the land they would control. Prime Minister Begin's solution was to provide the Palestinians with "administrative autonomy" within Eretz Israel. General Ariel Sharon has insisted on establishing the Palestinian state in Jordan. Extremist Meir Kahane's solution is to expel the Arabs from areas controlled by Israel to make their homes in Jordan or wherever they can go. These views of the "annexationist" camp in Israel about the shape of an eventual settlement cannot by themselves provide the basis for negotiation, because no Arab will negotiate an agreement that means giving up the West Bank, Gaza, and east Jerusalem to permanent Israeli control.

Palestinians cannot understand why any Israelis, much less their experienced leaders, would expect Palestinians to be satisfied with such arrangements as autonomy. They see Begin, who grew up with the autonomy of the Polish ghettos, spending much of his life fighting for an independent Jewish state. They cannot understand why Zionists, with their yearning for a state of their own, do not understand the Palestinian desire for freedom to shape their own state. Whatever the individual views within the Likud, none of them seems to include a view of a settlement that takes into account any Palestinians' views of themselves as equal partners.

In speaking of a negotiated settlement, I focus on the views of people who see a settlement as involving the exchange of land for peace—a central equation in United Nations Security Council Resolution 242. Key leaders of the Labor party, in contrast to their Likud colleagues, share a commitment to that equation. Even in the Labor party camp, however, differences in experience and viewpoint seem to have produced two different, though not conflicting, points of emphasis.

First, Israelis whose experience includes the private exchanges with King Hussein and the disengagement agreements before 1976 focus on negotiating a "territorial compromise" with Jordan. Under such an agreement, Jordan would resume control of a West Bank in which boundaries had been changed to improve Israel's security. Although they accept the two-stage negotiating process outlined at Camp David, these Israelis instinctively focus on the territorial arrangements in a final settlement. It is not clear how they interpret the memory that the Jordanians rejected their proposals in the earlier exchanges.

Second, Israelis whose experience includes the Camp David negotiations also cite the need to pay attention to the transitional process by which control would pass from Israeli military authority to Arab authority. Most important, they point out that it may be politically impossible for the leaders of both Jordan and Israel to address territorial compromise immediately because opponents of King Hussein will reject any but 1967 borders and opponents of Prime Minister Peres will reject any boundaries but the Jordan River. They further note that by concentrating on the functional aspects of transferring authority it may be possible to discuss withdrawal while leaving discussion of final sovereignty until the right political moment.

Can Jordan and the Palestinians Accept?

Even those Israelis who would be willing to negotiate an exchange of land for peace with King Hussein ask themselves at a minimum whether he has the political support to sustain an agreement that involves territorial compromise. They recognize that he has kept the Israeli-Jordanian border quiet since he expelled the PLO in 1970, and they believe that he personally wants peace. They know from exchanges with him in the late 1960s, however, that he has felt unable to accept any settlement other than Israeli withdrawal to the 1967 borders.

In addition to questioning King Hussein's ability to reach agreement, some Israelis feel that Hussein has made a series of critical bad judgments over the years, such as the decision to fire on Israeli forces in 1967, with the resulting loss of east Jerusalem and the West Bank, and flat rejection of the Camp David accords in 1978. These Israelis feel that, while his intentions may be good, he would be an unpredictable or indecisive partner in peace. Many were also concerned in early 1985 that Hussein was taking a grave risk in allowing the PLO to increase its presence in Amman, which might ultimately result in his loss of control in his own country.

Despite all of their doubts, Israelis are more familiar with Hussein than with any other Arab leader. They are constantly exposed to Jordanian television, which shows the king and his family almost daily. Whatever their reservations about his judgment or his political maneuverability, many Israelis respect him. Some also observe that television provides a ready-made channel for him to speak directly to the Israeli people in communicating a message of readiness to make peace.

In the mid-1980s, Israelis know that they cannot assess Hussein's ability to negotiate apart from the position of the Palestinians. Hussein's need to build a political base that includes the PLO complicates potential negotiations between Israel and Jordan. Like many Arabs, Israelis do not trust Arafat. That judgment aside, they do not believe, rightly or wrongly, that the main elements of the PLO are prepared to accept Israel. For a variety of reasons—some defensive and tactical, some reflecting genuine conviction—many Israelis believe or want to believe that the PLO is bent on destroying Israel. Continuing terrorist actions and the Palestinian National Charter contribute to their conviction. Whatever compromise the PLO might accept, many Israelis believe, would form part of an effort by the PLO to improve its base for achieving the ultimate destruction of Israel. This judgment of the PLO figures in the Israeli picture of the constraints on Hussein's ability to negotiate.

An equally fundamental issue may be whether Israelis can accept Palestinian acceptance of Israel. In addition to their basic fear of PLO intentions, Israelis may consciously or unconsciously feel that acknowledging a PLO claim in Palestine would be an admission that their own claim is less than absolute. Deep in some Israeli consciences may also be a personal fear of coming face to face with the people whom the establishment of the Israeli state has dispossessed and has made homeless and stateless. An objective analysis may conclude that the mainstream of the Palestine National Council and a large majority of Palestinians under military occupation are ready to make peace with Israel. Still, although Israel has acknowledged some Palestinian rights, Israelis do not hear—or do not allow themselves to hear—those voices fully enough to assess whatever they may be saying.

A critical question for an Israeli leader who wants to negotiate a settlement with Jordanians and Palestinians is how to enable Israelis to hear and assess open-mindedly what Hussein and the Palestinians are saying. The real obstacle to a settlement may no longer be the difficulty of arranging the technicalities of Palestinian recognition of Israel. The real breakthrough might come from mutual recognition of each other's suffering. Some Palestinians still carry the keys to the homes they have lost, and they ask by what just legal process present owners occupy them. By any reasonable standard, for whatever cause, they have suffered injustice. The Israelis still bear the searing wounds of the Nazi Holocaust and the pain of centuries in diaspora as a people without a real home. Because of their historical longing for the biblical land and because they saw nowhere else to go where they could be secure, they sought a national home in Palestine. In asking the Palestinians now to accept the reality of a reborn Jewish state, they are perhaps asking a concession unprecedented in history—one comparable to the depth of their longing for the land and the length of their exile. The issue may be whether that concession can be turned into an act of nobility on the Palestinian side, an act that could provide a meeting ground on which the two sides could accept a solution for sharing the land.

My thought of an act of nobility comes from remembering a visit I made to one of the Palestinian refugee camps near Jericho in early 1967. One of the Palestinian camp managers spoke to me as follows: "You have to remember how an Arab blood feud is settled. First, the person responsible for a wrong done must acknowledge that an injustice has been done. Second, a price is set to atone for the injustice. Third, the highest act of nobility is that the money is turned aside. You Americans and the Israelis have to recognize that we've been ill done to." I heard him saying: "I know I will not get my home back, but I want you to recognize my hurt and acknowledge the injustice I have suffered." I am told that psychologists see this as a classic formula for helping a victim to heal his wounds.

The question on the Israeli side would be how to pave the way for a response to such a Palestinian act—even to encourage such an act or to make it possible. When Israelis assess whether the other side can live with the kind of settlement that the same Israelis envision, they face three problems: analyzing the other side's position exactly; hearing that position as it is; and considering how they can politically open the doors to accept and communicate with that position. One obvious step is to increase face-to-face contact systematically at all politically relevant levels.

Power for Negotiation or Power for Digging In?

The Israelis have worked tirelessly since the mid-1960s and particularly since the 1973 War to build an unchallengeable military force. Security is Israel's overriding concern. As of the mid-1980s they must feel that they have succeeded, despite the shock of the setbacks at the beginning of the 1973 War. The issues in Israel in early 1985 were not whether Israel maintained military superiority but what effect defense expenditures were having on the economy and whether Israeli leaders had shown wisdom, for example in Lebanon, in using their military power. Although Israelis were watching Syria's military development with increasing concern, they seemed to feel confident about their security in the mid-1985 balance of forces.

According to the Israelis' own psychological self-portrait, their sense of security should contribute to a sense that Israel is in a solid position to negotiate, but either the self-portrait is incomplete or other interests complicate the picture. The imbalance of forces in Israel's favor often seems to have affected Israel in a different way. Israel's ability to conduct a number of military operations without serious opposition has, in some Israeli quarters, generated a sense that Israel can operate without limits or without a concern for consequences. The experience in Lebanon raised grave questions among Israelis about the appropriate uses of force, in terms of Jewish philosophy, as well as about the judgment of some of Israel's top policy makers—not about the effectiveness of the Israeli Defense Forces. Israelis have long debated the security and effectiveness of massive retaliatory attacks on Arab positions, some arguing for maintaining proportionality between threat and response and others justifying a show of overwhelming power. In Lebanon, many Israelis found it abhorrent that their leaders were sacrificing lives on both sides to achieve debatable political objectives beyond the defense of Israel and were creating an environment in which violence without limits seemed to have become a tolerable instrument of policy.

In that atmosphere the Israelis reacted to the massacre of a large number of innocent men, women, and children in the Beirut Palestinian refugee camps of Sabra and Shatila in September 1982. A commission of prominent Israelis—the Kahan commission—determined that some Israeli officials bore at least "indirect responsibility" for the massacres because they did not take steps to prevent an action that they should have anticipated. Although the commission could not go beyond that judgment on the basis of the evidence before it, some Israelis would acknowledge that some of their leaders in Lebanon had communicated the attitude, especially after the bombings of Beirut in the first two weeks of August 1982, that the unrestrained and indiscriminate use of force against Palestinians would be tolerated as an instrument of Israeli policy. Reacting also to mounting casualties, a large number of Israelis rejected such use of Israeli power, causing withdrawal of Israeli forces from Lebanon to become an objective on which the leaders of both the major political blocs agreed.

The relationship between Israel's superior military power and Israel's readiness to negotiate has acquired an internal dimension. Will Israel use its military strength for essential security, which includes demonstrating to the Arabs that there is no realistic alternative to accepting Israel and negotiating peace? Alternatively, will Israeli forces be used to subjugate an alien population permanently within Israeli boundaries? The prolonged existence of military government in areas under Israeli control worries Israelis concerned about the damage that the use of superior force can do to the soul of the Jewish state.

While the Palestinians in the West Bank and Gaza cannot match Israel's military strength, they can dramatize the ways in which Israel's military government demeans the dignity of individual human beings. Many Israelis would put on the negotiating scales the weight of political and moral argument such as the pressure that eventually forced the government to withdraw Israeli forces from Lebanon. Palestinians wonder whether enough Israelis will come to understand what is happening in the areas under military government before West Bankers move to create a continuing bloodbath of violence and repression—or are provoked to do so by hard-line Israeli settlers adamantly opposed to any compromise of territory.

Finally, it is impossible to write in the mid-1980s about the balance of forces without mentioning nuclear weapons. It is generally assumed that Israel has the capability to use nuclear weapons. Someday an Arab power will be able to do so. The question facing Israelis who think about the longer-term future is which position they would prefer for themselves when the day arrives: Would they prefer to try to defend their small land against nuclear weapons by means of technical military defenses, or would they prefer to address the threat in a political environment where peaceful methods had also been provided?

Elements of an Approach to Israel

Above all, people who want to approach Israel must make plain (1) that they recognize the unique suffering of the Jewish people, particularly in the Nazi Holocaust, (2) that they accept Israel as a state in the Middle East with the right to engage in the pursuits and relationships with neighbors that are normal to states at peace, (3) that Israel's security can be assured in those relationships, and (4) that they are prepared to negotiate peace on a reciprocal basis.

This position must be communicated convincingly to the Israeli body politic. Furthermore, the offer to negotiate peace must somehow be made so clear and compelling that Israelis will have no choice but to respond. Israelis could not ignore President Sadat's visit to Jerusalem.

That dramatic visit will not be replicated. Other ways to achieve comparable impact must be found—perhaps a direct television broadcast of a speech by Hussein to the Israeli people or an Israeli-Jordanian summit held privately or openly.

Friends—particularly the United States—must work with Israelis to develop limits in Israel's relationships. Some Israelis, including veteran senior military officers, criticize U.S. leadership and the Congress for damaging Israel by providing, almost unquestioningly, much of the money, most of the weapons, and most of the diplomatic support for which the Israeli lobby asks. These Israelis say Americans have made it impossible for Israelis to curb what they see as Israeli excesses—in lack of economic control, in the use of force, and in the failure to take initiatives in seeking a negotiated peace. Arabs ask for limits of a specific kind. Many say they are prepared to accept Israel if Israel will define itself. Even Syrians claim they would accept Israel if Israel would accept the pre-1967 borders, but Syrians accuse both Israel and the United States of being unable to put a map of Israel's proposed borders on the table as a basis for negotiating peace. Pressure and the introduction of limits into this relationship are not the same thing. Limits should be regarded as a necessary component of healthy normal human relationships, which depend in part on each party's understanding the other's limits of tolerance.

In approaching the Israelis, it is necessary to take into account particular psychological factors beyond the Holocaust—a historic sense of belonging in the biblical lands, the suffering caused by centuries of persecution, a special sense of victimization at the hands of history, the violence of the 1948 War for Independence, and the deep-rooted need for security and acceptance. In psychological terms, the aim is to approach the Israelis in a way that will open the door to mutual Israeli and Palestinian acknowledgment that each people has in different ways been the victim of history. If each side could be brought to acknowledge rather than deny the other's suffering, that mutual acknowledgment might remove one of the most formidable barriers to negotiation.

U.S. government officials must also remain alert to one other delicate element in the psychological relationship with Israel. The firm articulation of U.S. interests is natural for the United States when it speaks officially. American officials must be sensitive to Israeli and other Jewish feelings under the surface that the appearance of coercion by Gentiles can be read as a recurrence of cyclical anti-Semitism. One appropriate antidote is steady reassurance that the American government and people have an unchanging commitment to the enduring security of Israel. This reassurance is critical in dealing with the basic Jewish fear that "it can happen again." The fears that stem from this feeling partly explain Israeli caution—and even paralysis—in running risks for peace that may seem reasonable to other people. Sensitivity to Jewish memories of the Holocaust is critical in any productive relationship with Israelis.

4

Palestinians: Moving toward a
New Pragmatism

Ready to Take the First Steps?

In the 1970s we often felt that, if the Palestinian movement had to decide whether or not to make peace with Israel, the movement would split. In mid-1985 the movement was more sharply divided than ever. The fault lines were complex, depending on perspectives and issues. Portions of the Palestine Liberation Organization that were powerfully supported by Syria continued to reject any negotiating process in which they did not take part. Nevertheless, it seemed accurate to suggest in mid-1985 that perhaps three-quarters of the Palestinians, or at least a significant number of those living in the West Bank, Gaza, Jordan, pre-1967 Israel, at the PLO headquarters in Tunis, and elsewhere, were moving toward a more pragmatic position than ever before. They seemed ready to take the first steps toward peace with Israel, but difficult issues still constrained their leaders.

One division of the movement reflected the amount of face-to-face experience different Palestinians had had with Israelis—with their military government, their soldiers, their economy, their settlers, and even with their lawyers, their university community, a few of their journalists, and some private individuals seeking peace. The Palestinians who lived under Israeli military government had a greater sense of urgency about the need to make peace. They also had a more pragmatic sense of their real choices in negotiating an end to Israeli military occupation.

In February 1985 I asked some Palestinians in Damascus what their aim was. "An independent state, a place at the table under our own names," and sometimes "return to our homes," they replied. These Palestinians left their homes in 1948, have fought Israel as an enemy ever since, and have seen Israelis across the barriers of belligerency almost as abstractions—not as individuals building and functioning in a society and political system of their own. These Palestinians have also had little contact with the 2 million of their countrymen who have continued living face to face with the Israelis in the land west of the Jordan River. Nevertheless, their hopes and their voices demanded the attention of PLO leaders. The Palestinians who do not live on Palestinian land impose an almost weightier burden on PLO leaders than the Palestinians under occupation. The PLO was born as an organization of exiles.

I asked other Palestinians living under Israeli military government in the West Bank or Gaza whether their top priority was a state of their own. "No. Our highest priority is getting rid of the Israeli occupation." If the Israeli occupation were lifted next week, what would happen? "We would need a transitional period and interim authorities so we would have time to build our own institutions and our relationships with our neighbors." How long would that take? "Perhaps three to five years." What kind of interim arrangements might be useful? "The Egyptian autonomy"—the Egyptian proposal for the powers and responsibilities of a Palestinian self-governing authority that was put forward in the post–Camp David talks on autonomy for the inhabitants of the West Bank and Gaza. The increasing pragmatism of these Palestinians catches PLO leaders between their readiness to compromise to save part of Palestine and the uncompromising stance of the exiles who left the part of Palestine that is destined to remain Israeli.

When the PLO was split, partly by Syrian action, Arafat had to rely increasingly on the almost 3 million Palestinians in Jordan and in the land west of the Jordan River as his main constituency. Nevertheless, he continued to be deeply sensitive to the Palestinians who lived in dispersion. In connection with the Hussein-Arafat agreement, PLO leaders grappled with practical questions facing the Palestinian national movement: Shall we hold out for full recognition of the PLO by the United States and Israel and for an independent Palestinian state? Shall we demand agreement to these points at the outset of negotiations, or shall we adopt a more pragmatic approach? Shall we start realistically with the situation where we are now and take the first steps to begin working toward the freedom to govern ourselves as a separate people? If we adopt a more pragmatic approach, how can we protect the interests of the Palestinians who live in exile? Increasingly, PLO leaders seemed ready to move a step at a time, although they remain wary of any step that could jeopardize the PLO's place at the table and could divide the exile community from the people who are still on the land.

Palestinians' views reflect not only where they live today but when they left Palestine and what they have done since. Like the Palestinians in established positions in Damascus, those in Jordan who left the parts of Palestine west of the 1949–1967 armistice lines that defined pre-1967 Israel tend to take more rigid positions. They are older; bitterness has become part of them; they have become established in Jordan; they see little realistic prospect of recovering property they lost even for their children and none of recovering the years they have spent as refugees; many feel comfortable as belligerents standing on principle. Those who left the West Bank or Gaza because of the 1967 fighting and Israeli occupation may be younger; many have families living under Israeli military government with whom they maintain constant contact; they may have somewhat more hope that Israel will withdraw from that land and that a lasting Palestinian political identity will be established in those lands.

The Palestinians who left Palestine before 1967 include people who, from the time of their departures beginning in the late 1940s, sought identity in political action. Some took the lead in developing the philosophical underpinnings of Arab nationalism. Others in the 1950s focused on their own Palestinian identity, on articulating a Palestinian nationalism, and then on shaping political organizations to press the Palestinian cause. Fearful of separate Palestinian political power, Arab governments had worked to channel it into an organization where their own influence would be strong. The main point here is not that these Palestinians had their own difficult experiences with the principal Arab governments but that the whole lives of these Palestinians were committed to building an institution—the PLO—to wring recognition of the whole Palestinian people from the world and to win their independence.

Yasser Arafat and a handful of men around him have devoted thirty years, more or less, to the Palestinian cause. For them, the PLO alone represents the interests of all Palestinians, wherever they are. They recognize that the PLO is the only embodiment of Palestinian identity. It is understandable that they would vigorously debate any step that threatened to compromise full participation of the PLO in negotiations or a Palestinian state, which they would govern. Sometimes they seemed to put those goals ahead of ending the occupation, but that attitude may have reflected their concern with the interests of Palestinians living in exile. By mid-1985, Arafat and his closest colleagues seemed to be debating whether their only realistic hope lay in engaging in a negotiating process rather than in holding out for acceptance of all their demands first.

Since Israel ended the 1967 War occupying the West Bank and Gaza, an increasing number of Palestinians have debated the shape of their political future. More and more have argued that Israel is here to stay and that Palestinians should seek a state of their own in the land from which Israel withdraws. Since 1982, some Palestinians have taken a second pragmatic step in their reasoning. They have understood that Israel, the United States, and even Jordan are not ready to accept an independent Palestinian state. They have been willing to try to negotiate with Jordan terms under which they could be satisfied that they were exercising their right of self-determination by governing themselves within a Jordanian-Palestinian confederation. To have some chance of success, a negotiating process will have to provide those who urge this further evolution in Palestinian thinking with reason to argue that this approach alone can produce results. The debate is under way. The negotiating process could help shape its course.

These more pragmatic positions differ markedly from those we encountered after Camp David in 1978–1979. At that time, the widespread Palestinian position was that the United States should press for Israeli withdrawal to the pre-1967 borders and should then arrange for a totally free act of Palestinian self-determination in the land from which Israel had withdrawn. Because the Palestinians would vote for an independent state if they were given a totally free choice, they equated the principle of self-determination with an independent Palestinian state. Only recently have a number of Palestinians have come to share the realization that persuading the Israelis to withdraw depends partly on providing them with a picture of a settlement that includes the quasi-guarantee of involving a known element—Jordan. Some of them have come to recognize that an act of self-determination may itself have to be defined pragmatically by the context in which it occurs.

Israelis and other people will question whether this apparent Palestinian shift toward a new pragmatism is simply a tactic. It is a fair question, because PLO leaders are constrained by the complex realities of their own divided community and of shifting political sands in the Arab world. The only answer to the question is that the PLO may well be undergoing a serious transformation, but the only way to determine what it represents is to probe.

A Palestinian State in Part of Palestine

Some Palestinians define the problem in terms that acknowledge Israel as a part of the picture and take their present situation as a starting point from which to build a political expression of their own identity. Mainstream Palestinians define the problem in terms of gaining recognition of their right as a people to self-determination in the part of Palestine from which Israel withdraws. Other Palestinians seem mentally to turn the clock back to a time when Israel was not part of the picture. They continue to speak of the problem as how to reclaim all of Palestine and how to secure the right of Palestinians to return to homes they left in 1948. Their picture does not seem to include what has happened in the Israeli part of Palestine since 1948.

Many Palestinians recognize that Israel's statehood is, by virtue of its military power and economic development, an accomplished fact. They withhold recognition mostly as a tactic—not because they do not recognize that Israel will continue to exist. They say frequently that recognition is the "only card" they have to play, and they assert that they do not intend to recognize Israel as a state until Israel recognizes them as a people with a right to political expression of their identity. Whether or not they formally recognize Israel in public declarations, most PLO leaders speak from a map of the Middle East in their mind's eye that includes Israel. When they demand Israeli withdrawal to pre-1967 borders, they assume that Israel will exist west of those borders. When they speak of readiness to form a state of their own in land west of the Jordan River from which Israel withdraws, they assume peaceful coexistence with Israel.

Other Palestinians reject peace with Israel. Their picture of the problem starts from the Arab demand of the 1940s for one secular state in Palestine. This was still the position of the Palestinian movement in the 1960s when the Palestine Liberation Organization was formed and the Palestinian National Charter was written. In some minds that position had become part of a larger picture of the Arab world. Organizations such as the Popular Front for the Liberation of Palestine (PFLP) of George Habbash cast Palestinian objectives in almost Marxist terms that provided for pressing armed struggle to drive all manifestations of Western imperialism, including Israel, from the Middle East as a means of mobilizing the masses and mounting revolution in the region. In other minds, the PLO's position simply reflected a view that justice required restoration of their lost homes.

After the 1967 War, when Israel took control over all the land west of the Jordan River, some of the top leaders of the Palestinian movement concluded pragmatically that half a loaf was better than none at all. They continued to dream of a secular state in all of Palestine but set their sights more practically on a Palestinian state in part of Palestine. It is obvious why Palestinians in the West Bank and Gaza might settle for a homeland in those territories. It is much more complex to explain the process by which Palestinians who cannot return to their lands would accept the new realities. In effect, these Palestinians in some way seem to have transferred their dreams from the recovery of particular homes or farms to the recovery of their Palestinian identity. The establishment of a political expression of that identity has become in many minds the psychological vehicle through which the Palestinians may be able to let go of the past. In the exile community, a Palestinian passport and a Palestinian homeland to which they could look for an expression of their identity are the critical substitutes for recovery of all the land. Although this assertion cannot be proved quantitatively, the Palestinians holding this view in the mid-1980s appear to represent the mainstream.

Israelis see a threat in even this Palestinian position because most Palestinians will not recognize the *right* of the Israelis to a state in Palestine. Even the most moderate Palestinian will respond that it is asking too much of him to say that he must recognize the Israelis' right to live on land and in a home he regards as ancestrally his own. He will contend that it is enough for him to accept a historical statement of the problem—that Israel is an established fact and that the problem is to define terms by which Israelis and Palestinians can coexist with equal rights in the land west of the Jordan River. If the problem is to be defined in terms of Israel's right to live on their lands, Palestinians say, they will have to argue their rights, and the argument cannot provide the basis for a settlement.

If right to the land cannot provide the basis for a settlement, perhaps it is enough for each people to recognize—as the Israeli philosopher says—why the other people feel they belong in the land. Perhaps it is enough for each people to include in its picture of the problem an awareness of what the other side has suffered and why it feels unjustly treated. The Palestinians, for their part, feel aggrieved that history has asked them to cede part of the land that they have occupied so that it can be the site of a Jewish home for Jewish people who have been persecuted by others. Israelis seek acknowledgment of their suffering in the Holocaust and assert a four-thousand-year-old God-given claim to the land; Palestinians seek some understanding that they mourn the loss of homes and land. When each side incorporates the other's mourning into its own picture of the problem, there may be a starting point for developing a common life in the land west of the Jordan River.

For the Palestinians, peace is more than ever a powerful incentive to take the first steps. Peace would presumably mean an end of military government for most of 1.3 million Palestinians. It would mean the establishment of a homeland—even if in association with Jordan—and an opportunity for the political expression of identity. It would provide a psychological anchor for troubled Palestinians, whether in Lebanon's refugee camps or in the uncertain economies of the Gulf. The incentive to take the first steps grows as the situation in the Middle East deteriorates.

Time Creates Facts

The Palestinians in the past have believed that time was on their side, that Arab strength would increase with time and that Israel would eventually have to bow to superior Arab numbers in armed struggles and would withdraw at least from territories occupied in 1967. By the mid-1980s, the Palestinians, and especially those in the occupied territories, had begun to recognize that Israel was so steadily and so firmly entrenching itself in the territories that it would be increasingly difficult for Israel to pull back even if new Israeli leaders wanted to do so.

Americans involved in the peace process have found it difficult to understand why Palestinian leaders seemed to prefer to drift along with the steady and calculated extension of Israeli control in the West Bank and Gaza rather than engage in a process to arrest that extension. If we could understand the roots of this Palestinian preference, perhaps we could grasp one of the main obstacles to negotiation.

Answers apparently lie not so much in belief that the alternatives to negotiation are potentially more productive as in the conviction that negotiation is the ultimate capitulation. At best, the Palestinians are being asked to legitimize and perpetuate Israeli possession of land that they feel was once legitimately theirs. They are being asked either to engage in an act of generosity that is virtually without historical example or to accept their own defeat. In each case, they are also still denied the recognition of their identity that would come from recognition of the PLO or of their right of self-determination. Even Sadat had to erase the humiliation of the 1967 Arab defeat by crossing the Suez Canal in 1973 before he could negotiate—and he was negotiating to get *all* Egypt's land back. The challenge in bringing the Palestinians to the table is how to enable them to accept the loss of part of Palestine.

Our argument to the Palestinians after Camp David went something like this: Israel is too powerful to be conquered. Israel is steadily expanding into all the land west of the Jordan River. It is better to accept some formula such as the negotiations proposed in the Camp David accords, which would bring into being a Palestinian self-governing authority that would then negotiate a permanent relationship between Israel and a Palestinian political entity of a nature to be determined. This approach would give the Palestinian people for the first time in modern history one self-governing body elected by all the Palestinians in the West Bank and Gaza. By our logic that course of action seemed better than the alternative for the Palestinians of continuing to live either under military occupation or as an ethnic minority in other states. With the loss of any serious military option in Lebanon in 1982, negotiation of political alternatives seemed the only realistic route to take. We Americans perceived three possible explanations of why the Palestinians did not buy this argument.

First, the Palestinians were being asked to accept the Israeli nation, whereas neither Israel nor the United States would give the Palestinian people comparable acceptance and recognition as a people. When President Reagan spoke on September 1, 1982, against an independent Palestinian state and said the Palestinian problem would be resolved in association with Jordan, one Palestinian leader responded, "If the Reagan plan is improved by adding one word—'self-determination'—things would change completely."[1] Although his statement may oversimplify the PLO position, he seemed to say that, if the United States would see the Palestinians as a people with the same right of self-determination that the Israelis had exercised, the Palestinians could negotiate in dignity. The Palestinians still find it difficult to see how they will find expression of their identity.

Second, Palestinian leaders, whose roots lie mainly in the exile community, have naturally worried that a Palestinian settlement will focus on the Palestinians who remain on the land in the West Bank and Gaza and will ignore the interests of those Palestinians who have lived elsewhere. It is an interesting question in the mid-1980s whether either group could really trust the other to represent its interests in a negotiation. This fear that the interests of the exile community would be left out of a settlement was one strong reason for the Palestinians' rejection of Camp David. Whether or not they intended it to do so, their position sometimes created the impression that recognition of them as the Palestinian spokesmen was more important than taking the first steps toward a practical solution. In many cases this observation may be unfair, but the PLO leadership's ability to bring a deeply divided organization into peace negotiations seemed in some measure to depend on the leadership's ability to win a place for itself at the table. PLO leaders claim that they alone represent the 2 million Palestinians living outside the territories occupied by Israel in 1967, who have no alternative Palestinian leadership at all.

Third, although the 1.3 million Palestinians in the West Bank and Gaza have in the past elected municipal leaders, they also look to the PLO to represent them in peace negotiations. They have been unable to build even a regional political organization of their own. Some of their uncertainty resulted from the need to have the blessing of the full Palestinian movement in accepting the final partition of Palestine. In operational terms, they had no mandate from the PLO to negotiate on behalf of all Palestinians. Some of their uncertainty resulted from Israeli prohibitions against political meetings and from deportation of competent leaders, which the Palestinians did not feel able to challenge effectively. After Camp David, when I was discussing with a group of senior West Bank and Gaza notables how they might develop a mandate to participate in the Camp David negotiations, one of them threw up his hands in frustration after a fruitless conversation and exclaimed, "We are all sheep!" Yet every Palestinian in the room expected to be subject to deportation if he pressed positions that the Israelis rejected. These leaders might have felt differently if some international protection had been assured. In its absence, they felt safer leaving the problem to the PLO.

In the Palestinians' eyes, the alternatives *to* negotiation are known, and the alternatives *in* negotiation are seen as no more than imposing second-class status and the terms of defeat. They still see no avenue through which all Palestinians can find the expression of their identity. The issue is how to make negotiation seem more attractive than the alternatives that are already being tested. The Arabs can always take some comfort in the long view—that over a historical period the situation will change as the Arab states become stronger and as a 40 percent Arab minority within Israel exerts its effect on the character of Israel. At this point they see nothing else they can do until negotiation seems to promise them dignity and recognition rather than humiliation.

Partition, Confederation, and a Struggle for Leadership

The fundamental position since 1947 among Palestinians, as among other Arabs, rejected the partition of Palestine and the establishment of a separate Jewish state in Palestine. After the 1967 War, Palestinians began to move toward acceptance of partition and toward recognition of Israel's existence in part of Palestine on the condition that the Palestinians could have a state of their own in the other part of Palestine. I concede that some Palestinian leaders and organizations continue to reject Israel. I do, however, assert that the mainstream of the Palestine National Council and the portion of the PLO that Yasser Arafat consolidated in Tunis after the 1982 and 1983 expulsions from Lebanon take the position that peace can be made with an Israel defined by the 1967 borders provided that the Palestinians can exercise their right of self-determination in the land from which Israel withdraws.

This assertion will be challenged. The challengers will argue that the Palestinian National Charter still stands, that the Arab summit declaration from Fez in 1982 refused to mention Israel by name, and that the PLO in early 1985 still refused openly to accept Security Council Resolution 242. King Hussein in Washington in May 1985 stated, however, he was authorized to say, "The Palestinians are willing to accept United Nations Security Council Resolutions 242 and 338, and the principles they contain, as the basis for a settlement."[2] The proper response to this argument is not a textual one. It is simpler and more powerful: key Arab leaders work from a mental map of the Middle East in which Israel exists. The Fez Declaration, to which the PLO leaders were party, calls for Israeli withdrawal to the 1967 borders. What will exist west of those borders? Israel. When PLO leaders argued about the terms of the Hussein-Arafat agreement, they did not argue over the principle, stated in that agreement, of exchanging land for peace. Peace with whom? Israel. The PLO leaders who wanted to modify that agreement were concerned about the exact role of the PLO in negotiations and the exact relationship between the Palestinian political entity and Jordan. Negotiations with whom? Israel.

Some observers continue to doubt that the mainstream Palestinians are ready to make peace with Israel. The question is whether these observers are prepared to test through negotiation evidence that exists or whether they will try to denigrate the evidence and ignore it. The question that I would address to those who are not willing to test the evidence is whether they really want to negotiate a settlement with the Palestinians.

Let us assume, at least for purposes of discussion, that the main elements in the PLO leadership are prepared to see Palestinians living at peace with Israel in a partitioned Palestine. In early 1985, the real debate among the PLO leaders about the shape of a settlement began at this point. The real issues had become pragmatic ones. Exactly how would the Palestinians exercise their right of self-determination? Exactly how would political expression of their identity be worked out in a constructive relationship with Jordan? How exactly would the role of the PLO in negotiations be defined? Certainly Palestinians in the West Bank and Gaza would include on the agenda of questions: Exactly what agreements will govern the necessary continuing relationship with Israel?

For the first time, Palestinians are thinking in pragmatic terms about *how* to move from military occupation to political freedom and what forms freedom would take. In most of my previous discussions, Palestinians seemed to assume that recognition of the Palestinians' right of self-determination would resolve the problem. Now they are beginning to recognize that, even if the right of self-determination is assumed, it will still be necessary to negotiate about ways of exercising it so that Israel and Jordan can accept that the Palestinians' act of self-determination will not jeopardize their own right of self-determination and their security.

During the Jordanian-Palestinian talks that produced the Hussein-Arafat agreement, discussion of how Palestinian self-determination might be arranged reached a new level of practicality. The option of a confederation between a Palestinian West Bank and the Hashemite Kingdom of Jordan had been in the air for more than a decade. The details of such a relationship have not been fully discussed, but the February 1985 agreement recorded intent to seek a solution within that context—Palestinian self-determination exercised within a Jordanian-Palestinian confederation. This step reflects Palestinian focus on the shape of a settlement that could become the subject of negotiation.

The realism shown by some Palestinians in the West Bank about the need for time to build regionwide institutions in the West Bank and Gaza also reflects political realities of a different kind. It demonstrates recognition both that such institutions have never existed and that tension will sharpen between people who have lived in and governed the territories and members of PLO committees who may want to move in and govern.

The psychological significance to the exile community of identification with a Palestinian homeland and of determining how the exiles will relate to that homeland in practical ways—matters of passports, voting, investment, and property ownership—will become an important part of the process. The debate over the shape of the settlement within the Palestinian movement has become more realistic. Although it also seems to have become even more complex, the time has arrived when we can talk about these issues as more than abstractions.

The people who try to shape a negotiating process will need to take into account a Palestinian political process in which a major issue is the nature of the settlement within the Palestinian community. Who will play leading roles? How will a settlement deal with people who are left out? A major objection to the Camp David accords in the Palestinian community stemmed from the judgment that one purpose of the accords was to divide the Palestinians in the West Bank and Gaza from the PLO leadership and the rest of the Palestinians elsewhere. Movement toward negotiation will confront this obstacle again if it fails to take into account that part of the political process on the Palestinian side involves commitment to a settlement for all the Palestinians.

What Will the Arabs Support? Can Israel Accept?

For the Palestinians, there is more than just one "other side." They must come to terms not only with Israel but also with the other Arabs. This problem applies in a unique way to Jordan but is broader.

In the years between the armistice agreements of 1949 and the 1967 War when Jordan and Egypt controlled the West Bank and Gaza, the two nations made no move to create a separate Palestinian state. In fact, some Palestinians will openly say that they were given only refugee status by the Arab states generally. Jordan was the sole state to accord the Palestinians citizenship en masse, but even there the issue was discussed in terms of fuller participation by Palestinians in Jordanian political life and possible greater autonomy in administering their own communities. Although many observers in the Arab world may find it disturbing to be asked to discuss the issue, the fact is that any effort to resume the Arab-Israeli peace process must build in part on an Arab-Palestinian political process that may continue to define this relationship.

Although the Arab states formally support creating an independent Palestinian state, it is not at all clear how much any of them welcome the idea. It was 1974 before they finally acknowledged formally that the Palestinians should speak for themselves in a negotiation with Israel. Reports and actions over the years have indicated that both Jordan and Syria see a Palestinian political entity as relating to them in ways that would give them significant influence in determining the actions of that entity. They are clearly concerned about the impact on their security of a separate Palestinian state. Other Arab governments, especially in traditional societies such as Saudi Arabia, have feared elements of the PLO that have their early roots in revolutionary nationalist philosophies, some of them Marxist. Whatever the roots of the feelings, the fact is that the Palestinians can realistically hope to exercise their right of self-determination only in a context that has granted the affected states the opportunity to build into any solution whatever safeguards they can to protect their own integrity.

The Hussein-Arafat agreement was an important milestone in a longstanding series of efforts to define a workable relationship between the Hashemite Kingdom of Jordan and the Palestinian people. In 1972, King Hussein published his plan for a United Arab Kingdom in which Palestinians would govern themselves under the umbrella of a Hashemite government that would retain responsibility for defense and foreign affairs.[3] The agreement of February 1985 described the relationship as a confederation. Within the framework of an agreement defining the confederal relationship, the Palestinians would exercise their right of self-determination. Argument in the Palestinian community focuses on the degree of independent action that would be considered an adequate political expression of separate Palestinian identity.

In short, the first question before Palestinian leaders is: What arrangements will the Arab side accept and support? The Hussein-Arafat agreement was more of an Arab coalition agreement than a basis, in the first instance, for negotiation with Israel.

The Palestinians must also assess the chances of Israel's accepting the kind of settlement that the Palestinians envision. In early 1985, they had to start from the formal Israeli position: no withdrawal to the pre-1967 borders, no independent Palestinian state, no negotiation with the PLO. At the same time, they watched the strong negative reaction among the Israeli people to the Israeli military operations in Lebanon from 1982 to 1985. They maintain a dialogue with a few Israelis who see Israel's need for a Palestinian settlement. They seem increasingly willing to accept pragmatically the tactical necessity of establishing a negotiating position in a joint Jordanian-Palestinian delegation without initially forcing the issue of PLO representation. Nevertheless, most Palestinians believe that the Israelis are not likely to agree to any settlement that they can accept. More than previously, however, they seem ready at least to probe the Israeli position rather than to judge it unmovable and do nothing.

Violence or Nonviolence?

The Palestinians seemed to recognize, after their military defeat and expulsion from Lebanon in 1982 and the split in the PLO that Syria forced in late 1983, that they did not by themselves carry enough weight on the negotiating scales to assure themselves of a fair outcome. They needed some kind of coalition context in which to approach negotiation. Because of Jordan's geographical position and historical relationship to the West Bank and to Israel, a Jordanian-Palestinian relationship was the natural cornerstone of such a coalition. Egypt's relationship with Israel and the United States and its experience with the peace process have led the PLO to accept Egypt's involvement. Beyond the Arab coalition, the Palestinians have persistently sought to draw the United States into the process in support of the realization of Palestinian rights. Some of the small group of colleagues around Arafat may argue for keeping the door open for a return to a Syrian-centered coalition, but others see no alternative to Jordan because of its geographic and demographic involvement in the Palestinian problem.

The PLO never had a genuine military option that could threaten the integrity of Israel, yet PLO urban guerrillas managed to withstand the Israeli seige of Beirut. PLO rurally based guerrillas could threaten Israel's northern towns with occasional shelling, and PLO terrorists could organize the occasional hijacking or bombing of civilian targets that drew public attention. Much of this threat is even less effective in the wake of the Palestinian expulsion from Lebanon, although the Palestinians still hold in reserve the theoretical possibility that they could mount a systematic campaign of opposition to Israeli military government that could produce persistent violence in the West Bank.

In approaching a potential negotiation, the PLO has a nonviolent weapon it can employ in an effort to change the balance of forces. The PLO could declare a suspension of violence by organizations under its control during a negotiation. In taking that step, its aim would be to support the efforts of people in Israel who argue for a negotiation that includes the Palestinians. Such a declaration could appear, at the appropriate moment, to be the equivalent of Sadat's call for "no more war."

On the violent side of the ledger, the Palestinians know they cannot physically break the Israeli military government, but some of them are beginning to ask whether creating a bloodbath in connection with military repression could generate political pressures inside Israel for withdrawal. More basically, they fear that provoking violence would simply lead to mass deportations. Looking back, they see deportation as a major weapon in Israel's arsenal. They know that the Israeli security apparatus and control in the West Bank and Gaza are far superior to those in the Shiite areas of southern Lebanon, and they are not eager to turn their own society into a war zone. But some—particularly the younger individuals, who may be responding to the Islamic fundamentalist and Shiite inspiration—are beginning to regard violence as the only way to attract the attention of Israel and the United States.

A few Palestinians have shown interest in using nonviolent techniques in the West Bank and Gaza to build political pressure inside Israel for withdrawal of the military government, but as of early 1985 the idea did not have a significant following. To begin with, Palestinians note that reputable Israeli journalists and scholars who have written persistently about life under the military government have had no more than passing impact. Although a few are intrigued with the idea of using moral suasion rather than violence to change the balance of political forces inside Israel, they see no evidence except Israeli opposition to the invasion of Lebanon that such an approach would work—and the Lebanon operation involved Israeli casualties.

Elements of an Approach to the Palestinians

Recognition as a people with an identity of their own and with the right of self-determination is the fundamental objective of the Palestinians in 1985. The right of self-determination has become the symbolic vehicle for expression of Palestinians' identity as a people. Closely connected to it is a yearning for recognition that they have suffered an injustice. These aims have both psychopolitical and practical dimensions.

On the psychopolitical level, one of the principal obstacles to an Israeli-Palestinian negotiation is the Palestinians' unwillingness to offer full acceptance of Israel until the Israelis offer them full acceptance as a people. The Palestinians believe that they are being asked by history or by the world community to forfeit land and homes in order to create a national home for Jews who have suffered at the hands of other peoples and civilizations. Even as the Palestinians are asked to make a concession that is probably without precedent in history, they are treated as nonpersons, people incapable of feeling pain, loss, or indignity. The only way to elicit from them the full acceptance for which Israelis yearn is to recognize their humanity, their peoplehood, and their suffering. The Palestinians may come to the negotiating table from practical necessity to rid themselves of the Israeli military government; they may negotiate a juridical peace, recognizing Israel's superior power; they may even negotiate arrangements for normal relationships from considerations of economic interest or necessity. The kind of full peace Israel seeks, however, can come only when Israel is prepared to accept the Palestinians to the extent that it wants to be accepted by them. Israel has the opportunity to begin the process of normalizing relations and building peace by making its own Sadat-like offer of recognition.

On the practical level, a successful negotiation requires the participation of Palestinians who have the authority both to speak on behalf of the Palestinians and to deliver the performance from Palestinians that they promise. Two options for involving the Palestinians have been considered: The first is negotiation with the PLO; the second is trying to assemble a group of West Bankers and Gazans who would be elected to negotiate. The people in the West Bank and Gaza as well as the Arab governments prefer the PLO because it is the one Palestinian organization that is set up to cope with all the elements in the Palestinian community, including the people who reject peace with Israel and will try to sabotage any peace effort. The Palestine National Council, with the PLO as its executive arm, is the one organization that can confer legitimacy on any compromises that will need to be made in a negotiation. Without such legitimization even Arab governments feel unable to make concessions beyond recognizing Israel within the pre-1967 borders. They know that compromises will be necessary for security arrangements even if for no other reasons. If Israelis and the U.S. government are reluctant to deal with the PLO, and *if* they want a serious negotiation, they will have to determine how to provide legitimacy for the Palestinian negotiators and the agreements they reach.

The effort to legitimize Palestinian negotiators must recognize that the Palestinians are extremely sensitive to efforts to divide them. The Camp David approach foundered, in part, on the point that Palestinians, in the West Bank at least, felt unable to speak for all Palestinians. Those Palestinians had been elected to govern municipalities at most, and they were acutely aware of the need to represent the Palestinians who had lost homes and property in 1948 and had lived outside Palestine since that time. Otherwise stated, it is essential to help the Palestinians who would be willing to negotiate so that they can do so under auspices that provide the greatest possible legitimacy. By their own definition, such auspices will include some blessing from the PLO. This raises an ugly and probably unanswerable question: To what extent will members of the PLO leadership block Palestinian participation in a negotiation to assure perpetuation of their own individual power and influence? Perhaps if the possible gains from negotiating are made realistic enough and attractive enough they will generate pressures that will reduce the opportunities for individuals to operate from such motives. The fact is that the power struggle for control in the Palestinian community will go on; the issue is whether the people who want to advance the peace process will attempt to buttress constructive elements or will throw up their hands because there is a struggle. People who are prepared to compromise also know that they may be asked to pay with their lives.

Notes

1. *The Christian Science Monitor*, February 23, 1983, p. 1, "What Arafat Wants From Washington" by Trudy Rubin.

2. His Majesty King Hussein, Address delivered at the American Enterprise Institute for Public Policy Research, Washington, D.C., May 1985, p. 6.

3. Excerpts from the proposal for a United Arab Kingdom, in *The Search for Peace in the Middle East: Documents and Statements, 1967–1979*, Report prepared for the Subcommittee on Europe and the Middle East of the Committee on Foreign Affairs, U.S. House of Representatives, by the Foreign Affairs and National Defense Division, Congressional Research Service, Library of Congress, Committee Print CP-957 (Washington, D.C.: U.S. Government Printing Office, 1979), p. 271, appear in appendix III.

5

Jordan: Building an Arab Coalition

Can Jordan Lead?

In King Hussein's eyes, peace cannot be negotiated between Israel and Jordan without resolving the Palestinian problem, and the Palestinian problem cannot be resolved in the mid-1980s without Jordan. In theory, Israelis and Palestinians could negotiate their own peace agreement, but Israel is still politically unable to negotiate directly with authoritative Palestinian representatives. In theory, Israel and Jordan could negotiate Israeli withdrawal from the West Bank and Gaza, but Hussein concluded in earlier peace efforts that Jordan cannot act alone in agreeing on boundaries or on relationships in Jerusalem. Egypt could negotiate with Israel alone, but Jordan can act only from a broader Arab political base.

The PLO will play a central role in any Arab negotiating coalition. No Arab government any longer feels able to judge between the interests of the different factions of the Palestinian movement in relation to each other or to take responsibility for the concessions in Palestine that peace will require. The action of the Arab summit at Rabat in 1974, which authorized the PLO to speak for the Palestinians, came at a time when a first step in Israeli-Jordanian negotiations was being discussed, so Jordan feels a particular requirement to move toward negotiation only with broader Arab support.

At the same time, some Arab governments see their relationship with the PLO as one key to their own security and to their political influence in the Arab world. Syria believes protection of its interests requires a Syrian voice in the settlement of the Palestinian question. The destiny of Jordan is historically and geographically entwined with the settlement of the Palestinian question. In early 1985, shaping the Arab negotiating coalition was one of the critical first steps in advancing the peace process beyond the Egyptian-Israeli peace treaty.

Jordanians have judged that the starting point in building a coalition compatible with securing Jordan's future is to work out the framework for a long-term relationship with the Palestinians. From that base, they would try to build broad Arab support for such a relationship and then, with that support, to negotiate peace with Israel. The issue for King Hussein is whether Jordan can assume the lead in building the coalition and can sustain it in the face of a serious Syrian challenge.

Opening the seventeenth session of the Palestine National Council on November 22, 1984, King Hussein expressed his own convictions:

> Perhaps . . . the natural starting point would be to emphasize the special relationship which ties Jordan to Palestine, a relationship forged by purely objective factors of history, geography and demography, which have placed the two brotherly countries and peoples, since the beginning of the century, in the same boat of suffering and hope, of interest and harm, of history and destiny. The particularity of our relationship is not a whimsical self-description, but a scientific fact which has made the Palestinian question a daily and central concern in our lives and a basis of our defence, foreign and development policies. If to our brethren the Palestine question is one of their foreign and defence priorities, to us, as to you, it is the foremost priority. Consequently, Palestine has never been a political tool to serve our state objectives or our selfish ends.[1]

In establishing the identity of their people Jordanian leaders have also struggled to view the Jordanian-Palestinian relationship in the larger context of Arab identity. "Who are the Palestinians, the Lebanese, the Jordanians, the Syrians or the Iraqis, whether Christians or Muslims?" asks Crown Prince Hassan bin Talal. "Are they the descendants of those who led the Pan-Arab Renaissance Movement of seventy years ago and the recipients of its principles and ideals? If so, why is it that they seem to have forsaken all semblance of solidarity, let alone unity, in the face of adversity?"[2] Born into a family—the Hashemites—that played a major role in the Arab effort to define the modern character of the Arab people, King Hussein and Crown Prince Hassan have grappled with the problem of building a society, a philosophy, and an economy that can join in one state the people whose past lies on the east bank of Jordan and the Palestinians whose traditions lie west of the river. The survival of their ideals, and of their dynasty, rests on their ability to define and win political support for one political entity that brings together both of these peoples.

"There must be a clear-sighted definition of the goals set out by the Hashemite political leadership for more than half a century," Hassan continued. "There is a great richness in diversity. Pluralism in society and politics is a noble aim. It should not be a cause for disunity but a basis for the evolution of a well-integrated and harmonious commonwealth." He concluded, "The question that faces us is this: Do we still have a political will to overcome our differences and achieve a common identity based on a *terra media* of interests in an increasingly polarized world?"

Jordanian identity today faces strong challenges. The Palestinian population plays a rapidly growing role in the Hashemite Kingdom of Jordan. From extremist elements in Israel come statements that "the Palestinians have their state—it is called Jordan." The Ba'athist regime in Syria seems not completely content to allow the Hashemite regime to play the key role in defining the character of a Jordanian-Palestinian commonwealth. The Palestinians themselves are divided over their relationships with both Israel and Jordan.

Underlying these explicit challenges to the character of Jordan itself is a less tangible but potentially even more powerful longer-term challenge that is spreading across the Arab world. A generation of Arab youth is approaching adulthood disillusioned with the political and economic models of the Soviet Marxist-Leninist experience and also with the democratic Atlantic community's tremendous burst of energy. Rejecting these models—in some cases with brutal and even purposeless violence—the new generation is turning precipitously to Islam for its inspiration and guidance. A longer-term issue in the Arab world is whether the Islamic resurgence will take violent form and will replace current political systems with Khomeini-style Islamic revolutionary leadership or whether leaders will be able to modify traditional political systems so that they can respond to these pressures from a resurgent Islam without revolutionary upheaval. This challenge too gives shape to the present political objectives in Jordan.

The Jordanian search for peace involves the need to define not only Jordan's relationship with Israel but also the identity of Jordan in a relationship with the Palestinian people who seek to establish an identity of their own. Whatever larger Arab strategy may be pursued, the search for an Israeli-Jordanian settlement cannot be separated from the need to define the Jordanian-Palestinian relationship in precise political forms. As the opportunity for an Israeli-Jordanian negotiation presents itself, the process will inevitably begin in a Jordanian-Palestinian negotiation on the best way to achieve common political purposes while preserving separate identities in the shared political relationship that is essential to both peoples.

Any effort to revive the peace process must recognize the critical character of the political processes involved in building an Arab coalition for negotiation. The first such processes take place within Jordan and within the Palestinian movement—at times separately and then together, as they develop their relationship. As I indicated in chapter 4, it will be a complex set of tasks to determine how Palestinians in exile might relate to their counterparts in a Palestinian homeland and how a

Palestinian homeland and Jordan will relate. Additional questions arise about whether other Arab states—particularly Syria—will support them. A fundamental question remains in the establishment of an Arab coalition for negotiation: Can Jordan lead?

Preserving the Integrity of the Hashemite Kingdom

The problem, as the Hashemite dynasty in Jordan views it, is how to achieve a settlement with Israel and in Palestine that will preserve the integrity of the Hashemite Kingdom. The problem is defined less in territorial terms than in terms of minimizing the threat to that integrity from whatever source—Israeli expansion, political erosion from within, or Arab subversion from outside.

The Jordanian-Palestinian relationship, in Hussein's mind, lies at the heart of the problem. In the vocabulary of conventional security, Hussein told the Palestine National Council in 1984, "The defence of Palestine is a defence of Jordan, as the defence of Jordan is a defence of Palestine." In the vocabulary of human and political rights, he said, "The Jordanian people, above all others and to a greater degree than others, have shared with the Palestinian people their pain, their suffering and their sacrifice, just as they have shared their will, their hope and their determination to regain their legitimate national rights on the land of Palestine." Whether fearing it or not, Hussein spoke of "our common destiny." "If the picture I have presented is bleak," he said, "one reason is that Arab and Palestinian action has dropped from its calculations the special relationship which ties Jordan to Palestine. . . . your sacred cause . . . holds the same interest to us as it does to you, and its repercussions affect us as they affect you."[3]

After the 1949 armistice agreements between Israel and its neighbors, Jordan attempted to play the Arab role in the West Bank exclusive of other Arab countries and tried to negotiate peace with Israel. That effort came to an end when King Abdullah was assassinated. Jordan continued to administer the West Bank, including the large Palestinian refugee camps there. By the mid-1960s, after Palestinian nationalism had begun to assert itself more actively, the Jordanian government was beginning to discuss with leaders in the West Bank ways of giving the Palestinians fuller representation in the national government, but there was no significant discussion of an independent Palestinian state at that stage on either side.

After the 1967 War, King Hussein felt a special obligation to restore the West Bank to Arab, and particularly Jordanian, control. Despite the political risk he initiated exchanges with Israel in an effort to reestablish a Jordanian presence there. At the same time Palestinian nationalism gained momentum, and the PLO gained wider recognition. The PLO began increasingly to act in Jordan as a state within a state. When King Hussein could not tolerate this challenge to his authority and cracked down in September 1970, the Palestinians fought back, and the PLO was expelled.

Again seeking a basis for negotiating with Israel for return of the territory, the king in March 1972 announced a plan for the United Arab Kingdom.[4] Explaining his proposal in retrospect to the Palestine National Council in 1984, he recalled, "The formula was intended to strike a balance between our national obligation to persist in an international search for the restoration of the West Bank on the basis of Resolution 242 and the reassurance of our Palestinian brethren that Jordan recognized their national identity and did not covet their land."[5]

His 1972 proposal began with transforming the Hashemite Kingdom of Jordan into the United Arab Kingdom, which would consist of two regions—the Palestine region (including the West Bank and other Palestinian areas that wanted to join) plus the Jordan region (the East Bank). The king was to be head of state. Executive responsibility would rest with the king, who would be supported by a central cabinet. Legislative authority would be vested in the king and in an assembly where both regions would be equally represented. The king would command the armed forces. The central executive authority would be limited to international affairs, law and order, and general economic matters. Executive authority in each region would be assumed by a native governor general, who would be supported by a regional cabinet and a local assembly. "Our suggestions," Hussein said in 1984, "did not meet with approval at the time."[6]

In mid-1974 Hussein made a serious bid to negotiate the beginnings of a Jordanian return to the West Bank through Secretary Kissinger's mediation. After negotiation of the Israeli-Syrian disengagement agreement in May 1974, we did detailed staff work to prepare for an Israeli-Jordanian agreement that would have returned some Jordanian control to the West Bank. For some months negotiations were delayed for political reasons in Israel, the United States, and the Arab world. Before the negotiations could begin, Arab leaders had met at the summit in Rabat in October 1974 and had declared the Palestine Liberation Organization "the sole legitimate representative of the Palestinian people." Jordan seemed for a time to have lost its chance to reestablish a role in the West Bank. King Hussein nevertheless continued to see the problem in terms of Jordan's need to play a role, for the sake of its own security, in shaping whatever possible settlement emerged in the West Bank.

Opinion in Israel kept the "Jordan option" alive. Refusing to negotiate with the PLO or to consider establishment of a Palestinian state,

Israeli Labor party leaders considered negotiating the return of some of the West Bank to King Hussein. The Jordan option was central to President Reagan's speech of September 1, 1982: "So the United States will not support the establishment of an independent Palestinian state in the West Bank and Gaza, and we will not support annexation or permanent control by Israel . . . . it is the firm view of the United States that self-government by the Palestinians of the West Bank and Gaza in association with Jordan offers the best chance for a durable, just and lasting peace."[7]

The people who favored the Jordan option seemed not to take into account two factors in the king's position: (1) Even for the sake of establishing secure borders, Hussein was not politically able to concede to Israel land that the Palestinians, as well as Arab governments, regarded as theirs. The Rabat summit had declared that only the Palestinians could negotiate for themselves, and even in the secret exchanges with Israel well before Rabat, Hussein felt politically unable to accept any terms but total Israeli withdrawal to the pre-1967 borders. (2) Hussein's position has been that if he were to negotiate the return of territory he would arrange for the Palestinians to exercise their right of self-determination in that territory. Although the act of self-determination would take place within the context of a prior agreement on the relationship between the Palestinians and Jordan, the Palestinians would enjoy substantial autonomy. The Hussein-Arafat agreement of February 1985 provided for a confederation, but the details were not discussed, and pressure within the PLO for virtual independence remained strong.

In short, although Palestinian self-determination has become recognized as an essential ingredient of a settlement by King Hussein, his view of the problem still calls for a significant effort to assure as much as possible that whatever Palestinian entity emerges will be compatible with the continued existence of the Hashemite Kingdom of Jordan. In his view, the task remains how to build a pluralistic state that respects the separate traditions and character of each party's identity.

"Last Opportunity for a Peaceful Settlement"

King Hussein's deep concern about the damaging impact of the passage of time on Palestinian and Jordanian interests is clear. As he told the Palestine National Council:

> The question is: For how long will we allow time to serve a greedy enemy who every day eats up part of the remaining land while we dissipate our time in fruitless argument and recrimination?
>
> How long shall we heed those among us who say: Leave it to future generations? Is this not a clear abdication of respon-

sibility? . . . Can they stop time and progress for the enemy and still keep them moving for themselves? What wisdom or morality is there in leaving future generations a heavy legacy which is apt to become more onerous than to recede? And will the Palestinians, who are lost in a sea of suffering under occupation, accept this kind of argument when they know better than anybody else the impact of granting the enemy even more time and the resulting impact on their existence and future? . . .

It is not indefinite suspension but proper utilization that endows time with meaning.[8]

The king's argument of urgency has not always gone unchallenged in Jordan. When Jordan found after the 1967 War that it could not by itself make the concessions demanded by Israel, the alternative to negotiating—sitting tight and providing equal opportunity for the Palestinians in Jordan—seemed more attractive. Some observers even argued that Jordan had the best of all worlds: Israel controlled the Palestinians in Palestine; the PLO outside Palestine was charged as the sole negotiator for the Palestinians but was too divided to negotiate; and Jordan made its Palestinians full participants in the Jordanian economy and polity.

After the Rabat summit in 1974, King Hussein felt that he had been sidelined by the Arab leaders. He believed that they would one day need to reinvolve him because Israel preferred negotiating with him; because Jordan continued to have support in the West Bank, having underwritten some essential services there; because many Palestinians are Jordanian; and because a Palestinian entity could not survive apart from some relationship with Jordan. Nevertheless, he had to stand back and wait for time to bring them to this point of view.

Jordanian interests continued to require Jordan to keep alive the possibility of an Israeli-Palestinian settlement *in the West Bank* rather than in Amman. The alternative was all too pointedly stated by Israelis such as Prime Minister Begin and General Ariel Sharon—that Jordan was the Palestinian state. Despite Jordan's role as a moderate buffer on Israel's longest border, Jordan has seen these Israeli leaders exhibit little understanding of Jordan's interests—or, as far as the Jordanians can understand, of Israel's real interests—so there seemed no negotiating alternative to sitting tight and building for the future.

Following the PLO's loss of its military option, its expulsion from Beirut, and President Reagan's speech of September 1, 1982, Jordan once again saw a serious possibility of coming to terms with the Palestinians and opening the door to negotiation with the Israelis. After intensive but ultimately unsuccessful efforts to formalize an agreement with Arafat, Hussein issued a statement in April 1983 that placed the responsibility for negotiating back in the hands of the Palestinians. He did so when

Arafat was unable to demonstrate that his own Fatah executive committee supported the agreement the two of them had reached. Again, Hussein was forced to wait.

Then, in late 1984, after the PLO had split between the rejectionists in Damascus and the mainstream PLO, which seemed ready to work out a settlement with Jordan and Israel, King Hussein hosted a meeting of the Palestine National Council in Amman. From the discussions that led to it, his dialogue during the meetings, and negotiations that followed emerged the agreement between him and Arafat in February 1985.

In short, Jordan's immediate alternative to negotiation is manageable. The longer-term alternatives are increasingly dangerous for Jordan. As Hussein said in urging "a cohesive Jordanian-Palestinian stand" on the Palestine National Council, "History will record your answer, because in it lies the last feasible chance to save the land, the people and the holy places." After meeting with President Reagan and other senior American officials in May 1985, Hussein told a Washington audience, "There is one basic point on which we all agree: The world cannot afford to miss what might be the last opportunity for a peaceful settlement of the Arab-Israeli conflict."[9]

A Jordanian-Palestinian Settlement

For Jordan, the shape of a settlement between Jordanians and Palestinians is almost more important than the shape of a settlement between Jordan and Israel, although the two are inseparable. Hussein's approach to negotiation depends on defining the relationship between them.

First, Jordan cannot negotiate with Israel until it has a political base from which to do so. That political base depends partly on establishing a common purpose with the Palestinians. Second, Jordan cannot define with confidence the security arrangements that will be required in an agreement with Israel until it has reached agreement with Palestinians on the security arrangements that they are prepared to support. Third, Jordan cannot be sure of its own integrity unless it can define the relationship between the 1.3 million Palestinians in the West Bank and Gaza and the Palestinians who constitute almost two-thirds of the population east of the Jordan River.

King Hussein described the options to the members of the Palestine National Council this way:

> The international position at large is one that perceives the possibility of restoring the occupied territories through a Jordanian-Palestinian formula, which requires commitments from both our parties considered by the world as necessary for the achievement of a just, balanced and peaceful settlement. If you

find this option convincing—recommended further by our ties as two families linked together by a united destiny and common goals—we are prepared to go with you down this path and present the world with a joint initiative for which we will marshall support. If, on the other hand, you believe that the PLO is capable of going it alone, then we say to you "Godspeed: you have our support." In the final analysis, the decision is yours. Whatever it is, we will respect it because it emanates from your esteemed Council, which is the representative of the Palestinian people.[10]

Determining the shape of a settlement for Jordan involves determining the political forms that will permit the Palestinians to believe that they have achieved political expression of their own national identity while sharing in a constitutional relationship with Jordan that expresses the intertwining interests of both peoples. Since King Hussein published his plan for the United Arab Kingdom in 1972, the debate between the two peoples has focused on the exact nature of a possible confederation between the East Bank and the West Bank. One part of the debate concerns the classic issues of where powers and responsibilities for different functions will reside. Another part of the debate focuses on how the Palestinians can exercise their right of self-determination within a framework that protects the Jordanian and Israeli rights of self-determination.

It may be asked whether the Palestinian entity will have a symbolic "moment of independence" before entering a confederation with Jordan. The Jordanian position calls for preagreement on the form of the confederation so that the Palestinian state—not the "independent" Palestinian state—would be born into the confederation.

The alternative to such an arrangement would be an independent Palestinian state. It could be argued that an independent state would not threaten the integrity of either Jordan or Israel as long as both states remained strong in their own rights. The issue, however, is not the potential military strength of the Palestinian state but rather its political power to influence or subvert the Hashemite Kingdom.

Can the Other Sides Accept?

There are three "other sides" for Jordan—Israel, the Palestinians, and other Arab states. The Israelis and the Palestinians are deeply divided over the kind of relationship with Jordan they want.

Jordanians, as I have said, fear the extremist Israelis who would turn Jordan into the Palestinian state while maintaining Israeli control over all of the West Bank and Gaza. Many Jordanians believe that such individuals will be the controlling voice in shaping Israeli policy, even though they know that Prime Minister Peres and his colleagues in the Labor party would prefer a solution that returned most of the Arab population of the West Bank to Jordanian governance. Jordanians also know that even Peres, with his desire to withdraw from some of the West Bank, is not prepared at best to withdraw to lines approaching those of 1967. Jordanians seriously question whether, if they and the Palestinians present themselves for a negotiation, Peres can deliver the kind of Israeli decisions that the Arab side would regard as essential to a just settlement.

On the Palestinian front, Jordan also sees a divided negotiating partner. Hussein's readiness to make a new effort to develop a common position in late 1984 resulted from his judgment that the military defeat in Lebanon and the split in the PLO made it more likely that the mainstream of the PLO would be ready to move ahead both in negotiation with Jordan and in negotiation with Israel. The rejectionist portion of the PLO remained largely in Syria, not without influence but largely without a seat in the critical councils of the PLO with which Hussein was dealing. His purpose in 1984 was to make another effort to reach an accommodation with those Palestinians with whom he could deal.

Finally, Hussein had to be concerned with the support of other Arab states, especially Syria. Speaking to the Palestine National Council, Hussein described his views on seeking broader Arab support:

> If you decide to adopt the first option I presented, namely the Jordanian-Palestinian formula, allow me to share with you our understanding of how the present situation can be transcended and effective action set in motion.
>
> The existing facts in the Palestinian, Arab and international arenas require us to adhere to Security Council Resolution 242 as a basis for a just, peaceful settlement. The principle of "territory for peace" is the landmark which should guide us in any initiative we present to the world. This principle is not a precondition, but a framework within which negotiations will be carried out. As such it is non-negotiable. . . .
>
> Organizing the Jordanian-Palestinian relationship is a basic responsibility of the Jordanian and Palestinian people. No other party, be it foe, friend or brother, has the right to interfere or to decide for them, since such action would constitute an encroachment on Jordan's sovereignty and a blatant interference in the right of the Palestinian people to self-determination. . . .
>
> In our view, these broad lines may serve as the general framework for a Jordanian-Palestinian initiative to be presented to our Arab brethren for their support, in accordance with the Rabat resolutions. Then, together with our Arab brethren, we

could go out to the rest of the world and seek widening support until it is adopted by the entire community of influential states.[11]

The Political and Military Balance

Despite its well-trained and modestly equipped military forces, Jordan remains the weakest military power in the area. Its ability to negotiate depends heavily on its relationships with other key Arab nations. Its move toward the leadership of the PLO outside Syria in late 1984 was coupled with a resumption of relations with Egypt—the first Arab state to resume normal relations following the break with Egypt after the signing of the Egyptian-Israeli peace treaty. For similar reasons, Jordan was the first of the Arab states to support Iraq wholeheartedly in its war with Iran, thereby building a relationship with its eastern Arab neighbor despite the difference in political systems. The Jordanians have also repeatedly tried to reach out to the Saudis, but they recognize that the effort is complicated by the fact that one of the principal pillars of Saudi foreign policy has long been maintaining a close relationship with Syria, one of the main potential radical threats to the traditional regime in Saudi Arabia.

Once Jordan has developed the broadest possible political base among the Arab states and among the Palestinians, Hussein still faces the question of how to deal with Syria. His dilemma is that Syria, in order not to be excluded from a settlement, will fight for a role in negotiation, but Syria appears likely to press for a degree of control that might make a practical settlement impossible. For this reason Hussein has called for an international conference, including the five permanent members of the United Nations Security Council, as the auspices for peace negotiations. In this way he is trying to provide the Syrians with an umbrella under which to negotiate so that Jordan cannot be charged, as Egypt was, with making a separate peace. It is also his way of at least opening a channel through which Soviet influence might be exercised in constraining Syrian efforts to disrupt a course of negotiation that the Syrians believed did not serve their interests.

Sitting at the political and military crossroads on Israel's longest frontier, Hussein knows that his participation in the peace process depends on his ability to deal with the complex balance of forces that affects his freedom to negotiate. Since Jordan's integrity is a solid buffer between Israel and potential attackers, Jordanians wonder why Israeli—and sometimes American—leaders do not show more concern for enhancing Hussein's ability to shape an Arab political base for negotiation.

A day on the shuttle normally began with a morning meeting with Israelis, continued with a flight to the other side and back, and sometimes ended with a late-night meeting where the day had begun. The U.S. shuttle team under Secretary of State Henry Kissinger meets with the Israeli negotiating team under Prime Minister Yitzhak Rabin at the prime minister's residence in Jerusalem in August 1975.

One shuttle flight might begin with a helicopter or car ride from Jerusalem to Ben Gurion Airport, continue aboard a U.S. Air Force plane to an Arab airport, and end with another car or helicopter ride to the negotiating site. The U.S. shuttle team under Secretary Kissinger meets with the Egyptian negotiating team under President Anwar al-Sadat on the lawn of his residence near Alexandria in August 1975.

Elements of an Approach to Jordan

Any approach to Jordan must begin by showing recognition that survival of the Hashemite dynasty and the present character of Jordan depend on developing a mutually satisfying relationship between Jordan and the Palestinians. King Hussein and his colleagues are struggling to find ways of building a pluralistic society and polity that will give the Palestinians a sense that they have exercised their right of self-determination even in their relationship with Jordan. The challenge is great. It is more critical to Hussein than his relationship with Israel—except for the fact that only in making peace with Israel can he regain the territory in the West Bank and Gaza that is necessary for establishing a Palestinian entity.

A corollary point is that Hussein cannot negotiate a settlement with Israel without having authoritative Palestinian representatives at his side—representatives speaking and acting for the PLO. Knowing that a settlement will require the adjustment of borders, he needs Palestinians to take responsibility for the concessions. Knowing that a settlement in Israel's interests as well as his own will require agreement on security relationships with Israel, he needs Palestinians who can agree and can deliver on their agreement. It is a natural American and Israeli tendency to worry about the strong negative political reaction in Israel that greets any suggestion of PLO involvement in negotiation. The time may have come when Americans and Israelis need to consider Hussein's political requirements as well as those of the prime minister of Israel. Both Israel and the United States since 1967 have pressed the proposition that "the parties to the conflict must be the parties to the peace." Reiterating that principle in Washington in May 1985, Hussein asked: "If the PLO is not a party to the conflict, then who is?"[12]

As Hussein constructs the political coalition from which the Arab side will negotiate, the United States must think of ways to help him enlarge the incentives to negotiate that moderate Palestinian leaders can offer their constituencies. U.S. moves toward the Palestinians should be taken in consultation with Hussein so as to maximize his ability to lead in the peace process.

Consultations with Hussein about Syria's potential participation in the peace process will also be an essential element in any approach to Jordan. Syria will be ruthless in opposing any steps that will result in Syria's exclusion. Syria's opposition is a dangerous security threat to Hussein and leaders in his government. For this reason, in the first half of 1985 he pressed for negotiations under the umbrella of an international conference. He has proposed that conference not because he believes it would be workable to involve the five permanent members of the United Nations Security Council in it but (1) because he needs the legitimacy it would provide in the wake of Sadat's solo negotiations with Israel and (2) because he needs, if possible, Soviet help in restraining Syria.

While it may be difficult for outsiders to involve themselves constructively, Americans should be ready to discuss with Hussein and his colleagues the details of ways to define the political relationship between Jordan and the Palestinians and should invite suggestions on how the Palestinians in the exile community can relate to a Palestinian homeland within a Jordanian-Palestinian confederation so as to focus their sense of Palestinian identity.

In short, talk about the "Jordan option" is unhelpful to Hussein. Any approach to him must show sensitivity to his need for a broad Arab base, including the PLO, to negotiate an Israeli-Jordanian-Palestinian settlement. People who approach Jordan must show an awareness that the purpose of the negotiation is to produce a settlement that will provide for the fulfillment of Israeli, Jordanian, and Palestinian identities while respecting other Arab interests.

Notes

1. His Majesty King Hussein, Address delivered at the opening of the seventeenth session of the Palestine National Council, Thursday, November 22, 1984, Amman, Jordan, pp. 14–15. (Text available from the Jordan Information Bureau, 1701 K Street, N.W., Washington, D.C. 20006.)

2. Hassan bin Talal, *Search for Peace: The Politics of the Middle Ground in the Arab East* (New York: St. Martin's Press, 1984). The quotations in this and the next paragraph appear on pp. 1–2.

3. His Majesty King Hussein, Address to the Palestine National Council, pp. 2, 15–16, 18.

4. Excerpts from the proposal for a United Arab Kingdom appear in appendix III.

5. His Majesty King Hussein, Address to the Palestine National Council, p. 6.

6. Ibid., p. 7.

7. The text of President Reagan's speech appears in appendix VIII.

8. His Majesty King Hussein, Address to the Palestine National Council, pp. 13–14.

9. His Majesty King Hussein, Address delivered at the American Enterprise Institute for Public Policy Research, Washington, D.C., May 1985, p. 3.

10. His Majesty King Hussein, Address to the Palestine National Council, p. 18.

11. Ibid., pp. 18–20.

12. His Majesty King Hussein, Address at the American Enterprise Institute, p. 12.

6

Syria: A Voice in the Settlement

Preventing Syria's Isolation

Syria's participation in any political process leading toward an Arab-Israeli-Palestinian settlement is, in Syrian eyes, critical to Syria's security and central to its policy. People who would pursue the peace process must come to terms with the depth of Syrian feeling that it is imperative to prevent Syria from being isolated and with Syria's strategy for involving itself. In the eyes of President Assad, Syria can be secure only when Syria has a voice in settling the affairs of its neighborhood. What happens in Lebanon, Palestine, Jordan, and Iraq is in his view vital to Syria's future.

In dealing with Israel, Assad believes strongly that serious negotiation will be possible only if the Arab parties are united in approaching Israel or sit down at the table in a position of military equality. In the absence of either, Syria must demonstrate its ability to influence events, as it has in Lebanon. His disagreement with the United States in the peace process began in early 1975 when Kissinger began to move toward a second Egyptian-Israeli interim agreement instead of addressing the Palestinian issue and the Israeli-Jordanian front to complete the circle of partial agreements and to establish the base for a comprehensive settlement. If each of the other Arab parties has made its peace with Israel, Syria will in Assad's view receive nothing from either Israel or the United States.

Syrians did not view the second Sinai agreement, the Camp David accords, or the Egyptian-Israeli peace treaty as parts of a continuing process that would ultimately lead to a comprehensive peace. Syrians saw their exclusion after 1974 as part of a strategy to isolate and surround them. At worst, in the 1980s they have seen U.S. secretaries of state treat them as nonpersons or as enemies. They interpreted the Israeli-U.S. agreement on strategic cooperation in late 1981 as concrete evidence of a policy directed at them. At best, President Reagan's February 1985 telephone call to thank President Assad for Syria's role in helping one of the American hostages who escaped in Lebanon was a step in restoring a critical relationship.

Rebuilding a working relationship of mutual understanding and respect will demand that the Syrians and the Americans engage in a sustained dialogue to increase sensitivity to each other's purposes. Neither side at this point hears the other's position.

Syrian officials do not understand why Americans repeatedly say that they do not know what the Syrians want. They believe that they have stated their position on a settlement clearly: An injustice was done to the Arab people in Palestine when Israel was created, and many Arabs lost their homes. The Arab states have said that Israel must withdraw to the 1967 borders if Israel expects to end the war. Peace is a relationship that grows; it cannot be legislated. Syria has thus stated its terms; Israel has not put forward its own proposed borders. The Arab states see no reason to offer more formal recognition than they did in their 1982 declaration from Fez until Israel makes clear the borders within which it seeks recognition. Syrian officials are prepared to acknowledge Israeli sovereignty within the 1967 borders.

American officials find Syrians inflexible in stating their position without showing a willingness to talk about the political process necessary for getting there. According to Americans, the Syrians find it enough to declare as objectives Israeli withdrawal to 1967 borders and creation of a Palestinian state, to conclude that Israel will not move, and to terminate discussion of political processes by which an Israeli decision to withdraw might be influenced or by which Palestinians might build institutions of their own. Because of their inability or refusal to continue the discussion, Syrians are seen as blocking the peace process and as unwilling to make proposals of their own.

Arab governments, Israel, and the United States face two choices in dealing with Syria as part of an effort to relaunch the peace process. Concerned that Syria will block imaginative solutions that do not conform to Syria's positions, which are perceived as doctrinaire, the three groups think most readily about developing a political and diplomatic process that will involve Israelis, Jordanians, and Palestinians, leaving Syrians to join when they decide it is in their interest to do so. They believe that the Syrians, acutely afraid of being left out, may act ruthlessly to block any process that seems to be gaining momentum without them. They see Syrian willingness to split the PLO in 1983–1984 as an example of the lengths to which Syria will go to preserve its voice in a political process leading toward a settlement. They see no practical way to include the Syrians, however, in view of the apparent inflexibility of their positions. The alternative is to try, as Jordan has, to develop its own relationship with the Palestinians and prospect of negotiating with Israel and then to try to construct a negotiating forum that will include Syria in the opportunity to negotiate; Syria's absence from the negotiations would then reflect Syria's choice, not Syria's exclusion.

For Americans, if we are honest, the choice is complicated by recognition that an Israeli-Syrian negotiation would be very difficult. The Syrians will insist on total Israeli withdrawal from the Golan Heights. Those of us who participated in the May 1974 shuttle, which produced the Israeli-Syrian disengagement agreement, remember the intense opposition of the Israeli settlers at that time. By mid-1985, their settlements in the southern part of the Golan were much more fully developed than in 1974, and the opposition was likely to be even more vicious. It was one thing for Begin and Sharon to close the last settlement in the Sinai for the sake of peace with Sadat's Egypt; doing so for the sake of an agreement with a Syrian government, which is neither known nor trusted and is believed to be committed to Israel's destruction, would be politically much more difficult. American mediators see little prospect of eliciting help from Assad in that political process.

In addition, the psychological distance—we might say "hatred"—between Israel and Syria seems greater than between Israel and any other neighbor. Israelis feel that Syria has treated Israeli prisoners with greater cruelty than has any other adversary. Israelis cite the Syrian government's massacre of its own people as further evidence of "barbaric behavior." The barriers to peace may be higher here than on any other front.

Organizing Syria's Neighborhood

For President Assad the top priority in his definition of the problem is organizing his neighborhood in a way that is secure for Syria and for his regime. Each decision he makes must be understood in light of his aim to establish Syria's influence over the course of events. Given the enmity between the current leadership in Iraq and Syria, the uncertainty in Lebanon, and the military power in Israel, Syria cannot afford to stand by and see a Jordanian-Palestinian-Israeli settlement that leaves them out. Coupled with such a settlement, a rapprochement between Egypt and Jordan with Iraq as a partner would threaten to produce a Syrian isolation that the Syrians would regard as dangerous. In addition, resolution of the Palestinian problem without Syria would reduce the justification for continuing Saudi financial support, on which the Syrian government depends.

A second priority is settlement of the Palestinian problem. For whatever reason, Assad has shown a seemingly genuine personal commitment to resolving the problem. His interest may stem from a combination of reasons—some sense of Syria's historical relationship to Palestine, a simple sense of injustice, or concern about the effect on Syrian stability of integrating stateless Palestinians within his own body politic. Assad has stated repeatedly that, unlike Sadat, he would not sign an Israeli-Syrian settlement before the Palestinians have their settlement.

Although the Syrians do not often mention the Golan Heights because they do not want to seem to be begging, the recovery of that territory remains an important third objective. Loss of the territory did not displace a large population, and loss of its agricultural productivity was measurable but marginal. Still, the humiliation of the loss is a significant psychological factor for Assad, and the extension of Israeli law to the Golan—the so-called annexation in December 1981—was in Syrian eyes an extension of Israel's aggression.

Syrian officials see the Israeli-U.S. relationship as having special strategic consequences for Syria. They are blunter than Egyptians or Jordanians in noting that Arab acceptance of Israel's 1967 borders is already a major Arab concession. Whatever historical claims to the biblical lands the Jews may make, many individual Arab families lost their homes in Palestine to make a place for the Jewish state. Syrians see no moral or legal basis for justifying their loss. In their view, acceptance of Israel within 1967 borders demands recognition of this Arab concession by the United States, which should curb further Israeli expansion. U.S. failure to do so in Syrian eyes is evidence that the United States is less interested in a just settlement than in using Israeli military power to threaten Syria. In the analysis of one prominent Syrian, the Israeli-U.S. agreement on strategic cooperation in November 1981 almost caused Assad to give up hope in U.S. readiness to take a fair stand.

In mid-1985, Syria redoubled its efforts to bring Lebanese factions together and to institutionalize Syria's long-term influence in Lebanon. The question for policy makers trying to advance the peace process was to what extent Assad would press for the same kind of institutionalized Syrian involvement in the Palestinian political entity as it evolves. Would it be enough for Israel, the United States, and the other Arabs to concede Syria's special role in Lebanon, at least while Lebanon is reestablishing its internal unity? Or will Syria also insist on similar involvement in a Palestinian settlement?

In short, Syria's picture of the problem hinges on the perceived threat to its security that would result if it were excluded from the peace process. Moreover, the substantive picture is that the Arabs are making a fundamental concession in accepting Israel within 1967 borders, and that concession has been matched by neither Israel nor the United States in defining the extent of Israel's territorial ambition.

Syrian Aims Overshadow Urgency

The Syrians are less closely in touch with developments and daily life in the West Bank and Gaza than the other parties to the conflict, and they seem to think of the problem more abstractly. They view the steady progress of Israeli settlements in the territories as news or intelligence items. They do not have the constant intercourse with the people of the West Bank and Gaza that the Jordanians experience, so they do not feel the day-to-day weight of living under occupation. It comes as a revelation to even those Syrians prepared to discuss the subject quietly that the West Bankers and Gazans support the pragmatic efforts of Hussein and Arafat to negotiate their liberation rather than the posture of the Syrian government or the elements of the PLO that are in Syria. From this quarter, then, there is little sense of immediacy.

On the Golan Heights, Israel's occupation, settlement, and cultivation are a source of continuing irritation and embarrassment to the president of Syria. Neither the security of his state nor the stability of his government, however, is threatened by the Israeli presence on the Golan Heights alone, and he can live for some time with the present situation in the absence of a settlement there. This statement seemed especially true after Syria showed its increased influence by blocking an Israeli-Lebanese settlement in 1983 and 1984.

On the broader political front, the Syrians see neither a cohesive Arab political context from which to move soon nor an Israeli-U.S. relationship in pursuit of a fair settlement. Assad does not feel urgency from the Palestinians under occupation, nor does he see an alternative to taking whatever time may be required to build a military and political base from which he could approach a settlement in a position of strength.

An intolerable situation for Syrian leaders would apparently be one in which Syria lost its ability to influence the course of events in its immediate neighborhood. That situation seems unlikely to develop fully as long as Syria's presence appears necessary in Lebanon, as long as Syria dominates part of the PLO, and as long as Syrian military power grows. A peace process that seemed to be advancing *and* enjoying substantial Arab support might increase the Syrian sense of urgency. Syria would then face a choice between lashing out to destroy people involved in the process and seeking a constructive approach to achieving its own aims.

1967 Borders and a Palestinian State

I have already noted Syria's commitment to Israeli withdrawal and to an independent Palestinian state. This position is apparently rigid. Americans and Syrians differ in that Americans are prepared to talk of a political process in which trade-offs between security measures and borders could be discussed, while the Syrians see the settlement strictly in terms of implementing the principle of total withdrawal. They speak of the 1967 borders as an Arab "right." "Sovereignty is not negotiable," one jurist said. When asked what had given the pre-1967 armistice lines the character of sovereign borders, he responded, "Now that the Arabs are ready to accept Israel as sovereign within the 1967 borders, are you going to risk that by trying to change them?"

Americans do tend to overlook the fact that the Syrians are speaking of the 1967 borders as recognized borders of Israel. Assad spoke that way during negotiation of the Israeli-Syrian disengagement in May 1974, and Syrian officials speak that way today. They speak of agreeing on the "principle" of withdrawal before any negotiation can begin. The Arabs have put their map on the table; it shows the 1967 borders. Now, they say, let the Israelis put an equally precise map on the table. Then negotiations can begin. While the United States complains about not knowing what the Syrians want, the Syrians say there can be no mistaking their position. The United States, they complain, has never insisted that Israel put its proposed map on the table.

In this connection, it is also necessary to record that the disengagement agreement that the United States mediated between Israel and Syria in May 1974 began with these words: "This agreement is not a peace agreement. It is a step toward a just and durable peace on the basis of Security Council Resolution 338 dated October 22, 1973." Resolution 338 called for the implementation of Resolution 242 (1967) and for negotiations "aimed at establishing a just and durable peace in the Middle East."[1]

Four other points are worth remembering about the shape of a settlement that Syrian leaders envision. They are valid substantive points, but it is not yet clear how they can be made politically relevant.

First, in line with his personal commitment, Assad as of mid-1985 had kept the Golan disengagement lines peaceful for eleven years, virtually without incident of violence. Whether Israelis regard Assad as a leader whose intentions they trust is an important question for the Israeli politics of negotiation with Syria. A review of the record of the May 1974 disengagement agreement can produce only the judgment that that agreement has been scrupulously kept. Although more detailed and ambiguous analysis would be needed, a review of tacit Israeli-Syrian understandings on avoiding conflict in Lebanon might also make a case that even tacit arrangements with Syria have been maintained. For political reasons, the creation of a Syrian role in the peace process will require that ways of building on that record be found. Although it is a difficult point for the Syrians to accept in view of their feelings as an aggrieved party, in the eyes of potential mediators, the responsibility of finding ways to reduce Israeli suspicion is as much Syrian as Israeli.

Second, the Syrians are prepared to discuss the security concerns of both sides in a settlement. The position taken by Syrians in private conversation is that demilitarization of the border can be negotiated. They insist on demilitarization on both sides of the border—a position that the Israelis, despite their aversion to the principle, finally accepted in a symbolic way in the Egyptian-Israeli peace treaty but that would be much more difficult to achieve in view of the geography of the Golan and the Galilee. Nevertheless, the point remains that the Syrians can talk about the practical aspects of a negotiated settlement.

Third, while the Syrians have agreed to the goal of "a just and durable peace on the basis of Security Council Resolution 338," they do not yet state their readiness for normal relations with Israel. Sadat eventually agreed to an exchange of ambassadors with Israel, but he consistently argued that diplomatic and legal forms would not create the substance of truly normal relations between peoples until the political environment generated natural incentives for normal relations. Sadat eventually realized that agreement to the forms was critical in the Israeli body politic to decision making on withdrawal from the Sinai. He was sincere in hoping that continuation of the peace process between Israel and its other neighbors would gradually create a political environment in which a full range of relationships would become natural and normal. As of mid-1985, the Syrians seemed less ready to take the extra steps that Sadat had taken to help change the political environment in Israel, at least in the absence of visible signs of Israeli interest in negotiating a settlement with Syria.

Fourth, in the 1970s some reports suggested that Assad's aim was a Jordanian-Palestinian-Syrian confederation. It was never clear exactly what the details of such a relationship might be, and it is not clear in the mid-1980s to what extent Assad would press for Syrian partnership in the Jordanian-Palestinian confederation that Hussein and Arafat have been discussing. Given the present Jordanian-Syrian relationship and Syrian actions to split the PLO, such Syrian involvement seems unlikely, but how important it is to Assad will be a factor in determining Syria's strategy toward efforts to build a Palestinian settlement around a Jordanian-Palestinian confederation.

In short, Syria speaks of ending the war with an Israel defined by the 1967 lines. According to senior Syrian officials, when they are asked whether the Fez Declaration envisions a Middle East map that includes Israel, Israel will be sovereign within the 1967 borders. If the statement from Fez does not recognize Israel by name, they say, it is because Israel has not stated its demands. When Israel is more forthcoming, they state, we will be more precise.

Israel Will Not Withdraw

Syrians see no likelihood that Israel will accept the only terms that Syria regards as the basis for a just settlement. They focus on the statements of Likud leaders in Israel such as Yitzhak Shamir, who says that the West

Bank and Golan are parts of Israel, and on comments of Labor leaders, notably Shimon Peres, who states that the Jordan River is Israel's security border. They have heard American leaders say that they understand why Israel could never come down from the Golan Heights. Syrians ask incredulously how anyone can believe that Israel will withdraw to the 1967 borders.

Equally important, Syrians again and again cite instances in which the United States itself has not maintained even its own position that Israel should withdraw to "1967 borders with minor rectifications." They do not believe that the United States will support a just settlement. They say they are waiting for the United States to take its own position, one different from that of Israel, and to keep to it. They explain U.S. unwillingness to maintain its position in two ways: First, the United States, in their view, has a strategic alliance with Israel for several purposes, of which one is the isolation of Syria. Second, they conclude that the American political system is in the grip of the Israeli lobby.

In a word, Syrians regard the situation as "hopeless"—not because their position is mysterious but because they believe that Israel is unable or unwilling to state clearly what it will settle for and the United States stands impotent to stake out the common ground that it judges to provide the basis for a fair settlement.

United Arab Front or Military Parity with Israel

The Syrians more than the other parties to the conflict talk above all not about the substance of a settlement but about the balance of forces that would form the basis of an effort to achieve a settlement. Since they do not believe that Israel will negotiate voluntarily, they envision no negotiation until Israel has been confronted with power that leaves it no choice but to negotiate.

In 1973, Assad joined Sadat in launching a surprise war partly to involve the superpowers. The combination of a united Arab front and superpower support, they felt, would balance the scales against Israeli military preponderance. In 1974, he cooperated with U.S. mediation to produce the Israeli-Syrian disengagement agreement of May 1974. Assad for a time put his trust in the United States and left the Soviet Union on the sidelines because he hoped that the special U.S. relationship with Israel would make the United States more able than the Soviet Union to sway Israel.

When in early 1975 U.S. diplomacy turned to a second Egyptian-Israeli interim agreement rather than to the Jordanian-Palestinian front or to a comprehensive settlement, Assad stated his opposition straightforwardly: If Egypt and then Jordan were each to make a separate peace with Israel, neither Israel nor the United States would pay any attention to Syria, and Syria would never recover its lost territory. While he deeply disagreed with the U.S. approach at that time, he remained committed to preserving the relationship with the United States. In 1977 when the Carter administration pressed to resume the Middle East Peace Conference in Geneva, Syria's strongest efforts focused on organizing the conference around united Arab negotiating teams, addressing functional issues such as borders, security, and waterways rather than organizing Egypt-Israel, Israel-Jordan, and Israel-Syria negotiating groups. Again, Syria did not want to be isolated in dealing with Israel.

In 1984–1985, Syrians supported the Soviet call for an international conference to deal with the Arab-Israeli conflict in part because they needed Soviet influence to offset what they regarded as uncritical U.S. support of Israel. If the United States moved to a position that, Syrians judged, would permit the United States to act as a fair mediator, as in 1974, they would give serious attention to any U.S. proposal.

Assad bitterly opposed the Camp David accords in 1978 and the Egyptian-Israeli peace treaty in 1979 again because he saw Egypt decisively separated from the united Arab front. In addition to his bitterness at being deserted by a major Arab ally, he faced the prospect that the burden of confronting Israel militarily fell squarely on Syria. Assad's position gradually shifted until he stated that Syria would not be able to negotiate seriously with Israel until Syria achieved military parity with Israel. Standing alone, Syria could force Israel's attention only when it could threaten Israel militarily. After resisting for several years, he finally signed a friendship treaty with the Soviet Union.

In 1983 and 1984, Syria moved actively and with some success in Lebanon to curb the effectiveness of both Israeli and U.S. military power. The eventual withdrawal of the U.S. Marines in early 1984, in Arab eyes, demonstrated the impotence of U.S. policy. As Israel began withdrawing its own forces from Lebanon, Syrians and other Arabs began concluding that systematically organized guerrilla attacks on Israeli forces in southern Lebanon had produced the Israeli decision to withdraw. They inferred that the use of force in this way in the West Bank and Gaza, while conventional Syrian military power grows, is the only way of making Israel withdraw there.

Syrian experience with guerrilla and terrorist actions against the United States and Israel in Lebanon, against PLO factions supporting Arafat, and potentially against other Arab states creates a dilemma for Syrian policy makers. On the one hand, Syrian experience shows that such actions do produce results that sometimes enhance the Syrian ability to influence the course of events. On the other hand, for highly organized Iranian-supported Islamic fanatics to be allowed to run beyond Syrian control in Lebanon with the potential of gaining a toehold within Syria itself is inconsistent with the Syrian regime's own security interests. In addition, Syria's appearance of encouraging or acquiescing in such actions gives Syrian policy at least somewhat the character in Western eyes of ruthless rejectionism that cannot easily be dismissed.

Syria's attention to the balance of forces goes beyond the Arab-Israeli military balance to the political balance within the Arab world. Fearing isolation, Syria has maneuvered ruthlessly to block an Arab consensus behind an extension of the Camp David approach to the Jordanian-Palestinian front. Syrians regarded the Hussein-Arafat agreements of April 1983 and February 1985 as such efforts. Having divided the PLO and then watched as Arafat convened the Palestine National Council in Amman in late 1984, Syrians worked actively in February 1985 to undercut formal PLO endorsement of the agreement that Hussein and Arafat had worked out.

In the larger international arena, Syria will continue to seek a balancing Soviet role as long as it judges that the United States will not take an independent role based solely on its own interests. Assad knows that the U.S. political system will not permit the United States to provide military supplies to Syria—the U.S. Congress will not even support scholarships for Syrian students—and so he will have to rely on Soviet military equipment. He does not want to be left alone with the Soviet Union; he has kept open the American connection even at low points in the political relationship. Few competent analysts, even in Israel, consider Assad a puppet of Soviet policy. Soviet specialists themselves say, "You don't control Israel, and we don't control Syria." For the Syrians, the Soviet relationship is essential to building a balance of forces to which Israel will eventually have to respond.

Elements of an Approach to Syria

Any constructive U.S. posture toward Syria will have to communicate persuasively an understanding of Syria's concern that exclusion from the political process is part of a U.S. and Israeli strategy of isolating, surrounding, and weakening Syria. The United States will have to show understanding that Syria sees its isolation as a grave threat to its security. U.S. rhetoric and actions have done much to create the impression that the United States regards Syria as an enemy.

The only evidence that will be persuasive in Damascus is a sustained demonstration that the United States is pursuing an independent policy toward a settlement and that the Israeli-U.S. strategic relationship is designed neither for joint offensive military action nor for supporting nondefensive Israeli action. The Syrians do not expect the United States to stop supporting Israel; they do look to the United States to make its own judgments about what a fair settlement requires.

Damascus considers a forthright U.S. statement regarding the kind of settlement it would support as a necessary step in a serious dialogue. Although the Syrians are holding back to maintain room to bargain, the United States must in their view recognize that they have all but formally made the fundamental concession asked of them by Resolutions 242 and 338—acceptance of Israel as a state within essentially pre-1967 borders. Syrians expect the United States to understand their attitude that they have no reason for moving further until the United States has made clear to both Israel and the Arabs what Israeli boundaries it will support in a settlement.

Any U.S. approach will have to make clear—in act as in word—that we oppose the indiscriminate use of force either by conventional military units or by unconventional groups. The United States will live with its own military deployments against Syria from 1982 to 1984 and will be held partly accountable for Israel's actions. Only from that base will the United States make credible its point that Syrian participation in any political process cannot reflect Syrian support or toleration of guerrilla and terrorist violence.

The United States will have to press its argument that a settlement cannot be achieved apart from a political process among the parties to the conflict—among the Arabs, with Israel, and within Israel. At some point, when the shape of a settlement has been accepted, that process will have to involve negotiation.

As with the Jordanians, the United States will have to give serious attention in dialogue to meeting the Syrian concern that negotiations take place within an internationally based framework. It may not be practical to form a Jordanian-Palestinian-Syrian negotiating delegation. The question is whether some sort of Arab political steering group behind the negotiating teams could provide a coordinating mechanism and the sense of legitimacy that some Arabs seek in a large international conference. An alternative to be explored with the Syrians is whether such an approach, plus a symbolic informal meeting with the United Nations secretary general and even representatives of the Security Council, could provide the necessary international legitimacy.

Note

1. The text of Resolution 338 appears in appendix IV.

7

Egypt: Peace, Poverty, Population, and Food

A Vision of Peace

In the 1970s we came to regard the peace process in terms of visits, meetings, shuttles, negotiations, agreements, and relationships between Egypt and Israel. Although some people feel that President Sadat was willing to settle for getting only Egypt's territory back, Sadat's purpose reached far beyond recovering the Sinai with its defensive space and its oil. Sadat's objective was a comprehensive peace. He fell short not in his design but in his inability to rally Arab political support and to bring an Arab coalition to the peace table. In dealing with Israel, he made the same judgment that American presidents have made, rightly or wrongly: He judged that Israel is more likely to move in the context of a political process than of confrontation.

On Sunday evening, September 17, 1978, Carter, Sadat, and Begin flew by helicopter from Camp David to the White House. They came to sign, before television cameras and the world, the two agreements that they had laboriously written in thirteen grueling days of negotiation behind closed gates. One agreement was the framework for peace between Egypt and Israel. The second was "A Framework for Peace in the Middle East Agreed at Camp David"—the design for a multi-stage negotiating and political process that was intended to result in peace between Israel and Palestinians and Jordanians and eventually with Syrians and Lebanese.

The three men were waiting in the smaller room next to the East Room. I took in the signing copies to show them where they would put their signatures. When each man had examined the documents, President Carter handed them back to me and said sternly, "The 'Framework for Peace in the Middle East' must be put on the table first, signed by all three of us, and removed from the table. It must be off the table before the Egyptian-Israeli document is put on the table to be signed." He looked me squarely in the eye for emphasis and concluded grimly, "President Sadat insists on it." Sadat was seeking symbolic dramatization that the peace treaty would be negotiated only in the framework of a comprehensive peace. The design for peace at Camp David was a design for peace between Israel and all its neighbors. After peace between Egypt and Israel, peace between Israel and the Palestinians and Jordanians was to be at the top of the agenda.

The craving for peace, as Sadat felt it, was rooted deeply in Egypt's soul. As he told Kissinger in their first meeting in November 1973, ending the war with Israel was the first step in dealing with Egypt's chronic problems of poverty, overpopulation, and a shortage of food and jobs. Sadat was a man of vision, and that was the vision. He was the architect. He relied on others to be the engineers, but he did not make the job of building a broader Arab political base for peace easier. He assumed that the other Arabs would have to follow Egypt, and viewed in a historical perspective, that statement may prove to be true. In the short term, it was not.

Any Egyptian when asked in the mid-1980s, "What is Egypt's highest priority?" would invariably answer "The economy." Pressure to deal with the human problems of Egypt—engineering economic growth to stay ahead of an uncurbed population explosion—pervades Egyptian politics and policies at all levels. Since Anwar Sadat became president of Egypt in 1970, progress toward a peaceful settlement of the Arab-Israeli-Palestinian conflict has become a centerpiece of Egypt's policies, a key to freeing resources for domestic growth, and a test of Egypt's traditional position of leadership in the Arab world. Some Egyptians say that Egypt could not have kept pace in economic development with population growth since the 1973 War if it had not been able to reduce defense expenditures substantially.

Peace, growth, military and economic security, pride, and the Palestinian problem are intertwined in Egyptian minds and politics. Egyptians feel strongly and sometimes bitterly that they have paid disproportionately in lives, equipment, and stunted economic growth for five Arab-Israeli wars. Accurately or not, they have equated peace with a chance to lighten the burden of poverty. They have erroneously even expected more immediate benefits from peace than were possible, and disappointment has become a factor in Egyptian politics.

When Egypt signed its peace treaty with Israel in March 1979, other Arab states broke relations and cut the flow of aid. For a time, a critical question was whether the Egyptians employed in other Arab countries would be dismissed and sent home. Their earnings were a top source of foreign exchange for the nation. Their return to Egypt would have swelled the ranks of the unemployed. In the end they kept their jobs because they were needed, but they had to live in a political environment where they heard Egyptian policies vilified daily in the press and on radio. The injury to their pride as Egyptians could not but be transmitted to families and friends in Egypt.

Egyptian political leaders see in resumption of the peace process the potential for vindication of their first steps in the 1970s toward a comprehensive peace, and in the mid-1980s for new steps toward restoration of their leadership in the Arab world, toward revival of national pride, and toward opening the door to renewed Arab economic assistance. At the same time, they see little prospect of increasing Egypt's foreign exchange earnings from workers' remittances, oil, Suez Canal tolls, or tourism. Peace is now part of the political fabric of Egypt. It may not be explicitly articulated as a first issue at the roots of the political process, but it underlies the political leadership's ability to cope with poverty and disillusionment.

Beyond the economic factors that affect all Egyptians, as conversations grow franker and blunter, thoughtful Egyptians again and again voice latent outrage over the injustice suffered by the Palestinians. Their judgment of their government's peace policy is colored by their outrage, and their judgment of the United States reflects it. They have no time for the Soviet Union after more than a decade of close economic and military cooperation. They are concerned about Islamic fanaticism but understand how a moderate return to Islam is a refuge for the disillusioned young in a rapidly changing world. Progress toward peace could become part of their inspiration and pride. Stalemate could fuel anger and rebellion.

Peace is a critical element in the background of Egypt's current politics and future direction. Sadat offered a vision of peace. It remains for his successors to make it realizable for all the parties to the Arab-Israeli conflict.

Regaining Momentum for a Comprehensive Peace

The problem since Sadat went to Jerusalem has been how to keep the other Arabs involved in the peace process. Since the 1973 War, Sadat's readiness to move faster than the others was at odds with the need to build the base for a comprehensive peace. It had been agreed in Resolution 242 in 1967 that the aim of negotiations would be to resolve the Arab-Israeli conflict once and for all, in "a just and lasting peace." The objective of a comprehensive peace was not the issue. The issue was how to achieve it. In 1967 and 1968 we spoke of a "package deal" that would resolve all outstanding questions. After 1970, the people involved began to think that a comprehensive peace could not be instituted all at once and that we should address manageable parts of the problem one step at a time. When "step-by-step diplomacy" became the watchword after 1973, the problem became how to keep alive a sense that all issues would eventually be resolved. That remained the problem in the mid-1980s.

Regaining momentum for a comprehensive peace is the objective of Egypt's leaders. Unlike some Israelis, Sadat intended the Egyptian-Israeli peace treaty to be the beginning, not the end, of the peace process. According to the terms of "A Framework for Peace Agreed at Camp David," and according to the terms of the treaty, which the Egyptian National Assembly ratified, the treaty was to be followed immediately by negotiations that would result, first, in the Israeli military government's replacement in the West Bank and Gaza with a Palestinian self-governing authority through a transitional period. Then, within three years, negotiations would begin on a durable peace and on relationships among Israelis, Palestinians, and Jordanians. The Egyptian objective remains essentially the same, and Egypt recognized the need to do what was not done after Camp David—to involve Palestinians and Jordanians in the negotiating process.

Egypt's leaders face the political necessity of regaining momentum for a comprehensive peace. Beyond the struggle for leadership, to which Syria aspires, at least in its neighborhood, Egyptians believe their success would strengthen the forces of moderation in the Middle East and would blunt the spread of radicalism and fanaticism. Having reoriented its strategic relationships from Moscow toward the West under Sadat in the early 1970s for economic as well as political reasons, Egypt believes that U.S. interests are heavily involved because their success or failure will, in part, shape the political map of the Middle East at least until the close of the century.

The Egyptians—at least Sadat—seemed to understand the politics of the peace process more clearly than other Arab leaders. Sadat became a master in dealing with the American political system; by the time he died he had received more than two-thirds of the members of the U.S. Congress in Cairo. He also understood how to reach the Israeli body politic. His dramatic visit to Jerusalem unleashed pressures for peace in Israel that the United States could not have aroused. Sadat defined the problem as first a political problem of removing the barriers to negotiation and only afterward as a negotiating problem. Egypt's leaders in the mid-1980s also understood that the peace process could not regain momentum until the Arab political base for negotiation had been broadened.

In operational terms, the Egyptians realize that the peace process cannot be resumed until an Arab coalition—principally Jordan and the PLO—is ready to offer to negotiate peace with Israel. The Camp David accords did not envision an exclusively Egyptian-Israeli negotiation about peace between Israelis and Palestinians. They envisioned at first an Egyptian-Israeli-Jordanian negotiation with Palestinian representatives in the Jordanian or Egyptian delegations and with full U.S. participation to bring into being an elected Palestinian self-governing authority. Representatives of that authority would then form their own delegation to join the others in negotiating the final status of the West Bank and Gaza. Only at the last moment at Camp David was the question addressed: What if the Jordanians and Palestinians refuse to join the negotiations? Sadat answered: "To ensure the implementation of the provisions related to the West Bank and Gaza and in order to safeguard the legitimate rights of the Palestinian people, Egypt will be prepared to assume the Arab role emanating from these provisions, following consultations with Jordan and the representatives of the Palestinian people."[1]

By May 1979, when the negotiations on autonomy for the inhabitants of the West Bank and Gaza began, only the Egyptian-Israeli-U.S. team from Camp David met in a hall at Ben Gurion University in Beersheba for the ceremonial start. Negotiations continued in working groups and in ministerial plenaries, with some interruptions through the remaining year and a half of the Carter administration. Much work was accomplished. The makings of an interim step for replacing the Israeli military government with a Palestinian self-governing authority are evident in many of the working papers from that negotiation. Important issues remained unresolved, but political leaders addressing them today would have the option in mid-1985 of settling for the minimum in order to take a dramatic symbolic political step quickly. As the autonomy talks proceeded, the Egyptians found themselves less and less able to make that choice in the absence of the Palestinians. For that reason, in 1985 they, like King Hussein, define the problem of regaining momentum for a comprehensive peace in terms of building an Arab coalition to negotiate with Israel. For that reason, too, in February 1985 President Mubarak's representative played a critical role in crystallizing the agreement between Hussein and Arafat.

Time without Progress Erodes Peace

Egyptians view the passage of time as eroding their ability to sustain the peace process as far as it has gone. Disillusionment with the Egyptian-Israeli peace treaty already runs deep in Egypt, as it does in Israel. The Egyptians are bitter about Israeli good faith, believing that the Israelis haggle over every detail in implementing the treaty. The Egyptians are also bitter about the Israeli invasion of Lebanon in 1982, the continuing steps to tighten Israeli control in the West Bank and Gaza, and the dispute over Israeli withdrawal from Taba.[2] As with the mirror image of these feelings in Israel, Egyptian leaders believe it is essential to restore faith in the reliability of signed agreements.

Many times at Camp David and after, Egyptians explained to Israelis that the quality of the normalization of relations between them would depend on the quality of the continuing peace process. If Egyptians felt proud that their leadership in peace was bringing the benefits of peace to the Palestinians and other Arabs, they would want to build that relationship. If they felt cheated, they would not. The impact of the Israeli invasion of Lebanon on this process cannot be overstated. Instead of making it easy for Egypt to develop normal relations, Israel's attack on the Palestinians in Lebanon dramatized to the world that Egypt was no longer able to defend Arab brethren under attack. In some ways, the humiliation was akin to that of 1967. In Egyptian eyes, Israeli actions as time passed after Camp David made it more difficult instead of more natural for Egypt to continue the process of normalization.

Moreover, Egyptians have recognized the importance of 1985 as a critical year. The unusual coalition agreement in Israel made 1985 the year in which Shimon Peres would have to move if he were to take advantage of his tenure as prime minister before relinquishing the post to Yitzhak Shamir. Egyptians also seemed to believe widely that a second-term U.S. president must move early in the term to be most effective. Finally, as they considered their own economic problems, they wanted to move as quickly as possible in order to resume normal relations with the other Arab states.

Although Egyptian leaders have critical reasons for wanting to regain momentum in the peace process before time further erodes it, they no longer control the timing of the next move. When Sadat saw the momentum of the Carter administration's efforts flagging, he gave the process a political jolt by going to Jerusalem. When other Arabs criticized him for breaking ranks with them, he decided to press the process forward with the conviction that progress would change the political environment in ways that would make it possible for the others to join the process in due time. In mid-1985, Egypt's options are limited to using its political influence to bring others together to advance the process.

The Aim Is a Comprehensive Settlement

For Sadat, the exact shape of a settlement was less important than the process of achieving it. From the beginning of the peace process in the 1970s, Sadat understood more fully than other leaders in the Middle East that the political conditions for peace must grow; they cannot be decreed. He understood that the foundation for building a relationship normal to states at peace was a political environment that would encourage the pursuits of peace. He understood that political acts are necessary to change the political environment.

As signers of the Camp David accords, the Egyptians understand better than the other Arab parties why Israeli politics make it necessary to allow for a staged approach to the Israeli-Palestinian conflict. They are committed to the concept of a transitional period and to interim political arrangements for the Palestinians. They recognize pragmatically that Israel must have time to adjust to withdrawal and might be more flexible on final arrangements in the West Bank and Gaza after experiencing a relationship in which the Palestinians demonstrated their ability to maintain, order, and conduct relationships in a peaceful and responsible way. The Egyptians also agreed at Camp David that the final status of the West Bank and Gaza should be negotiated. They endorsed a realistic understanding of how the right of self-determination would be exercised within three to five years.

Beneath that pragmatic approach lay one bedrock requirement— that the shape of both the interim and the final settlement in the West Bank and Gaza must reflect continuing commitment to a comprehensive peace between Israel and all its neighbors. Egypt argued at Camp David and during negotiation of the Egyptian-Israeli treaty that development of a peaceful relationship between Egypt and Israel must be linked to movement toward peace on the Israeli-Jordanian-Palestinian front and that Syria must eventually be brought into the process. Specifically, at several points in the negotiations, the Egyptians argued for direct links between stages in the Israeli withdrawal from Sinai and steps in the inauguration of a Palestinian self-governing authority in the West Bank and Gaza. They tried to negotiate a linkage whereby the eventual normalization of Egyptian-Israeli relations would coincide with implementation of an agreement on the final status of the West Bank and Gaza.

In retrospect, it can be argued, even from the Egyptian viewpoint, that formal linkage would have been unwise. It would have given those Israelis who did not want to withdraw fully from the Sinai the option of slowing negotiations about the West Bank and Gaza and then deferring the Sinai withdrawal because no agreement had been reached. Nevertheless, Egyptians see resumption of the peace process in the mid-1980s as a way of proving their commitment to a comprehensive settlement. Whereas the Arabs once demanded abrogation of the treaty as the price for resuming relations with the Arab states, Egypt has resumed relations with Jordan and, if the peace process resumes, will gradually reenter the Arab world, bringing the peace treaty and the Egyptian-Israeli relationship with it.

How Can the Other Side Be Moved to Accept?

Egypt has already negotiated its treaty, so the issue is not so much Egypt's judgment about Israel's readiness to negotiate. The important contribution that Egypt can bring to further negotiations is its decade of experience in dealing with Israel and in trying to influence Israeli political processes as they affect a negotiation. Other Arabs may argue that Sadat's strategy for dealing with Israel failed, but they must acknowledge that Egypt successfully negotiated the return of every inch of land lost in the 1967 War. The Arabs' eventual judgment of Egypt's approach will depend on whether the peace process that Egypt did so much to launch is picked up by other Arabs and continued.

In the mid-1980s, Egypt can still influence Israeli thinking about the peace process positively or negatively. Despite the disillusionment of many Israelis with Egypt's implementation of the treaty, Israelis still value the fact of peace with Egypt. A first step in reviving the broader peace process is to put the Egyptian-Israeli relationship back on the tracks. Disillusioned Israelis say, "If this is peace, who needs it?" Showing that the relationship is still alive and can grow in the context of a larger political process that involves Israel and its eastern neighbors could help create a political environment in which Israelis could assess other opportunities to negotiate against the background of a positive experience.

I have no means of apportioning blame for the state of the normalization of Egyptian-Israeli relations, nor is it my purpose to do so. Still, resumption of the process could reopen the door to dialogue about the politics of the peace process. Egyptians strongly feel that Israel's invasion of Lebanon violated the spirit of the peace process—that each side would pursue peace by peaceful means. They feel that Israel's settlements in the West Bank and Gaza demonstrated lack of Israeli good faith in honoring the Camp David commitment to leave the question of sovereignty in those territories open. Israel has its own complaints. Resumption of measured normalization would provide both a lift to the process and an opportunity for Egypt to speak openly and directly with Israelis within Israel about the effect on normalization of a continuation of the larger process.

At a moment when the Israeli prime minister wants to negotiate but presides over a divided cabinet and a divided country, Egyptian understanding of how to relate to the Israeli body politic is important. Even during the period of coolness in the relationship, contacts between the two nations continue at a variety of levels. Some of these contacts were deliberately established between political parties so that the Egyptians could maintain contact with the Labor party leaders who favored some

102

Israeli withdrawal from occupied territories. The ongoing party contacts provide an opportunity for politicians to compare notes informally.

Since Sadat's death, Egypt has slowly and patiently but steadily begun again to play its influential role in Arab politics. With Syria doing everything in its power to undercut Arafat's leadership of the PLO and to gain some control over the Palestinian movement, Egypt's support for the PLO is critical. Egypt's threat in February 1985 to limit its support if Arafat and his colleagues again retreated from agreement with Jordan may have been decisive in producing the Hussein-Arafat accord. While Sadat was still alive, Mubarak was assigned to maintain the relationship—such as it was—with the other Arabs. He recognized then as now the importance of maintaining a broad Arab base. He has waited long enough so that he could move back into the Arab world with the Israeli treaty intact. Now that Egyptians are again advancing, they can help Arab colleagues understand how to present choices to the Israelis while also using their own relationship to influence the debate in Israel.

Politics in the Balance of Forces

President Sadat recognized that the balance of forces that affects a negotiation is not only a military balance. He found other instruments for changing the political environment so as to make it more favorable for negotiation. Sadat did not go to war in 1973 to destroy the Israeli Defense Force or even to regain the Sinai. As we have noted, he went to war (1) to erase the humiliation of the Arab defeat in 1967 so that Egypt could negotiate from a position of restored Arab honor and (2) to draw the superpowers into a stronger mediating role. He did not go to Jerusalem in 1977 to press for a negotiating position. He went to Jerusalem to lower the political and psychological barriers to the kind of agreement that would be necessary for a negotiated peace. He openly told the people of Israel to urge their leaders to struggle for peace.

By the mid-1980s, the Egyptians had recognized that negotiations could not proceed until the political base for them in the Arab world had broadened. During the post–Camp David negotiations to establish a Palestinian self-governing authority in the West Bank and Gaza, the Egyptians tried to negotiate on behalf of the Palestinians but realized that their ability to make arrangements for others was limited. They recognized the need to build the Arab negotiating group with Jordanians and Palestinians that we Americans had failed to assemble after Camp David. By late 1984, they had made progress in paving the way for their own reentry to the Arab world.

The Egyptian moves coincided in late 1984 and early 1985 with King Hussein's renewed initiatives to develop an understanding with Arafat, to resume diplomatic relations with Egypt, and to draw Egypt and Iraq closer. Not only did Egypt play an important role in the Hussein-Arafat negotiations, but President Mubarak also made his own proposals for drawing the United States back into the negotiating process by proposing U.S. meetings with a Jordanian-Palestinian delegation. Egypt also recognized its special role in helping build support in Israel for further negotiations by doing its part to restore the Egyptian-Israeli relationship.

Egyptian leaders realized that Egypt's gradual resumption of its leadership role in the Arab world would add to its political weight in dealing with both the United States and Israel. It might compensate for its lack of military power relative to Israel by means of its ability to broaden the political base for Israel's peace with its neighbors.

Elements of an Approach to Egypt

Egypt was a leader in the peace process and is a traditional leader in the Arab world. The interests of peace would be served if Egypt resumed its normal position of leadership in the Arab world with the Egyptian-Israeli peace treaty intact. Although details of an Israeli-Jordanian-Palestinian relationship will need to be developed on their own merits, progress on that front would strengthen Egypt's position and ability to proceed further with the normalization of Egyptian-Israeli relations.

An effective approach to the Palestinian problem is also critical to enhancing the stability of the political and economic systems in Egypt. We understand the disaffection of the liberal opposition in Egypt because the Camp David accords and the Egyptian-Israeli peace treaty seemed to be a separate peace without a commitment to progress on the Palestinian problem that could be enforced. We understand also that rightist opponents can use the more general political disaffection, together with Egypt's chronic economic problems, as issues on which to attack the government.

Although the United States increased its economic assistance to Egypt as an addendum to Sadat's leading role in the peace process, U.S. support for Egyptian development is far more important than a simple economic reward for good behavior toward Israel, as some observers in the United States have seemed to construe it. Since the early 1970s, Egypt has shifted its orientation from Moscow to the West and has made its economic and political future dependent on moving the Arab-Israeli conflict toward resolution and on potentially changing the political map of the Middle East, including acceptance of Israel. Solutions to its economic problems are central to that future. Without arousing excessive expectations, the United States is prepared thoroughly to review its

104

assistance program in order to make it as effective as possible and not subject to the ups and downs of the Egyptian-Israeli relationship.

Notes

1. *The Search for Peace in the Middle East: Documents and Statements, 1967–1979*, Report prepared for the Subcommittee on Europe and the Middle East of the Committee on Foreign Affairs, U.S. House of Representatives, by the Foreign Affairs and National Defense Division, Congressional Research Service, Library of Congress, Committee Print CP-957 (Washington, D.C.: U.S. Government Printing Office, 1979), p. 28.

2. Taba is the site of a hotel that the Israelis built near Eilat on land that, according to Egypt, belonged on the Egyptian side of the boundary after Israel's final withdrawal from the Sinai under the terms of the peace treaty. Israel asserted its claim to remain there. This surprise issue became a symbol on each side of the other's unwillingness to implement the treaty with generosity of spirit.

8

The Role of Third Parties and the Superpowers

Looking to Outsiders for Solutions

Conceptually, we can consider the Arab-Israeli peace process a political and negotiating process among the parties to that conflict, but third parties have been intimately involved since the beginning. Outside powers have acted in shaping the Middle East's modern history and political map. The peoples and governments of the region—from habit, from necessity, or to avoid responsibility for their own problems—still look to outsiders for solutions.

Third parties are familiar participants in many negotiating processes. Third parties in the Arab-Israeli peace process have played three roles:

First, they have been go-between, catalyst, facilitator, mediator, and full partner. In the period since the 1967 War, we have seen a continuing tension between two arguments. On the one hand, the Israelis have pressed, almost as a matter of doctrine, for direct, face-to-face negotiation. They have interpreted Arab readiness to meet and negotiate in the same room as a symbolic Arab act of recognition and acceptance. They have also argued, as has the United States, that the give-and-take of negotiation offers the most practical way of measuring each side's willingness to negotiate seriously and also the best way of developing politically realistic trade-offs in reaching agreement. On the other hand, we have addressed Arab unreadiness to take the symbolic step of accepting Israel and both cultures' traditional reliance on the go-between as an essential actor in settling differences and shaping solutions. In addition, we have learned—for instance, from the chemistry between Sadat and Begin at Camp David—that, at some moments, negotiating face to face hardens positions instead of leading to creative solutions. In this situation, parties traditionally turn to a semi-outsider for help.

During the intense shuttling of the mid-1970s, Sadat coined the phrase "full partner" to describe the role that the United States was playing. There is always a question about the role of the third party. Will that party be simply a mailman, carrying positions back and forth between the two sides? Will he inject ideas of his own for the solution of difficult problems? Will he even favor one solution rather than another and risk appearing to take sides? Sadat's phrase was intended to indicate that the United States would be expected to do all of these things and more. As Sadat and Begin wrote Carter on March 26, 1979, regarding their plans for further implementation of "A Framework for Peace Agreed at Camp David": "This letter also confirms our understanding that the United States Government will participate fully in all stages of negotiations."[1] The experience in the peace process during the 1970s led the parties in the conflict to regard the active and effective engagement of at least the United States as a source of ideas and as a catalyst in the effort to crystallize agreement.

Second, third parties are a factor in shaping the balance of forces that underlies a negotiation in the Middle East. They influence the balance of power that affects how parties negotiate.

At the simplest level in the negotiations, it is impossible to distinguish between the role of the "full partner" in helping fashion solutions and both sides' perception that the partner's support for one solution or another is a form of political pressure. Even at the nuts-and-bolts level, the third party becomes a factor in shifting the balance of forces behind the negotiation.

On the larger political stage, experience during and since the 1970s reveals the obvious struggle by each party in the peace process to shift the United States to its side of the balance. Arab parties try to enlist the United States to put pressure on Israel. Israel presses the United States, first, to maintain its position of allowing the weight of Israel's superior military power to be felt and, second, to demonstrate unequivocally that the United States will not allow Israel to be destroyed.

On the global stage, the states of the Middle East have consistently seen relationships with the big powers as a normal part of the regional political scene. They have turned to the big powers to strengthen their own military and economic as well as diplomatic positions. They have tried to exploit the rivalry between the superpowers to increase support for their own positions.

On the Arab side, there has been a predominant concern with building their own military strength to offset that of Israel. Some Arab governments have turned to the Soviet Union for arms. Others, in which traditional regimes govern, have recognized that the Soviet Union's long-term view of the development of the political map of the Middle East is not necessarily compatible with their survival. They also recognize that, in the Arab-Israeli context, even the limited U.S. ability to influence Israel is greater than the foreseeable influence of the Soviet Union.

On the Israeli side, the overriding concern has been to build Israel's strength to a level where Israel's security will not have to depend on any other nation, but there has also been a less willingly articulated recognition that Israel would not want to be without the ultimate security guarantee of the United States. In the early 1980s, much was made of the strategic alliance between Israel and the United States, in which Israel was painted by some as the defender of U.S. interests in the Middle East. The validity of that position is debatable, especially in view of the complexity of Israeli relationships with the superpowers whenever the Soviet Union offers to resume relations with Israel and in some informal way implies that the quality of Jewish life in the Soviet Union and opportunities for Jewish emigration could be discussed.

Third, the parties to the conflict look to some combination of third parties to fulfill functions that are normally the responsibilities of the international community. One such function is to provide an umbrella of legitimacy or even international pressure for their efforts to negotiate peace. Another is to uphold and apply principles judged to be essential in building a peaceful world.

The international community has been involved in the Palestine problem simply because no one party could resolve it. History early placed the Palestinian problem and then the Arab-Israeli conflict in the hands of the international community. The Palestine Mandate was formed under the League of Nations and became one of the early problems placed before the new United Nations Organization. Since that time it has returned again and again to the Security Council because Arab-Israeli tension posed a threat to world peace. The world community has faced a dilemma: it cannot impose a solution, but the parties to the conflict have not been able to find a solution for themselves. It is accepted that "the parties to the conflict must be parties to the peace," yet the parties to the conflict have been unable or unready to make peace and have consistently drawn outsiders into the efforts to achieve a settlement.

Political leaders trying to persuade constituents often find support in citing larger principles or pressures from the international community as the reasons why they must enter negotiation. It is easier for them when they can share the responsibility or lay blame on some other doorstep. The Middle East Peace Conference in Geneva, for instance, met only in December 1973 under the auspices of the secretary general of the United Nations and the cochairmanship of the Soviet Union and the United States. Two of the three interim agreements signed in 1974 and 1975, however, explicitly stated that they were negotiated "within the framework of the Geneva Conference." Two provided for talks on implementation in Geneva working groups.

Each of the participants in the peace process has his own political reason for looking to some international umbrella. Arab participants have found it important to state symbolically that they were not negotiating a separate peace with Israel, forsaking their Arab partners. Israelis have often said they are indifferent to the views of the international community because those views are overwhelmingly pro-Arab as expressed in the United Nations votes. Nevertheless, Israel over the years has invested substantial effort and resources in broadening international recognition and support for the acceptance and security of Israel.

Beyond the practical political usefulness of an umbrella of legitimacy lies the difficult-to-define role of principles of international justice and order in a political process. The world community is also involved because principles of international order that they have enshrined in the United Nations Charter are involved. Members of the world community who are committed to a better world feel an obligation to involve themselves. The Arab-Israeli conflict perhaps places this obligation before the international community in a unique way. The Arab-Israeli conflict may be without precedent in history. Consider the situation at the end of World War II, when the victorious powers confronted the problem of how to respond with compassion and justice to the plight of the Jewish survivors of the Holocaust. Leaders of the Western democracies were faced not only with the survivors of one of history's most massive and unbelievable crimes against humanity but also with the experience of literally centuries of persecution of the Jewish people. Those leaders made a decision unique in two ways. Not only did they decide to support creation of a new nation as a haven for the Jewish people; they also asked another people to forfeit their homes and lands to make room for that state. The principles of justice and peace are being uniquely tested in the resolution of this conflict. Third parties in an unusual way represent the world community in applying the principles of international order.

The Superpowers

I have analyzed the roles that third parties play in the peace process. The superpowers are a special case. How they play the third-party role will be determined partly by their own global designs and partly by the relationships between them.

In Washington, some of the most frequent questions posed about the Arab-Israeli peace process are: Does the United States have an interest in "legitimizing" Soviet presence in the Middle East by including the Soviets in the negotiations? Can a lasting peace be achieved if the Soviets are excluded? Two camps in Washington would exclude the Soviets from the process. One camp would do so from a general ideological uneasiness about the morality or safety of working with Communists even on parallel paths. Another would exclude them from a strategic interest in preserving a center-stage position for the United States as the only nation with the power to influence the course of history in the Middle East. Apart from either of these groups, a third would apply a factual test to determine involvement: A superpower that actually contributes to building common ground for negotiation among the parties will in fact be involved in the peace process.

In Moscow, two concerns are uppermost in policy makers' minds. Since the early 1950s the Soviets have had a basic strategic interest in moving hostile military forces and bases in the Middle East away from Soviet borders. Soviet targets have included alliances of Middle Eastern states formed by the United States to block Soviet expansion, U.S. missile and air bases as well as intelligence stations, and U.S. naval forces in the Indian Ocean that could carry the U.S. strategic threat to the Soviet Union's southern front. A second area of concern has been psychological and political in the global context. "We are your nuclear equals," the Soviets say in one conversation after another. "You must treat us as your political equals." Treating the Soviets as political equals, it quickly becomes evident, involves inviting them to join us as equal partners in the peace process. The Soviet purpose may reflect a combination of resentment, as if the United States regarded Soviet society as inferior, and the geopolitical aim of being seen as coarbiters of the world's future course.

The nature of third-party involvement, I think, should be determined in part by a pragmatic test of the contribution that the third party is able and willing to make to the negotiation. In the particular case of the superpowers, the Soviet Union and the United States both have legitimate interests in the Middle East, although they are not symmetrical. The policies of each in the Middle East are tied partly to its interests in preventing the other from gaining a predominant position in the area, but in bilateral relations both have a vital interest in reaching agreement to prevent the use of nuclear weapons. The issue in the Arab-Israeli peace process is how much political capital either nation is willing to spend in encouraging the Arab and Israeli parties toward serious negotiation and compromise.

Each nation must deal with the political constraints that grow from its relationships with friends in the area. Moscow knows that it cannot play an equal role in the peace process as long as it has no serious relationship with Israel. It has told the Israelis that it would resume relations when a peace process begins, but it also has the option of

The first of the five Arab-Israeli agreements signed between 1974 and 1979 was a disengagement agreement to separate Egyptian and Israeli forces after the 1973 War. Egyptian and Israeli teams signed that agreement under UN auspices in a desert tent at Kilometer 101 on the Cairo-Suez road in January 1974.

Much of the work during the Kissinger shuttles was done in flight. The author confers with Secretary Kissinger during the shuttle in August 1975, which produced the second Sinai agreement between Egypt and Israel.

The Camp David accords were signed at the White House on the evening of September 17, 1978. Late that afternoon, after the understanding was reached, President Carter, Secretary of State Vance, National Security Adviser Brzezinski, and the author met at Camp David to plan messages informing world leaders of the agreement.

encouraging the process by opening a serious private dialogue to offer Israel concrete advantages in a relationship. Yet Moscow must weigh the fact that developing such a relationship would cost the Soviets something in Arab quarters that are important to them. The United States recognizes that continuing its role will require dialogue with the PLO but knows that such dialogue will produce a sharp negative reaction in Israel. Either power will pay a short-term price for trying to advance the peace process. Each must assess the price in terms of the possible longer-term gain from genuine progress toward peace.

What interest does either superpower have in settling the Arab-Israeli conflict? It is commonplace to say that the United States has significant interests in peace, whereas the Soviet Union just wants to "keep the pot boiling." It is a fair analytical question to ask to what extent leaders in either country have acted as if an Arab-Israeli settlement had high political priority. The answer is different in each case and may be different in degrees at different times within the administration of a particular leader or under different leaders. Political leaders' priorities in pursuing interests change with shifting circumstances, obstacles, and opportunities.

The analytical community in Washington has argued consistently over the years that the United States has a critical interest in an Arab-Israeli peace. Peace would create an environment for constructive development, and moderate regimes would have a better chance to strengthen themselves. Perpetuation of the conflict will give extremist forces a major issue with which to attack existing regimes. A just peace brought about under the influence of the United States would not only strengthen the United States' geopolitical position but would help recapture some of the lost image of the United States as a power that genuinely stands for the principles it helped write into the United Nations Charter. A secure peace would enhance Israel's prospects for survival without presenting the continuous specter of confrontation possibly involving the superpowers.

In contrast, people in the United States often characterize Moscow's aims by saying that the Soviet Union has an interest in "pursuing a policy of controlled tension." Discussion with Soviet analysts produces a different picture. These analysts say that the Soviet Union has an interest in movement toward a settlement of the Arab-Israeli conflict because the Soviets do not want another Arab-Israeli war in which they will be asked to send troops to prevent another Arab defeat. Although that seems a reasonable statement of the Soviet interest, it is not clear exactly what steps Moscow has taken to move toward peace. Soviet analysts do not mention that continuous social, political, and economic change in the Middle East will provide an adequate field for pursuit of Soviet influence in the societies of the area without the danger of major military setbacks

112

to their friends or the hazard of potential confrontation with the United States.

Each side's judgment of its interests is most plainly evident in the political capital each is willing to spend to influence the political environment in which Arab and Israeli leaders will make the decision to negotiate. A sometimes significant difference between the approaches of the two superpowers—depending on how far the United States is willing to go in engaging itself at a given moment—is the notion each has about how to move the peace process forward. The two attitudes may reflect different instincts about the use of power in the current world. Whereas the Soviets seem to rely mainly on a contest of power to produce a negotiation and a result, the United States tries in addition to build on the superior military power it has helped Israel develop by encouraging a political process that would evolve into a negotiation.

I do not mean that the Soviets do not attempt to work in the broader political environment of the Arab-Israeli area. Still, although the Soviets maintain their contacts with Egypt and Jordan and seem to have urged the PLO to accept Israel, they have not established meaningful contact with Israel. Generally, Soviet policy seems to entail advancing a proposal for an international conference and waiting for governments to respond to it. It is unclear to what extent the Soviets stand behind friends in the area, such as the Libyans and South Yemenis, in rejecting peace with Israel. It is equally unclear to what extent they stand behind the Syrians in trying by any means to block negotiations in which they are not involved. They have not, however, been actively engaged with all of the parties to the conflict in trying to help them generate a political process that might improve the environment for negotiation.

Although U.S. execution often shows shortcomings, the United States works with parties on both sides of the line in trying to find a basis on which to build political support for negotiation. The United States, like the Soviet Union, has learned that it cannot force a negotiation simply by throwing its weight around. Because the United States alone has maintained a relationship with Israel and because of its own unique political relationship with Israel, it is particularly conscious of the need in the modern world for big powers to find a substitute for unusable raw power in influencing smaller nations. The United States during the intensive negotiations of the 1970s found that pressure in the classic sense of threats to withhold aid, for instance, was not useful. Helping each party in a negotiation to analyze the pressures—the advantages and disadvantages—inherent in the situation, on the other hand, was useful. The United States could help design a political-diplomatic process that each side could see as advancing its interests in a measured and safeguarded way. In short, the United States came to see that creating superior power in a situation would not by itself lead to a solution, that it was essential to generate a political process with its own incentives and pressures. That operation is the peace process, and it is not clear that the Soviets are prepared yet to participate.

Judgments in both Moscow and Washington about how the United States and the Soviet Union will deal with each other in the context of the peace process will be made partly on the basis of what the overall bilateral Soviet-U.S. relationship permits. It is worthwhile to consider this question at least partly in terms of whether or not cooperation would make possible progress in the peace process that would not otherwise take place. If so, then another factor is added to the scales of judgment. At the end of the day, there may well be larger political reasons for cooperating or not cooperating, but policy makers should know precisely what they will and will not stand a chance of deriving from the cooperation before they make that judgment. The judgment itself should reflect thoughts about the exact nature of the contribution that each side is able to make and the political limitations under which it will operate. In the end, the appropriate question is not: Should we bring the U.S.S.R. into the peace process? If the Soviet Union takes steps that contribute to negotiation, it will be a participant in the process as a matter of fact. The same statement applies to the United States.

Note

1. "Joint Letter to President Carter from President Sadat and Prime Minister Begin," in *The Search for Peace in the Middle East: Documents and Statements, 1967–1979*, Report prepared for the Subcommittee on Europe and the Middle East of the Committee on Foreign Affairs, U.S. House of Representatives, by the Foreign Affairs and National Defense Division, Congressional Research Service, Library of Congress, Committee Print CP-957 (Washington, D.C.: U.S. Government Printing Office, 1979), p. 49.

9

Shaping the Political Environment: A Framework for Action

The Peace Process as a Political Process

In chapter 2, I wrote about the judgments that leaders make in deciding whether to try for a negotiated settlement, but now we must look at the practical politics of that process. What goes on in a leader's mind is one thing; what the leader does in the political arena is another. The peace process is in the end a political process. Without political support, leaders cannot negotiate. Before they negotiate, they seek to shape the political environment so that the moment becomes ripe for negotiation. When the moment ripens, their problem is to take steps toward the other side that will influence the political environment there so as to make a negotiation happen. When leaders negotiate, their purpose is to reach an agreement that will change the political environment to support implementation and to open the way for the next steps in building a new relationship.

I described the five parts of the peace process analytically in chapter 2 in order to make two points: (1) Since the Egyptian-Israeli peace treaty was signed in 1979 and focus shifted to the Israeli-Jordanian-Palestinian-Syrian fronts, we have moved back to the early stages of the peace process. We have returned to the period that precedes leaders' political commitment to negotiation. The job to be done in this period is different from what needs to be done when representatives are gathered in the negotiating room. (2) To bring the parties to active negotiation, we must identify the substantive and psychological issues with which political leaders grapple as human beings in reaching their own personal decisions to negotiate. In chapters 3–7, I considered in detail how each of the parties to the conflict defines the problem and judges time's effect on its interests; whether it sees a settlement that it could live with; how it views the adversary's readiness to negotiate; and whether it thinks the balance of forces would make possible a fair settlement.

Now in this chapter we must think about how leaders act in the political arena while this analytical process is going on in their minds. In doing so, we are not suddenly walking away from the analytical framework for the process. Instead we are turning our attention to how leaders bring their bodies politic into line with their own reasoning. What steps can they take to translate their thoughts into political action? Until they feel they have a supportive political base, they are unlikely to risk negotiation. Even when a leader has decided to negotiate, he cannot try to negotiate a formal agreement until he has shaped a political environment that will support him in negotiating—that will even press him to negotiate.

Such analysis of the peace process suggests ways of formulating aims in the early stages that are different from those stated in the usual diplomatic options paper about how to launch a negotiation. The two approaches are different but complementary. The steps in this part of the process are more natural to the politician than to the lawyer or the diplomat. The diplomat is not suddenly excluded, but his job is changed. His task at this stage is not just to develop the terms of reference for a negotiation but also to help devise ways of shaping the political environment.

The objective in the early stages is to generate a political process that will support—will even demand—negotiation. The political foundation for a negotiated settlement is produced in the minds of people in the political arena, not first around the negotiating table. A strategy for shaping a political environment differs from a strategy for constructing a negotiation. It involves political debate and maneuver. It involves changing people's minds.

The issue for leaders who want to negotiate peace is how to shape that political process. Prudent policy makers will sit back and ask themselves whether the moment is ripe for any movement toward a negotiated peace at all. Bold ones will also ask how—or at least whether—they can help the moment ripen.

Peacemaking is not simply a matter of negotiating agreements but is also part of a continuous political reshaping of the political environment. The question is not whether the political environment will change, but who will shape that environment as it changes. If the process of change is continuous, leaders who will engage must play a continuous role. The process does not stop with one negotiated agreement or another. Peace, like politics, is never finished; it is always in the making.

Peace, like politics, also encompasses the full range of human experience. Peacemaking builds from the pain of conflict; it reaches for the joy of reconciliation. It offers the leaders of men and women a creative framework within which to improve the human condition. The issue is whether and how they will shape that framework.

The issue for a potential mediator is a special one. In a normal situation, parties to a negotiation would interact directly in the process. In the Arab-Israeli conflict the parties for the most part do not talk directly with each other. In the traditional manner of their cultures, they have turned to go-betweens to bring them together. As Americans who have played the mediator's role, we survey the process under way in each political arena with an eye not only to how each political process will develop but also to how all of them can be brought together. I have written the present chapter from that American perspective.

In order to understand how a leader translates analysis into political strategy, we must consider the moment when the leader asks himself: "How do I start the ball rolling? What are the first steps?" In chapter 2 we examined all five stages of the process, paying greatest attention to the first two stages, before a commitment to negotiate is made. There and again in chapters 3–7 we concentrated on the questions that a leader asks himself as he struggles to define the problem and to decide whether to try to negotiate a change in the present situation. In this chapter we shall think in operational terms as distinct from the analysis and decision-making judgments on which we focused in chapter 2. In this chapter, we are talking mainly about how, in the critical first and second stages of the process when a leader decides to try for a negotiated settlement, he acts to persuade his constituency to share his judgments.

Operationally, it may be useful to think in terms of functions to be performed in three areas.

• *Exploration.* An extended period of exploratory exchanges, mostly private, will mark much of the period before negotiation as leaders decide whether to try to negotiate a peaceful settlement. During this period, they will begin to test their thoughts against political reality, both in their own bodies politic and in those of their adversaries. They may explore in a number of directions, even across international boundaries into the other camp. The main characteristic of actions during this period is that the leader keeps himself in a highly flexible position so that he can change course at minimum political cost.

• *Political engagement.* At some point, even during the period of exploration, leaders will begin to add a public political dimension to the process by taking first steps aimed at changing the political environment. They will initially try to influence their own bodies politic as they become more confident of their own analysis and instincts. The public will see trial balloons and, gradually, a picture of a leader with an increasingly obvious intention to negotiate. Most leaders will leave themselves political room to change course at any moment with the least possible political loss, but at this point a leader will be actively trying to bring his people with him into negotiation. As leaders accumulate domestic support, they will begin thinking about how to communicate positions to the other side to change the political environment there to one more supportive of a decision to negotiate.

• *Making negotiation happen.* When serious effort to try for agreement has begun, leaders and mediators will look for ways of making negotiation happen. These are steps necessary at least to formalize one side's decision to negotiate and to define concrete actions designed to bring the parties together in efforts to arrange a negotiation.

Underlying actions in each of these stages there will be questions about the role that third parties can play in the evolution of the process. A potential mediator seeks as complete a picture as possible of what needs to be done to advance the process to its next stage. The mediator will also feel responsibility to understand how the interaction between the superpowers may figure in the politics of the peace process.

Let us consider each part of the political process in turn. Again, I do not group actions under headings to say that one phase will be completed before the next begins. The groupings are intended solely to help us concentrate on the main jobs to be done at each step of the way.

The Exploratory Phase

The exploratory phase is not only a period when leaders are deciding whether to negotiate but also a period when they are asking themselves how they can persuade their bodies politic that it is time to negotiate. Leaders are asking, in other words, how they can generate the same analytical process in the body politic that they have gone through in their own minds. Much the same debate will already be under way in many parts of society if the issues are as deeply embedded and as important to survival and identity as are those in the Arab-Israeli conflict. The leader's concern will be to devise ways of shaping the debate to arrange the conclusion that he would most like to see.

It is virtually impossible to define the boundaries of the exploratory phase. To begin with, as the peace process continues, the exchanges in one phase form part of the prelude to another. Furthermore, the lines between exploring and actually negotiating are not firm. During the exploratory phase the leader will need to test his own judgments on a wide range of issues. He will talk with a lot of people within his own body politic and will try to learn as much as possible about views on the other side. Much of the exploration across borders may be done unofficially or through third parties, but sometimes it may even involve officials in secret discussions of the principles of a settlement, as did the clandestine meeting in Morocco between emissaries of Sadat and Begin before Sadat decided to go to Jerusalem in 1977. The simple fact of exchanges between potential negotiating partners blurs the line between exploration and negotiation.

The exploratory phase is distinguished by its tentative character. During this period the leader need not politically defend a clear commitment to negotiate. This phase precedes the conspicuous decision to attempt written agreement and the submission of that decision to public judgment. More important than identifying the exact moment when the exploratory phase ends is recognition of the difference between exploring the desirability and feasibility of negotiating and actually taking steps that join political debate in ways that risk the leader's political position.

The initial job of a mediator during this exploratory phase includes not just confirming that a leader is addressing the full range of analytical questions that must be answered in a decision to negotiate but also helping each leader focus public debate so as to produce political support for attempting negotiation. Involving ourselves as mediators in a foreign leader's political strategizing is plainly neither easy nor natural for the American diplomat or even for a secretary of state. The professional diplomat is told that politics is not his business and that he must not interfere in another leader's politics. Yet without an effective political strategy, negotiation may never begin.

Ultimately, the mediator will help shape political steps in each body politic so as to have a constructive impact on the parallel debate in the body politic of the potential negotiating partner. The mediator must then act in such a way as to help one leader time or formulate a step so that it will also help shape debate on the other side. An effective mediator in a complex situation such as the Arab-Israeli conflict will have no choice but to engage in the political strategizing necessary to build political support for negotiation.

As each side's *picture of the problem* is explored, two central issues become apparent: (1) Each side has political groups whose picture of the problem does not acknowledge the other side as having a share in the problem. Palestinians and Israelis have claims and histories in the same land, but many on each side act as if the other people and their claims do not exist. (2) Each side's picture includes a judgment that the other side cannot accept it as part of a solution to the problem in ways consistent with its identity and dignity. How many times we hear each side say that the other "will never negotiate seriously"!

In the exploratory period the aim is not immediately to remove these barriers but simply to identify them as parts of the problem that will block progress toward a solution if they are not dealt with. Later, as a strategy is developed, steps will have to be devised that will begin changing the picture within the leader's own camp. Then steps will be considered that will give the leaders and people on the other side reason

119

to begin reexamining their own pictures of the problem.

The main focus in this part of the exploration is to identify steps that would help each side begin thinking of the other side as a group of human beings who, if reality is accepted, are part of one's own problem.

• The more Palestinians recognize that Israel is here to stay, the more Israel becomes part of a realistic Palestinian picture of the problem. The daily reality of living under Israeli military government and watching Israeli road and housing development has brought home this realization for the third of the Palestinians living in the West Bank and Gaza. The more Israelis must confront what it means to be an occupier and their choices in dealing with the Arab element, which amounts to nearly 40 percent in the population west of the Jordan River, the more they will recognize that the Palestinians are part of their problem. The question is whether Israeli leaders will wait for sustained violence to make these points or whether they will find nonviolent ways of dramatizing them.

• The more the two peoples have opportunities to meet as individuals with normal human, professional, and business concerns rather than as occupier and occupied, the more difficult it will be for each side to treat the other as no more than a faceless mass. Particularly, the more each human being knows individual human beings on the other side who have their own suffering and pain, the more difficult it will be to dismiss each other from mind. The more each side is able to recognize the injustice that the other has suffered, the more each side recognizes the humanity of the other. In an age where each side watches the other's television, ways are readily available to enlarge that exposure quickly and many times. Face-to-face meetings are more difficult to organize and involve smaller numbers, but they are critical.

• The more each side shows by meeting that it is prepared to do business in a normal way, the more difficult it is to maintain a picture of the other side as unwilling to move toward a normal relationship.

• The more each side is willing openly to foreswear the calculated use of violence as a policy instrument, including official or police violence, the more the other side will begin to believe that mutual respect for security might be achieved in a settlement.

• The more each side is willing to speak openly of a peace that includes the other, the more difficult it will be for each side to maintain that the other side will not negotiate seriously.

• The more each side is willing to use an exploratory period to learn which gestures would be important in changing pictures on the other side, the more the other side will begin to change its own picture. One way to achieve this goal is to listen carefully to the debate on the other side to understand what the real issues are. Another is to ask each leader

120

directly what his counterpart on the other side can do to help him build a political base for negotiation.

In short, it is important to learn through exploration what could be done to expand each side's picture to include pictures of the other side as human beings who have a part share in one's own problem. How can Israelis come to accept a definition of the problem that includes identity, justice, and security for the Palestinians as well as for themselves? How can Arabs come to acknowledge the magnitude of Jewish suffering and the fact that Jews feel they belong in Palestine? How can Israelis and Palestinians speak of the problem as one in which they both must deal with each other on the basis of respect for each other's suffering, mutual acceptance, common claims, and a reciprocal commitment to work out a coexistence in which each side could enjoy the full and secure exercise of its rights as a people? How can Israelis and Palestinians assure Jordan that Jordan's integrity is respected? How can all parties assure Syria that its interests are seen as part of the problem and that it could maintain a voice in the settlement?

Another objective in this period is to explore the ways in which parties to the conflict see *the influence of time on their interests* if a situation continues. If the facts warrant, one aim at this stage is to assure that the full consequences of doing nothing are assessed. Questions must be asked in diplomatic discussion that are often not raised or, if they are, are not probed to the point of producing candid answers. Leaders do not easily talk outside a limited circle about the pressures they face. As a leader draws his own conclusions about the effect on his interests of the passage of time, he must begin thinking about how these considerations can be introduced into the public debate to lead people to the same conclusions.

- Some Israelis have asked reflectively whether a bloodbath will be needed on the West Bank to bring to a politically significant pitch the uneasiness some Israelis already feel over prolonged military occupation. Some young soldiers have refused to serve in the occupied territories, whereas other Israelis have voiced concern that the continued occupation is eroding Israeli values. There is a broad national abhorrence of what came to be regarded as an excessive use of force for the wrong objectives in Lebanon. A leader must ask how to direct that feeling against further prolongation of the military government.
- Palestinian leaders must ask themselves how to dramatize to their own people the fact that continued Israeli occupation restricts the ability of the Israeli government to negotiate freely about the Palestinian future there. One of the leading figures from the West Bank was assassinated in

Amman in early 1985, partly because he advocated negotiating a settlement with Israel before Israel's grip becomes irreversible. Would determined petitions from those Palestinians living in occupied territory broaden support in PLO councils for negotiation before too much time has passed?

• King Hussein deals regularly with Palestinians from the West Bank, whereas President Assad does not. The need to move seems much more urgent to Hussein, and he must think a great deal about how to bring Assad face to face with the problem so that he cannot treat it as a distant abstraction. Are there ways to equate support for the Palestinians with support for urgent movement in the negotiations?

Simply taking time to focus on these questions may draw attention to the questions that ought to be dealt with in debate together with the question of whether to enter a negotiation. Questions such as these are often bypassed, and the result is that diplomats try to arrange a negotiation without full political support.

An often neglected corollary is that, as leaders think through how time will affect their interests, they must be able to see clearly the doors that are closed as well as the doors that are open or could be opened. In some cases they must be helped to understand the limits of their resources—military, economic, political, and diplomatic. They must be helped to understand the political limits on the other side with some precision. Limits include the Palestinians' loss of a military option, the Jordanians' sense that they cannot negotiate alone, and the Israelis' realization that no nation can expect a blank check where political, economic, diplomatic, or military support from any other nation is concerned until it has demonstrated that it has done all it can for itself. "Doing all it can" means that each side must give the other a sense that it recognizes the needs and the humanity of the other as part of establishing a base for negotiation.

A third aim in the exploratory phase is to begin discussing in general terms *the shape of a possible settlement* that a leader could live with politically. Thought must be given not only to the settlement that the leader would most like to envision but also to the elements of a settlement that would most appeal to the broadest constituency and would be the most popular issues on which to confront opponents. Often, a leader will need to think not only about the shape of the settlement itself but also about the shape and sequence of issues to be dealt with prior to the settlement. In mid-1985, leaders had to consider issues such as the following:

• An Israeli leader had to consider that the Knesset approved negotiations with the Palestinians after Camp David, but negotiations with the

122

PLO are widely opposed. He might recall that even the Likud under Menachem Begin agreed to a first step in negotiation about the West Bank and Gaza that would lift the military government but would defer decision on the issue of territorial compromise. He would improve his tactical position if he could separate the issue of security from the issue of Israeli settlements.

• A Jordanian leader would improve his position more if he could show that he was able to win Palestinian participation in the negotiating process than he would if he had to defend himself right away on the issue of territorial compromise. He would improve his position more by achieving some rollback of the Israeli military government than he would by having an early confrontation over the powers of a Palestinian state within a Palestinian-Jordanian confederation.

• A Palestinian leader might consider the consequences of giving more immediate political priority to assuring some recognition for the PLO than to beginning negotiation. Having lost part of the PLO in the split of the organization, he might give greater weight to representatives from the West Bank and Gaza and might be able to use them to greater advantage than before. He might gain more politically from showing involvement in negotiation than from doing nothing at all. Progress toward relaxing or removing Israeli military government could elicit political support from more Palestinians than talking about armed struggle to achieve an independent Palestinian state.

In short, the issue during exploratory probes is not just the normal diplomatic effort to develop pictures of a settlement that could be negotiable but also the extra effort involved in putting those pictures together in such a way as to win political support and to blunt opposition.

A fourth concern during the exploratory period is to ensure enough understanding across boundaries to enable each leader to make judgments about *whether the other side could buy the kind of agreement he could live with.* Not only does side A need to think about side B's views and positions; side A needs to think about how its own actions can influence side B's judgments about side A's ability to conclude an agreement side B can live with.

The evidence that will contribute to such judgments will come from a wide variety of areas.

• One leader will want to know whether the other is in control politically. Can he deliver what he may negotiate? Can he make difficult political decisions and make them stick?

• What sensitivity has one leader shown to another's political problems? Even though an Israeli prime minister may prefer negotiating with the Jordanian leader to negotiating with the Palestinians alone, does he show sensitivity to Hussein's judgment that he cannot negotiate openly with Israel alone? Can an Israeli prime minister speak in some way that is politically possible for him but will also help Hussein enhance his credibility with the Palestinians? Can a Jordanian leader act to strengthen an Israeli prime minister's credibility when he states that Jordan is prepared to negotiate peace and can produce Palestinians who are also ready to make peace? How can a Jordanian leader persuade Israeli leaders that, with Palestinian participation, he can make compromises that he could not make alone when he exchanged positions with the Israelis after the 1967 War and in 1974?

• Is one leader in speaking to his own constituencies prepared to describe a picture of the problem that reflects understanding of the other side's most basic needs?

The issue is not a simple comparison of positions but an inquiry as to whether one political leader judges that he can count on the other to move in the same direction and that he can be prepared to help him, where possible, to deal with his own political problems.

Finally, the dialogue must explore *how to develop a balance of forces that would allow a fair deal if they negotiate*. Not wanting the risk in negotiating to be any higher than necessary, leaders do not want to walk into a negotiation where they feel the cards are stacked against them and the risk of failure is high. The Arabs particularly fear the consequences of coming away from a negotiation empty-handed. Leaders will consider an array of factors:

• Their first consideration will be the balance of political forces within their own political environment. For an Israeli leader, that environment includes the State of Israel and, to some limited extent, influences from the world Jewish community, although those seem unlikely to be decisive. For an Arab leader, that environment includes both constituencies within his own country and the configuration of alliances among those Arab states and movements with an interest in the situation sufficient to cause them to act. Optimally, leaders would like to position the issues so they will at least appear to be under pressure to negotiate. In any case, they will need to judge that they have a reasonable chance of winning political support for entering negotiations.

• They will consider the power of their adversaries. Usually, leaders will not come to the table when they are seen as so much weaker than their adversaries that they have no choice but to negotiate a settlement at almost any price. In some cultures, negotiating when one has no option of using force is seen as a wise course. Leaders will take into account the classic balance of military forces. Although the oil weapon seems to have faded from the picture for a moment, in 1973–1974 it provided one of the century's outstanding cases of the impact of economic power on political judgments.

• The stand taken by major powers in relation to the negotiation is also a major factor in a leader's calculations about the balance of power. It is not just that the provider of economic assistance and military supplies holds power of a limited sort. The much more important fact is that the Arab world sees Israel as existing largely because of American support, and indeed Israelis—though they hate the dependence—know that international support for Israel has dwindled since 1967 until the only power on which they have a reasonable chance of counting is the United States. Arab states have looked to the Soviet Union for military supplies and to offset in some way the otherwise seemingly uncritical U.S. support for Israel.

• Leaders will also realize that unspoken and even unrecognized coalitions for and against negotiation cross national boundaries. Sadat's appeal to the people of Israel is a dramatic recent example, but the number of meaningful human relationships that have grown between Israelis— even influential members of the Knesset—and individuals in the Palestinian movement has created a political factor that might be used to political advantage.

• Finally, a leader will look to the balance of forces within the negotiating arena itself. For years, Arabs have feared going into the negotiating room because they feared that the Israelis would outmaneuver them. Some Israelis have feared that entering a negotiation with some Palestinians would amount to surrendering some of their legitimate claim to a position in Palestine. They have also preferred direct negotiation—in addition to the act of recognition involved—in order to maximize the impact of their own power and to minimize the opportunity for a third party to insert itself into the balance.

At this point, it is appropriate to say a word about pressure. The greatest pressures are those inherent in the overall political, economic, and strategic situation that the parties to the conflict face, not those in the hands of an outside power. Israel, for instance, faces two long-term riskfull options: One is to batten down the hatches and try to survive in a fortress Israel, knowing that the Arabs will achieve the capacity to turn their numerical superiority into a military victory at some point in the future, perhaps with nuclear weapons; the other is to risk trying to build peaceful relationships with their neighbors. Pressures can be unleashed simply by causing leaders to understand the consequences of different courses of action and by prompting people to see a possibility of peace where they saw none before. President Sadat put more pressure on the government of Israel by his visit to Jerusalem than the United States could have by withholding billions in aid.

In the discussion of pressure, a particular word must be said about the role of the United States. The widespread assumption in the Arab world is that the United States could force Israel to agree to any solution on which the U.S. insisted. It is true that the U.S. could influence Israeli decisions far more than it does if it chose to exercise that influence in proper and compassionate ways. It is not true that the United States can force Israel to do anything; nations do not sell their futures to anyone. It is true that the Israeli lobby in the United States is uniquely strong and uniquely pervasive, particularly when working in the Congress, but it is also true that a president of the United States maintaining a reasonable stand for a secure and just peace can probably count on broad political support in the United States, including much of the Jewish community.

Although the influence of the United States is limited, the United States does have the capability—even the obligation—to demonstrate to regional parties that no major international power will support them in a violent resolution of the conflict. They must believe that active major powers will support a fair settlement. In addition, the United States has the option of making clear its stand on specific issues. It is sometimes argued that we as a great power have an obligation to leave our friends in no doubt about our position when our self-respect and interests are involved.

In short, the subjects of discussion in this exploratory phase entail reshaping people's pictures of the problem, an acute awareness that the consequences of drift will be greater harm and pain, a sense that solutions are available, a demonstration that adversaries are prepared to seek political solutions, and a sense that no party to the conflict will have unlimited support from any major power for other than a peaceful settlement. This is the language of heads of government and political leaders. Dialogue can take place on all levels, but experience has demonstrated that it cannot produce a national commitment to negotiate until political leaders are themselves committed to that dialogue and to a peace process.

Steps to Shape the Political Environment

At some point a leader will move toward political engagement. He will pass beyond exploration and will take at least tentative steps to begin building political support for negotiation. The first moves will normally be made within his own body politic. Even in taking those steps as he begins to operate publicly, he will be aware that he is communicating at least indirectly with the constituents of his potential negotiating partner. When he feels some political support is accumulating at home, he will take steps to communicate directly to people on the other side in hopes of bringing them closer to negotiation.

At home, his first steps will probably be taken within his own political inner circle. He will need to gather around him quietly those political allies most likely to share his thinking and to begin building consensus in that group. IIn high political circles, even bringing a small group of close advisers together around a course of action may not be easy. These are strong-minded individuals, sometimes with sharply differing political styles and senses of strategy. Some are more patient with a strategy of grinding away at a problem; others are impatient and want to take the bold step regardless of the uncertain political reactions that may result. They may have slightly different experiences with the problem and strong preferences about ways of attacking it. Personal chemistry among individuals may sometimes make it difficult for them to agree even when they are substantively close.

As the group talks together or as the leader talks with subgroups separately, a plan for moving into the larger political arena will begin to form in their minds. A leader will need to form a sense of how much political support each of these immediate supporters can deliver and what roles he can count on each to play. Other members of this group will not be direct players in the political arena but will be staff advisers experienced in sensing or measuring how the body politic defines issues and divides over them.

At some point, the time will come to broaden the political circle and to try to build wider support in the body politic. This can be done in a variety of familiar ways that need not be detailed here. The key in this step will lie in formulating the issues for public presentation so as to appeal to the largest segment of the constituency. At the right moment, some specific step will need to be framed that will begin to crystallize a concrete body of support and will give the leader means for assessing the extent of his support.

An important example of this kind of step in the Arab world was the Hussein-Arafat agreement announced on February 11, 1985. This was not, as it was judged in some quarters, a document on which to base an Israeli-Jordanian-Palestinian negotiation. It was first a coalition agreement between Jordanian and Palestinian leaders and second an instrument for Arafat to use in building support in his own inner circle in the executive committees of the PLO and Fatah, the largest organization under the PLO umbrella and Arafat's own base. The agreement was designed to become the focus of political debate and to identify the most sensitive issues in the relevant bodies politic that had to be dealt with to gain broad political support. Another device in the larger Arab world has been the communiqué from the summit meeting of Arab leaders, such as that issued from the summit in Fez in September 1982, which recorded, albeit imprecisely, the Arab leaders' readiness to accept a settlement predicated on a map that included Israel within pre-1967 boundaries.

In Israel, a political leader will start from the knowledge that the electorate will divide on steps toward peace according to the way the issues are presented, according to the way the trade-offs are formulated, according to what security they can realistically expect to achieve, and according to the price they will be asked to pay. The leader will know that the support he can develop will depend heavily on how he presents the issues, on the sequence in which he presents them, and on his ability to convince his people that the adversary is genuinely ready to negotiate a peaceful relationship. In the 1970s, the two disengagement agreements in 1974–1975 persuaded Israelis that they could negotiate with Egypt agreements that would be kept. Sadat's visit to Jerusalem in 1977 persuaded the Israelis that Sadat was serious about negotiating a peace based on the acceptance of the Israeli state. On that basis, the prime minister felt he could find support for a peace agreement based on Israeli withdrawal from the Sinai if he could deal adequately in negotiation with security issues and with the Israeli settlements in the Sinai.

When a leader begins to shape the debate in his own country, he will become increasingly conscious as time passes that he must consider how that debate contributes to the other side's readiness to negotiate. He will have to meet first the political imperatives within his own body politic, but he will recognize that, where he has latitude, he must show concern about the influence of his own society's debate on the ability of his potential negotiating partner to negotiate on terms that could lead to agreement. At a minimum, he must demonstrate abroad, as at home, that he is in charge and can deliver decisive political support when necessary. He must particularly show that he is able to overcome known opponents to a settlement on terms that the other side could seriously consider. He must also demonstrate that he can maintain political support while talking about the issues to be negotiated in a way that recognizes the other side as part of the problem. Adversaries will look for symbolic gestures intended to show sensitivity to their concerns, even when those gestures are made largely in a domestic context.

Ultimately, when a leader begins to develop some confidence in his own political base, he may feel able to take actions specifically directed at the sensitivities of the other side. The process will be enhanced if he begins to think about what he can contribute to bringing these separate political processes together so that they begin to reinforce each other in making a negotiated settlement seem possible, more attractive than drift, and even imperative. That Menachem Begin rarely thought in these terms was a major disappointment to Sadat. Other Israelis such as Moshe Dayan and Ezer Weizman at the height of the Camp David and peace treaty negotiations did think in terms of the other side's political needs. It was one of Sadat's most important contributions to the process that he learned how to appeal to the people of Israel and the United States in ways that strengthened their leaders' ability to negotiate and mediate in directions he regarded as constructive. Many individuals struggling with launching the peace process again in the 1980s have thought in terms of how to devise a "Sadat-like act" appropriate to present actors and situations.

When leaders address the constituencies of their potential negotiating partners, they should particularly focus on two points. First, they must demonstrate that their picture of the problem includes the other side's deepest fears and concerns. For both Israelis and Palestinians, the withholding of recognition has been their most potent weapon in dealing with the other. It has been potent because it strikes at the other side's most basic human need—assuring its own identity. Sadat's powerful message to the Israeli Knesset was not one of diplomatic recognition but one of accepting the Israelis as a people and as a potential partner in peace. Sadat made clear that the peace he wanted for the people of Egypt had to include peace and acceptance for the people of Israel.

When asked what act would be most likely to move the Israelis toward peace negotiations with the Jordanians and Palestinians, most Israelis will answer, "A real Arab peace offer." The Palestinians regard withholding recognition of Israel as the "only card" they have to play in negotiation. Similarly, even Israelis who want to negotiate peace with the Palestinians cite as their reason for not wanting to negotiate with the PLO the Palestinian National Charter's stated premise that creation of a state in Palestine would end the existence of Israel. Many Israelis believe it is not enough for Palestinians to recognize that Israel is here to stay; they believe the Palestinians must recognize that Israel has a "right" to exist and is a part of the Palestinian picture of the world.

The operational question is how each side can insert itself constructively into the other side's debate. In Israel and among the Palestinians, a major debate would take place before either side would decide to negotiate because alternative viewpoints about each side's future would be at stake. The issue is how the debate could be precipitated in a constructive way and how each side could take steps that would help the other side see its peaceful alternatives. For Palestinians and Israelis, the issue is whether there are ways for each side to reach into the other's constituency to let it be known that a common or complementary definition of the problem is possible.

Examples from Israel might include statements in the Israeli debate that the Israeli state cannot be built on the obliteration of Palestinian rights and that Israel is ready to talk with Palestinians about how they can exercise their rights without endangering Israel. Such statements would be taken more seriously if they were underscored by a relaxation of some of the military government's most restrictive practices, by permitting political leaders to meet quietly, or by returning deposed elected mayors to their positions. Examples from the Palestinians might include endorsement by the Palestine National Council of Jewish-Palestinian dialogue and a slight elaboration of the 1982 Arab summit call for guarantees of the security of all states in the region to add the words "including Israel." Examples among the Arab states could include both readmitting Egypt into the Arab League with the Egyptian-Israeli peace treaty intact and adoption of a statement that explicitly mentioned negotiating a settlement with Israel.

Second, leaders must convince leaders and people on the other side that they are prepared to make some of the concessions that would be necessary to produce an agreement with which both sides can live. To put the point another way, each side must convince the other that it is ready to negotiate seriously about all outstanding issues. The most devastating fallout from Israel's policy of placing and expanding settlements in the West Bank and Gaza is its role in convincing Arabs that Israel does not intend to negotiate all outstanding issues—that, to use the words of the Begin government, Israel is "creating facts that will be irreversible in a negotiation."

Making Negotiation Happen

When a leader has developed a strategy in his mind and feels he has built some political support, he will begin developing concrete steps to engage the other side in working toward negotiation. The problem he faces is how to translate his inclination to negotiate into steps that will actually bring about the first meeting to arrange a negotiation. Leaders on opposite sides can reach a moment that seems to the analyst to be ripe for negotiation without being able to make negotiation happen. They may be unable to devise or take steps that can be matched by steps on the other side that will actually lead to the negotiating table.

Steps that may be taken can cover the full gamut of political actions. Some may be unilateral steps that can both help to change the political environment and give the other side a specific glimpse of concrete changes in the situation that might result from negotiation. These steps may seem as much a part of the exploratory effort as part of an effort to make negotiations happen, but they will have the added character of seeming to start the negotiating process with an implicit or explicit invitation to the other party to join. A second range of actions may be developed by a mediator—a proposed approach with which each side independently concurs. Kissinger's shuttle negotiations in 1974–1975 worked in this way. After extended talks with each side, Kissinger described a way of proceeding and the shape of the agreement for which the parties would aim. His proposal, which grew informally from those consultations, was the instrument for joining the negotiation. A third range of actions may be steps taken by the parties individually or in series—by prior agreement or by actions on independent tracks—that will in fact gradually engage them in a common scenario leading to the negotiating table.

As with other parts of a political process, actions do not fall neatly in one category or another. An astute politician will operate on several levels at the same time. Any significant action may have several purposes, or the hope may be that a first step taken with a modest objective may evolve into a second step with a larger purpose. The purpose in characterizing steps is not to limit opportunities for trying to get the ball rolling but to identify them.

One key in formulating these steps is the concept around which they are built. If they are to be effectively designed, they must address the political and psychological barriers on both sides that were identified during the exploratory phase. Leaders have to present proposed moves so that their constituencies will see the possibility that their needs will be met at a price they are willing to pay. After the 1973 War, as the United States helped crystallize such steps, the idea was the disengagement of forces—first for the purpose of reducing the likelihood of resumed conflict and then for the purpose of beginning a process of negotiation that would anticipate the withdrawal of Israeli forces and peace. In early 1977, with three interim agreements on the record, the concept at the beginning of the Carter administration was resumption of broader peace negotiations in the Middle East Peace Conference at Geneva, with the aim of achieving a comprehensive peace. Exploratory talks were aimed at defining terms of reference from which the parties were willing to start those negotiations.

My purpose here is not to lay out a plan of action for a particular time or situation, nor is it to examine a comprehensive list of all possible steps and their variations. Rather I wish to highlight the characteristics of steps that a leader can take in trying to get the ball rolling toward negotiation and to underscore the importance of designing those steps as much to erode the political and psychological barriers to negotiation as to provide a substantive base for negotiation.

The following menu was devised to include examples of: (1) unilateral steps that could serve as an invitation to negotiation; (2) steps a mediator might take to start a negotiating process; and (3) steps the parties themselves might take. Some of these actions could fall in two or three groups, depending on their arrangement and on the nature of their evolution. This menu was appropriate in mid-1985. As the process moves on, other examples may replace these.

Concerted effort to broaden private dialogue. In the Arab-Israeli context today, private contacts and a small number of private dialogue groups already exist. The simplest of these contacts involve Israelis and Palestinians in the West Bank and Gaza. They happen often. In addition there are more structured meetings involving some combination of Egyptians, Israelis, Palestinians, and Americans, usually in Europe or the United States. A leader on either side who met quietly with some of those groups or with individual members to signal a strong personal interest in the dialogue would not be making himself politically conspicuous. A leader could also begin to share the outlines of his thinking so that it could be conveyed with whatever authority he authorizes to individuals on the other side as a preview of positions he might advance in a formal negotiation.

A systematic effort of this kind would serve at least two purposes. Increased direct human contact would help the leader in his own efforts to paint and broadcast a picture of the problem that takes into account the humanity and the pain on the other side. A carefully conducted campaign of this kind would begin to build a record on the other side that would support belief in his own readiness to negotiate seriously. The more developed a program of this kind became, the more it would be possible to bring individuals who had experienced such contacts before the television cameras for a wider audience.

To be specific, an Israeli prime minister and defense minister or Jordanian leaders have the option at any moment they choose of injecting a fresh message into the large network of contacts that already exists on both an informal and an organized basis. Since Jordanian television is watched nightly in Israel, Jordanian leaders also have the option at any moment of helping Palestinians and Jordanians in every walk of life develop a personal approach to the Israeli people on a human basis. The television is not a substitute for direct contact because the individual who presents feelings on television should be someone who has learned in private dialogue with Israelis to speak in terms that show sensitivity to Israeli concerns while making vivid his own.

A unilateral Israeli move toward increased Palestinian authority on an interim basis would result from Israeli decisions simply to pass on to Palestinian officials in the West Bank and Gaza more responsibility for managing their own affairs. Such a step, if taken by the Israelis alone, would aim to create on the other side a picture of movement toward a new situation with the implication that the other side could become part

132

of further steps in the process. The same unilateral step could also be taken after consultation between the two sides to enable each to take maximum political advantage of the move in building the base for a tentatively agreed next step. If no one on the Arab side is able to help design such arrangements, Israel could do it alone or with the United States alone or after informal U.S. consultation with Jordanians or Palestinians.

Even as a unilateral step without prior consultation, such a move would have two substantive aims. It could demonstrate to Jordanians, Palestinians, and other Arabs an Israeli readiness to move on the Palestinian issue. To be effective it would have to be clear that this was designed as a step toward a final settlement—not as the final settlement itself. It would be important in removing from the Arabs' picture of the problem the image of an intransigent Israel. By taking a step within the framework to which Begin agreed at Camp David, an Israeli prime minister might hope to avoid dividing his own electorate with his first move. A formal broadening of authority could be preceded or enhanced by Israeli decisions to allow Palestinians in the West Bank and Gaza to resume the activities of groups that once attempted coordination by Palestinian municipal officials throughout the territories. It would also be enhanced if the Israeli decisions were accompanied by a call for free elections in the West Bank and Gaza.

This approach has several disadvantages. It is not clear that a broad coalition in Israel would support such a step in the absence of a clear-cut Arab negotiating partner, as was envisioned in the Camp David accords. It is also not clear that West Bank leadership would respond to this challenge by participating or by running for election. The Israelis could increase the likelihood by lifting the restrictions now imposed on officials and allowing the deposed officials to return to their homes and offices.

Designate a particular group for substantive discussion. One step beyond injecting positions into private contact groups would involve each government's or organization's designating an individual or two to meet directly or with a mediator to hold preview discussions of substantive issues. This procedure would differ from the informal dialogue groups because authorities on each side would have given specific blessing to the participants to explore solutions on their behalf—though not to negotiate—with an indication of readiness to move the talks to the formal level if agreement seemed possible. Such meetings would fall short of secret official contacts in that the individuals would not necessarily be officials of government or at least would not be speaking for governments. They would be authorized to explore within limits that governments would impose on them informally, but they could not

133

commit their governments to agreement. The unilateral alternative is for a private group to meet with more official involvement by one government than by another.

Whenever a prolonged impasse exists, private groups appoint themselves to meet under private auspices to hold discussions of this kind. They meet and talk as representatives only of their cultures and countries to see whether they can generate ideas that could open the doors to official agreement and formal solution. Responsible private groups with the particular purpose of exploring the ways and substance of negotiating can be useful in developing new concepts and new ways for two sides to approach each other. They can put new ideas in the air and can help change the political environment over time. Individuals in these groups may have more or less substantive ties to their governments.

These private groups, however, differ from the kind of meeting I am describing here in two major respects: First, they are self-appointed, whereas I am suggesting a quasi-private meeting taking place at the initiation of governments. Second, the group I am talking about would meet with an explicit understanding that the discussions will stay generally within broad limits set by governments with their "representatives" and will be reported to governments for eventual judgment about more formal negotiation. An important purpose would be to use the meetings to convey to one or both sides that agreement may be more possible than they thought.

Drafting a new document. Going beyond unilateral steps and informal dialogue to steps specifically designed to convene formal negotiation, a new document might be developed by the United States as mediator in secret discussions. It could build from the elements that are common to Resolutions 242 and 338, the Camp David accords, the Reagan initiative, the Fez Declaration, and the Hussein-Arafat agreement. The purpose of engaging in such an exercise would be to provide either a political rallying flag or the basis for negotiation.

The advantage of this approach is that it would permit a fresh effort for the first time to bring together common elements reflecting a broader Arab consensus than was possible following the Camp David accords. In some instances, the act of developing such a document itself becomes the vehicle for communicating readiness to negotiate and can suggest other approaches not previously thought possible or useful.

The disadvantage of such an approach until political dialogue is well advanced is that pulling together words on paper will not by itself be sufficient. In addition, any mediation effort must go to the heart of those political obstacles that prevent leaders from building political support for negotiation. Concentration on drafting often lulls participants into avoiding thought about the political steps that are prerequisite to negotiation.

134

The draft might be kept under constant development, however, as a sort of "rolling draft," using it more as the focus for continuing discussion than as a finished document.

Invitation to negotiation. A classic step in trying to precipitate a negotiation is to draw up terms of reference in the form of an invitation from a third party to meet and negotiate. This was the device—formulated by Kissinger and issued by the United Nations secretary general—that convoked the December 1973 meeting of the Geneva conference.

A variation would be a joint declaration issued more or less simultaneously by individual parties stating each side's intention to negotiate a settlement. Agreement on language to describe the objectives of the negotiation could be used to change public perceptions on each side of the usefulness of negotiation. Such a statement could be evolved directly or through an intermediary. In either case, the purpose of the exercise is to make impending negotiations a political reality to which people must adapt, thereby changing the political environment in which the negotiations will take place.

Such a document has wide possibilities. The parties could agree in advance, for instance, that sitting down to negotiate together could constitute an act of recognition, and the exact nature and general conditionality of that recognition could be spelled out. The document could not resolve the issues that can be dealt with only in negotiation, but it could remove some of the barriers of nonacceptance. In form, the document could be impersonal, or it could be directed at the government and people of the potential negotiating partner. If such a document were developed between two parties, each would experience more flexibility in tailoring the terms to their individual needs than in working with a general invitation to a larger conference.

International conference. In the mid-1980s, the call for an international conference to negotiate a comprehensive Arab-Israeli peace won widespread support in the Middle East and rejection in Israel and the United States. Some of the Middle Eastern parties seemed genuinely to believe that such a conference was essential, since they did not believe the United States was any longer able or willing to serve as an impartial mediator. Despite such feeling, many of them did not necessarily want such a conference. They supported it either as a last resort or as a means of pressing the United States to play a more active and impartial role.

A fundamental question in dealing with the proposal for an international conference was the function that it would serve. For Jordan and Syria, it seemed important as a demonstration of legitimacy—that the parties were seeking a comprehensive peace and not just an agreement to serve their own purposes. They sought to avoid the isolation Egypt experienced after Camp David and after signing the Egyptian-Israeli peace treaty. For Jordan, an international conference may be a means of blunting Syrian opposition. For the Soviet Union, it was a device for overcoming Soviet exclusion from the peace process in the 1970s. The issue was whether those political needs could be met in some other ways; most of the parties recognize that such a conference would be cumbersome and would not provide the most effective negotiating format.

Secret communications and meetings among officials or emissaries. The history of efforts to achieve an Arab-Israeli peace reveals its fair share of secret meetings among officials or officially designated representatives. Most of these efforts took place at times when such contact would have posed high political risk but when the situation had become shaky enough to require some palliative measures or to offer some opportunity for movement. Some of these efforts—such as Nasser's exploration of negotiations with Israel in the mid-1950s—were designed simply to explore whether solutions or improvement in conditions were possible. Others—such as the Dayan-Touhami meetings in Morocco in 1977—explored a formula that led to direct negotiation. These meetings are distinguished less by the substance discussed than by the fact that the meetings have an official character and carry greater political risk because they cannot be disavowed as easily as the informal unofficial group.

In my experience, the first important consequence of such contact between two potential negotiating parties is that it will be read as an expression of intent to explore seriously the possibility of negotiation. I once asked one leader what a leader on the other side could do to help him persuade his own inner circle to consider negotiation. The answer was, "establish an authoritative channel of communication and dialogue." Through that channel, once it has been established, messages can be passed explaining unilateral actions as intended signals of good faith. When direct secret meetings become possible, discussions can cover the full range, from discussing steps to prepare bodies politic for negotiation to discussing formulas for resolving critical issues and arranging next steps and a forum for formal negotiation. Such meetings can be arranged through direct channels or through intermediaries.

Talks on transitional political arrangements in the West Bank and Gaza would be one step beyond a unilateral Israeli move to establish greater Palestinian authority. Discussion of transitional measures to show movement even before agreement to a final settlement could take place would build trust in negotiation and would help develop broader political support for negotiation.

This approach would have the advantage of picking up a series of talks in 1979–1980 that have already produced solid material on solutions to important problems and some measure of agreement. Whatever happens in moving toward an overall settlement, laying the groundwork for putting a transitional Palestinian self-governing body in place in territories occupied by Israel in 1967, except around Jerusalem, would be a step toward producing a more normal relationship between Israel and its Palestinian neighbors. Such talks would not need to take place formally under the Camp David banner. They would address practical steps that could be useful whatever the framework for negotiation.

The disadvantage in considering this approach is that it is difficult to determine who would negotiate with Israel. Egypt reached a point where it felt unable to speak for the Palestinians and seemed unlikely to resume its role as the Arab negotiator inn the absence of some broader Arab mandate. No such Arab mandate seems likely for any negotiation that would appear to keep the Camp David banner aloft. Everyone, from the Arab leaders at Fez in 1982 to the inhabitants of the West Bank and Gaza, however, recognizes the need for a transitional period and for interim arrangements to allow the Palestinians time to build their own institutions.

Mutual and simultaneous recognition between Israel and some grouping of Arabs, including the Palestinians, could be a step arranged to help break down the last barriers to negotiation on each side. From the recent unofficial discussions between Israeli citizens and individual Palestinians has come the suggestion that both sides issue statements at more or less the same time indicating respect for each side's right to self-determination in the context of a negotiated peace.

The advantage of this approach is that it would require some agreement to emerge from quiet dialogue that would begin to build trust. The mutuality and simultaneity would diminish some negative political reaction on each side. Mutual recognition would begin to meet each side's most basic needs for acceptance by the other, and the word "self-determination" would have special meaning in recognizing the Palestinians' identity.

The disadvantage of this approach is the difficulty of knowing what Palestinian spokesman would have a positive impact in Israel or on the Palestinian side and whether an Israeli statement that recognized the Palestinian people but not the PLO would have the necessary impact. One way of reducing the disadvantage might be to discuss a statement by a small coalition of Arabs, including Jordan, the PLO, Egypt, and perhaps some other Arab leaders acting individually.

A dramatic act or series of acts may be an essential part of any scenario. Two questions arise: (1) What act might have sharp impact on the political environment and increase support for serious negotiation?

Another way of putting the question is to ask what might constitute a "Sadat-like act"—a political act that could change the political environment as did the 1973 War or the precedent-shattering 1977 visit to Jerusalem. (2) If no party seems able to take such a dramatic step, are there combinations of lesser acts that might have the necessary environment-changing effect? With these questions in the background for discussion, options for a series of dramatic acts may be placed in several categories.

An Arab offer of peace could be conveyed in a well-advertised address by King Hussein to the Israeli people via Jordanian television, which many Israelis watch. The absence of an Arab negotiating partner ready to accept and make peace with Israel reinforces the position of people in Israel and the United States who argue against any Israeli or U.S. initiatives. A directly delivered Arab offer to negotiate peace with Israel on a reciprocal basis reflecting Resolution 242 would provoke serious discussion in Israel and in the United States. Such an address could recognize human suffering and the shared problem of providing dignity and justice for the Palestinian people "who live among both our peoples." Hussein could explain what Palestinian self-determination means to him and how an act of self-determination might take place within the framework of a Jordanian-Palestinian confederation and peace between the confederation and Israel. He could also make clear the nature of Palestinian support for his initiative. The move would be stronger with broader Arab political support and with prior coordination of timing with Israeli leaders. The key to this move would be a direct, eye-to-eye address to the people of Israel.

Israeli readiness to make peace with the Palestinians. The absence of clear-cut Israeli readiness to recognize the Palestinian people as a people with rights to political expression of their separate identity in Palestine leaves Palestinians and other Arabs without hope that a fair settlement of the Israeli-Palestinian conflict is possible. Steps Israel could take to begin overcoming that obstacle fall into two categories. Smaller steps to increase confidence that Israel will negotiate seriously about sharing the land west of the Jordan River with the Palestinians might include allowing more independent Arab economic activity in the West Bank and Gaza, restoring elected officials to office, or permitting political consultations. More dramatic steps could include Israel's declaring a freeze on new settlements, calling free elections in the West Bank and Gaza for municipal offices, or offering to negotiate with Jordanians and Palestinians on the basis of Resolution 242, which would suggest Israeli acceptance of some withdrawal. Any such step would raise questions about whether the coalition government could make or survive such a decision, and steps would have to show that the prime minister could deliver what he negotiates.

U.S. initiative. As a third party, the United States has more flexibility in choosing the vehicle or the channel for making its impact on the political environment. At some point, the parties to the conflict need to make some public demonstration of seriousness and recognition to lessen suspicion on the other side. The United States will not necessarily best accomplish its purpose by acting in public at each stage; often public moves by the United States serve only to unite all parties in reacting negatively to the big power.

In some circumstances, the U.S. influence is most effectively exercised in private with leaders, allowing them to put the U.S. position into political play in a way that will strengthen political support for negotiation. When the U.S. position is stated publicly, it is most likely to produce positive results if the timing and presentation echo the views of individuals within the body politic.

The first aim of the United States may be to put in the hands of leaders some instrument that will strengthen their position in going to negotiation. Such an instrument may serve as a positive inducement, as in an offer to stand fast in supporting certain positions or as in an offer of economic or security assistance, or it may inject limits. At a minimum, the United States has an obligation to make sure its friends know where it stands so that they will not be surprised or undercut by positions that the United States may decide to take. At a maximum, the United States, by stating what it will not support and how it will make that lack of support known, can limit a party's resources in pursuing its own aims. In addition, it is appropriate for the United States to let others know when its principles and interests are negatively affected. These interests, and the consequences of undercutting them, must be made a factor in the calculations of policy makers with an influence in the situation.

• *With Israel,* the United States has the option at some moment of clarifying the seriousness of the U.S. conviction that a lasting Arab-Israeli peace must be based on a just and secure sharing of the land west of the Jordan River between Israelis and Palestinians. That position is not compatible with the position of the Likud party in Israel. The United States also has the option of making clear among all parties to the conflict that it supports negotiation about all outstanding issues. That position contrasts with the policy of some Israeli authorities who refuse to negotiate with some Palestinians and who create facts on the ground by building settlements in the West Bank and Gaza that will be irreversible in a negotiation.

The U.S. purpose in clarifying its position is not to exert pressure to force Israeli acceptance. The purpose is to do what is necessary to protect the health of any human relationship—to establish the limits of each party's acceptance and tolerance so that there can be accommodation based on mutual respect. When a relationship is a one-way street, resentments fester like a cancer that could one day destroy the relationship. Because Israel and the United States have been working from diverging premises since 1977, the relationship has developed the beginnings of a deep but hidden cancer; a clear understanding of each other's positions would heal the relationship and destroy the cancer.

How the United States conveys its position will be important in determining its impact. Apparent U.S. pressure tends to unite Israelis in resisting; widespread knowledge in Israel that extreme Israeli positions jeopardize solid American support in a negotiation would strengthen the hand of people who would negotiate from middle-of-the-road positions. Important communication on such issues can take place only at the highest political levels. Since the late 1970s no U.S. president and Israeli prime minister seem to have had a profound discussion on the road we are traveling together.

• *With the Palestinians,* outsiders must ask what they can do so that Palestinian leaders who wish to negotiate can build political support for doing so. "If the Reagan plan [President Reagan's speech of September 1, 1982] is improved by adding one word—self-determination—things would change completely,"[1] said one Palestinian leader in early 1983. The formal U.S. position on Palestinian rights has been not to use the word "self-determination" because that word has been widely misdefined in the Middle East as meaning "an independent Palestinian state." In early 1985, the Hussein-Arafat agreement spoke of self-determination in the context of a Jordanian-Palestinian confederation. The commonly stated U.S. position has been a pragmatic one—that an act of self-determination can take place in a number of ways and may have a number of outcomes, not necessarily an independent state. With Arab leaders using the word in this pragmatic way in early 1985, the United States had the option of supporting the Palestinian right of self-determination through negotiation either through private dialogue or, when it would have maximum political impact, in public declarations. Use of that word would mean much to the Palestinians, since it carries with it acceptance of the Palestinians as a people. By using the word either the United States or Israel could change the Palestinians' picture of the situation to include the possibility that they could achieve recognition of their identity through negotiation.

• *With Jordan,* it is important to support King Hussein in his efforts to build an Arab coalition to negotiate with Israel. If, for instance, the

United States decided to speak openly of the Palestinians' right of self-determination, Hussein would appear in a stronger light if he seemed to the Palestinians to have delivered the United States on this issue. In addition, Jordan needs a close relationship with the United States and clarity about the U.S. position. Since the 1967 War, Jordan has increasingly wondered whether it could count on the United States to show determination in pressing for a fair settlement. "The economic and strategic importance of our region to the West is self-evident," wrote Crown Prince Hassan in 1984. "Yet, we are puzzled, confused, disoriented and disillusioned at the lack of direction and decisiveness in the formulation of Western, especially American, policy."[2]

No single act by itself is likely to change the political environment. Such acts in the context of a broader dialogue could lead to pre-understood responses, and the cumulative effect could begin to produce a new environment.

Notes

1. *The Christian Science Monitor*, February 23, 1983, p. 1, "What Arafat Wants From Washington" by Trudy Rubin.

2. Hassan bin Talal, *Search for Peace: The Politics of the Middle Ground in the Arab East* (New York: St. Martin's Press, 1984), p. 4.

10

A Leader's View
of the Peace Process

A Frame of Mind

I have spoken of the peace process as a political process. I have spoken of politics as an art that comes more naturally to the leader than to the lawyer or diplomat. Among leaders, policy is not a technician's blueprint of next steps but a frame of mind, a viewpoint, a perspective, a posture, a sense of direction. In the following summary statement, my purpose is not to repeat the many suggestions for action and approach that I offered in the final sections of chapters 3–7 and in chapter 9. They will stand on their own. Instead I want to distill an attitude that I hope leaders might bring to the peace process.

Identity

Fundamental to any definition of the problem in approaching the Arab-Israeli-Palestinian conflict is the need for each of the parties to find and be secure in its own identity. Other than life itself, few possessions are more vital to individuals separately and collectively than their sense of identity. Before two peoples can begin to build a peaceful relationship, they will need to be confident of their own identity and to find ways of making clear that each recognizes and accepts the other's. Steps that Israelis and Palestinians each take to recognize the pain and injustice that the other has suffered will be part of that recognition and acceptance. Such steps would enable Palestinians to recognize the enormity of the Jewish experience in the Holocaust. They would enable Israelis to recognize Palestinian peoplehood, the unique concession the Palestinians have been asked to make in accepting the Jewish state in Palestine, and the losses the Palestinians have suffered. Acknowledgment of each other's humanity and pain and acceptance of the other party in relation to one's own integrity would provide common ground on which to meet. Those of us who are neither Jews nor Palestinians cannot share equally in their experience, but as human beings we can join in mourning their losses.

If my words sound too abstract, stop and realize that I am talking about nothing more or less than how a political leader in his next speech will talk about the problem. A people's picture of a problem is shaped by how political and opinion leaders talk about it. Israelis' picture of their problem has been shaped over the decades by Arab leaders' threatening rhetoric. Arabs' picture of the peace process after Camp David was shaped by Begin's rhetoric. Is it too much to hope that leaders on each side will help their people find nobility in an identity that transcends narrow positions and particular borders? Sadat gave his people and the people of Israel hope in a future without war. Some Israelis describe the Jewish experience in a modern state without linking their vision to one border or another—security, yes, but borders, no.

I know of no negotiating formula that can embody the healing and reconciling political acts necessary to clear common ground. The stage must be set for an act of nobility on the Palestinian side that cedes land for the Jewish state in return for the land, the flag, and the passport that the Palestinians have never had, which would provide concrete expression of their identity. On the Israeli side, the incentive for conceding a territorial expression of Palestinian identity is acceptance by their Arab neighbors that they have a reason—they would say a "right"—to feel they belong in that land. On both sides, the overriding incentives are peace and security in the political expression of a confirmed identity. Assurance that peace and security are possible will be found first in the political arena, not at the negotiating table.

The stage must be set for these two peoples to come to each other saying: "We are both the victims of history. We initially intended no harm to each other. We cannot turn history back. Can we now recognize the suffering and injustice each of us has experienced and somehow find a way to build peaceful and productive lives together?"

A Mounting Sense of Urgency

Each side must come to feel an increasing sense of urgency, and a leader has the responsibility of focusing the feeling that time is not on the side of peace and security. Analysts can afford to sit back and feel wise in passing judgment that the time is not ripe for progress. Leaders must explain to future generations why they missed an opportunity to shape an opening to move toward peace. Attitudes will change; the only question is who will shape the change.

The keenest sense of urgency is felt by the people who face daily the consequences of allowing a situation to drift. Geographic proximity does not ensure that people will face the realities and consequences of a situation. Many Israelis in Jerusalem know little about daily life over the hill in Jericho. Some leaders in Damascus have little sense of the thoughts and feelings of Israeli settlers on the Golan Heights a few kilometers away. The art of political leadership is to bring constituencies face to face with the consequences, fears, and hopes in the leader's mind.

Television and the written press can remove distance that is mental as well as geographic. Leaders can speak to people in their homes. The agonies of violence and of indignities suffered daily over time can be dramatized in people's living rooms. The day-to-day experiences of Palestinians living under military government and the experiences of the Israelis who staff the military government daily in face-to-face exchanges with those Palestinians are the places in which two peoples meet and test each other's souls. Are leaders—Arab, Israeli, Palestinian—proud to accept responsibility for what they see? If not, can Israelis who have considered the consequences for the Jewish state and values of permanently governing an Arab minority that constitutes 40 percent of the population find ways to sharpen debate on those consequences with Israelis who have not? If not, can Arabs who believe a first step toward Palestinian self-government is better than waiting for promise of a distant "return to their homes" find ways of dramatizing the importance of change now?

Leaders of the United States are not exempt from judgments regarding the wisdom with which they have used their time. At a minimum, they have an obligation to explain what they will and will not be able to support.

A Shared Land

Every major international expression of principle on the Palestinian question since the Balfour Declaration has rested on the premise that a Jewish state could be created and could endure only if the rights of the Arab inhabitants of Palestine were respected. The questions are how to consolidate Arab acceptance that there should be a Jewish state in the Middle East and how to build Jewish acceptance that peace depends on their sharing the land with the Palestinians. The time for answering these questions, after almost forty years of Palestinian statelessness and Jewish insecurity, is now. The diplomats' debate over the exact way of shaping a settlement—difficult as it is—is less difficult than persuading people on either side why a peaceful settlement requires each to accept less than its ideal solution and its full hopes.

It is the task of leaders to shape the public discussion of these questions. Each leader will have to find the issues that will convince his people that a settlement would end the weariness of a half century of fighting, would bring peace and normal relations, and would permit full realization of identity. Genius in the politics of the peace process at this stage lies in building consensus around a two-people solution in Palestine.

The diplomat can play a critical role at this point in picturing for the political leaders specific steps on the ground that could work and could win political support. Opportunities for collaboration between politician and diplomat abound if the two will learn to work together. The art of tailoring steps for political manageability requires the insights of both. The art of formulating hope for the ultimate settlement without closing doors or heightening expectations unrealistically requires the realism of both. Support cannot be won for the shape of a settlement until a picture is painted that is realizable without being frightening. Visualizing the steps for reaching a destination may be as important as knowing where that destination is.

Making Peace Possible on the Other Side

The political question is not just whether the other side can accept but what one side can do to make it easier for the other side to accept. The essence of the peace process—and what separates the people engaged in moving it forward from mere observers—is the objective of changing the political environment so that what was impossible yesterday may become possible tomorrow.

In looking toward any negotiation, leaders draw a fine line between "hanging tough" to let the other side move closer and not "hanging tough" so long that they miss the moment of opportunity when the other side is ready to move. An even finer calculation involves determining when the other side is on the brink of moving and whether an initiative could help precipitate that move. Any reasoning of this sort presupposes that a leader has an interest in moving.

A Word to the President on Peacemaking and Power

In the mid-1980s, the main options for shifting the balance of forces in favor of a peaceful settlement are options for shifting the balance of political forces and argument. Although Syria's military buildup continues, the military balance as it affects a potential negotiation will remain essentially unchanged in the foreseeable future. In the longer term, Israel must look to a time when Arab forces—at some point equipped with nuclear weapons—will be able to challenge Israel's superiority, but that time is not now.

145

In most of this book I have focused on steps that the leaders of the Middle Eastern parties to the conflict can take to generate a political process that will lead toward peace. I would like to conclude with a word to the president of the United States and to my compatriots about the place of the Arab-Israeli peace process in American foreign policy making in the closing years of the twentieth century. The five Arab-Israeli agreements that the United States mediated in the 1970s had shortcomings, to be sure, but they uniquely demonstrated how determined American political leadership and creative diplomacy can steadily alter the course of history. If power in one sense is the ability to influence the course of events, the United States in its grueling persistence, in its imagination, and in its leadership showed its power.

While abhorring a purposeless interventionism, I believe the position of the United States as a world power in the remaining years of the century and beyond will depend in part on our ability to sustain over time a constructive engagement in dealing with the world's conflicts and problems where our interests demand that we be involved and where we can make a difference. It would be senseless to say that we have the knowledge or the resources to solve the world's problems and by ourselves to bring peace to the world. It would not be senseless to say that the United States has the capacity—if it chooses to exercise and develop that capacity—to grow as a power that the world can respect because it is prepared to engage and persevere in the pursuit of justice and peace.

The United States in the last two decades of this century needs to give at least as much attention to strengthening its diplomatic and peace-making arsenal as to ensuring its military power. We must continue to develop our military strength; we have no choice in that. We do have a choice, however, whether our leaders develop a vision of real peace as a part of our national objective. We can as a nation decide whether or not to insist that our leaders demonstrate the same abilities in the pursuit of peace that we have honored in the military heroes of the past. We know that our adversaries often proceed through a policy of confrontation. We must be prepared to meet them from positions of strength, and we must help our friends to do so. I am not proposing an alternative to advancing from such a position; I am proposing an addition to our arsenal.

Some readers may object that this statement is not hardheaded enough or is unrealistically idealistic. Those of us who have participated in the Arab-Israeli peace process will disagree sharply. The five Arab-Israeli agreements mediated, negotiated, and signed in the 1970s have produced concrete changes on the map and in the political environment of the Middle East. Representatives from the leading capitals of the world came to Washington to find out what was going to happen next. The United States suffered criticism in some quarters—but more for not going far enough than for what it did accomplish. When the United States produced change, we gained in respect and influence. We helped shape the course of history constructively. That is an achievement to make Americans proud.

1991 Epilogue:
The Politics of the Peace Process
in a Global Perspective

Seeing the World through New Lenses

All around us are the elements of a shift in the conceptual framework we use to understand our world and to act in it. We are working to develop a prescription for new lenses to bring a rapidly changing world into sharper focus. Experience and study tell us that familiar concepts do not fully explain what is happening around us, and the traditional instruments of statecraft do not reliably produce the results we expect of them.

For some in the 1970s, experience in the Arab-Israeli peace process or in Soviet-U.S. detente provided early insight, while academic colleagues were beginning to explore increasing interdependence among nations. Many of those insights now find deep resonance in a global context. As this book was first published, Mikhail Gorbachev was taking hold as the new Soviet leader. "New political thinking" in Moscow began to replace rigid ideology and to incorporate thoughts from earlier experience and writing. As I write this Epilogue, we are still absorbing the events of May and June 1989 centered in Beijing's Tiananmen Square and the dramatic changes in Eastern Europe later in the year. All of these experiences caused us to question a view of the world rooted in mechanistic theories of states and governments; they reinforced interest in the workings of civil societies and the organic interaction between bodies politic.

We are all standing on a bridge between two conceptual frameworks—one paradigm that no longer fully explains and one that promises to be rich in insight but is not yet sharply in focus. As we all stand together on that bridge gathering insights for a new conceptual framework—each from her or his particular vantage point—it may be helpful to consider how we became uneasy about parts of the

148

old one. Reflect with me for a moment, please, on the perspective of five centuries of Western thinking—familiar to us all—about how nations relate.

The rise of the sovereign nation-state produced a world with no central authority in which each institutionalized national unit relied on its own power to protect its security and to pursue its interests. The practice of seeking a balance of power became the system for blocking aggression, limiting war, and regulating competition. In this state system, rulers and philosophers sought some "objective" order. To curb the most destructive uses of power, statesmen developed "rules of the game" based on experience over time. Philosophers of law and ethics proposed principles to define just and unjust wars.

In the twentieth century, two world wars and nuclear weapons caused men and women to question a philosophy of states using power unilaterally to pursue their own interests. More and more, they refuse to accept that the world can work only through the clash of power and the use of force. While most people do not yet see sovereign states fading away, a growing number observes that national sovereignties are increasingly limited in what they can accomplish by themselves, and argues that genuine influence comes decreasingly from the use of raw power alone—that the nature of power and influence has changed.

Changes in the global context. As experience affirms that the old paradigm does not adequately explain the present, three observations about our changing world suggest thoughts for reconceptualizing relationships among nations. All of us will have our own ways of formulating these observations. I state them here not because they are new but because of the conclusions I would like to draw from them.

First, more and more problems confront nations that no one nation can deal with by itself. Only by cooperating can nations deal adequately with them. This is true partly because these problems cut across national borders—nations are interdependent—and partly because there are more centers of influence today that affect events—the world is multipolar. This observation causes nations to reflect increasingly on the nature and limits of national power used unilaterally outside a relationship with others who are concerned with a particular situation.

In the past, nation-states have been perceived as rational institutions in which leaders amass power to pursue objectively defined interests in a strategic chess game with other states. In that image, states resolve problems by the use or threat of military or economic power and by formal negotiation.

Today unilateral action seems less and less effective. Three examples illustrate this point.

To begin with, governments acting alone may no longer be able to meet one of their most basic responsibilities—providing security for their peoples against external threat—by building their own power. In East-West relations, the concept of "common security" has come to connote the paradoxical recognition in a nuclear world that each party to a conflict has an interest in the other's sense of security and that neither can be secure unless the two cooperate. The point is not limited to East-West relations. The destructive capacity of sophisticated weapons amassed in the Middle East approaches making war prohibitively costly. Some people there also understand that real security may come only from building new relationships with their neighbors.

Beyond those new problems in providing physical security, a global economy and ecology dramatize the permeability of national sovereignty and changing threats to national security as well as the opportunities for cooperation posed by economic and environmental changes that cut across national borders. These require new ways of thinking about economic power, competition, and cooperation. Nor can any one nation deal with many of the medical and resource issues that threaten humankind.

Finally, mounting attention to the rights of individual human beings within sovereign states has steadily become a factor affecting relations among states. Governments still jealously guard the principle of noninterference in relations between them and their people. Yet the legitimacy of one government's concern for the rights of individuals in another sovereignty has been established in such interstate agreements as United Nations documents and the Helsinki accords and in the watchfulness of such nongovernmental organizations as Amnesty International. Questions about the rights of Soviet Jewry, Palestinians under Israeli military occupation, blacks in South Africa, or protesters around Tiananmen Square affect relations between states.

Second, underlying the proliferating centers of influence is evidence of a broadening participation of people, both in the governance of nations and in the relationships between nations. Change more often seems to swell from the bottom up rather than to fall from the top down. Focusing on the political energies and interaction of communities of people—not just on state institutions—causes us to think in different ways about concepts such as the national interest and national policy, and about the causes and resolution of conflict.

Increased popular involvement has resulted partly from revolutions in communication, transportation, and information. These days what one leader says or does in her or his own country can be heard, seen, and assessed within hours by another's constituencies. Beyond leaders, peoples in many nations are more aware of one another as human beings and not just as institutional abstractions.

This phenomenon is far from universal. People from developing nations often remind us that most of them—as well as many of the poor in what we usually think of as economically advanced countries—are far from enjoying the luxury of this kind of interaction. Although they are sadly right, radio and, increasingly, television have begun to reach across even those barriers to international interaction. In many of the poorest countries, rebellion against government does not depend on expensive travel.

Increased popular involvement reflects a widely growing belief that relationships between governors and the governed are much less productive than they should be. People ask whether government is failing—or even whether government is dead. Nowhere was the question posed and answered more vividly than in Eastern Europe in the closing months of 1989. More and more, people feel they must harness their own political power in new ways to tackle chronic social and political problems. To accomplish this, they are thinking about politics in creative, noninstitutional ways. Looking beyond their own borders in this world with sophisticated weapons, where people are more aware of dangers from day-to-day interactions and are more in touch, citizens ask whether governments are capable of providing security and building peace. Dialogue among citizens on these issues is proliferating.

In important nations, leaders, too, are realizing that solutions lie beyond the power and proficiency of government. They also lie in new ways of practicing politics that turn loose and then help focus the energies of people in resolving their own problems and building their own futures. The power of individual incentive is recognized now in China and the Soviet Union after years of reliance on central planning and direction.

Governments have encountered the consequences of an increased popular role in other ways. Israel has had to deal with an essentially unarmed popular resistance in the West Bank and Gaza, a problem that military leaders say has no military solution. Both the U.S.S.R. and the U.S. have seen their aims thwarted by popular movements in Afghanistan and Vietnam. They saw the strategic balance between them shift following the popularly based Khomeini revolution in Iran. Soviets worry about the potential interaction between Islamic movements in Iran and Afghanistan and the Islamic peoples of Soviet Central Asia; Americans worry about a potential flood of refugees from south of their border if conditions there become intolerable. In the 1980s, popular movements changed East-West relations. The democracy movement in China, widely televised in the U.S., and the military crackdown around Tiananmen Square damaged Sino-American relations.

As more people experience or affect international relationships, incentives mount to understand nations and governments at least partly as collections of people. Understanding requires that we de-institutionalize and humanize our analysis of how nations relate. Increasing involvement of people in domestic and international politics demands new awareness of the human roots of interests, priorities, and conflict in relationships among nations. As this book suggests, fear, suspicion, rejection, mistrust, hatred, and misperception are often greater obstacles to peace than inability to resolve technically definable problems. In this century the behavioral sciences have deepened insight into what moves human beings and influences their interaction.

As the role of people increases, interaction between public agendas in civil societies plays a larger part in relationships between nations. Those agendas reflect the "gut reactions" of the citizens of one nation to the perceived character and intent of other nations. In different ways in different systems, they can impel or constrain policymakers. We begin to look beyond an abstract state system and to question the proposition that states are to be analyzed as institutions quite different from the groups of human beings who influence, make, implement, and sustain their policies.

Third, traditional instruments of statecraft often do not reliably accomplish what is expected of them. We have normally listed these instruments as including the exercise of various forms of military and economic power to gain what nations want or, as a nonviolent alternative, negotiation. More recently, we have added those opinion-shaping programs that fall under the rubric of "information" or "propaganda." Now, as we observe the broadening involvement of publics, we must focus on political instruments used in the political arena for changing the perceptions that shape political environments. Reshaping the political environment—the context in which publics decide and act to change or sustain national policy—is often a first step in changing the course of events.

Today the most powerful weapons the world has ever known

152

cannot be used by leaders of conscience, and even when force is used, it does not produce the expected results. The American and Soviet experiences in Vietnam and Afghanistan are not unique. Israel learned that superior weapons could not exterminate the Palestinian national movement in Beirut—a city mainly defended not by the armed forces of Lebanon but by the armed men of the PLO and local political militias. In the winter of 1987–1988, changes in the Israeli-Palestinian relationship came not from the armed power of a state but from the civil disobedience and sometimes violent resistance of an unarmed people. Television screens depicted Palestinian youths throwing stones at Israeli youths wearing the uniform of the Israeli Defense Force; cameras captured those Israeli soldiers beating Palestinian youths on the ground with stones, not fighting with planes and tanks.

In addition to continuing debate over the effectiveness of economic sanctions in places like South Africa, nations recognize challenges to their power and security from the economic arena. Rapid globalization of economic exchange has produced new mechanisms of cooperation and competition that cause economists to seek new understanding of ways to pursue economic interests.

Negotiation, normally considered the peaceful alternative to force, may depend more on political leaders working to change the political environment than on the skills of negotiating teams in finding technical solutions. The following observation is as relevant to the summit talks between Soviet and U.S. leaders as to the Arab-Israeli peace process: Negotiation does not initiate change. Change is initiated and shaped in the political arena. Negotiation may define, capture, crystallize, and consolidate change that has already begun. But until political leaders have transformed the political environment, negotiators are unlikely to succeed. Even if they do reach a technically sound agreement, it may not be fully implemented or have the intended consequences.

Moreover, traditional government-to-government negotiations have normally assumed that two parties who are at least equal in status and legitimacy, if not in power, meet to engage in a joint effort to resolve conflict by agreement. In the Israeli-Palestinian conflict, Israel is a state; the Palestinian movement—although it declares itself an independent state—is not a fully constituted state controlling its own territory. Individuals in both bodies politic point out that the conflict is not between states but is an intercommunal conflict. Because the issues at dispute are indivisible issues such as existence, survival, identity, and recognition, they may not at the outset be negotiable. Such issues may need to be resolved in the political arena through reconciliation, recognition, and commitment to peaceful co-existence so that the practical arrangements defining a new relationship can be spelled out in negotiation.

When I speak this way, some diplomatic or academic colleagues say: "I'd like to think the world has changed, but I just don't see it. Force is still widely used, and most nations do not reflect citizens' views in making foreign policy." Elsewhere in the Middle East they cite Iraq's 1990 invasion of Kuwait.

I understand that the world has not changed completely. But the evidence of change has been all around us for some time. Standing on the bridge between two paradigms, we would be unwise not to act in recognition of elements of the future that are already with us and not to begin developing a world-view that will enable us to act creatively in that future while we go on dealing with the present. When old pictures blur and old tools do not always work, the time comes to say "enough" and to search out more effective ways of thinking and acting. Even in the most difficult of military confrontations, it would be tragic not to explore all avenues for a peaceful political settlement.

The Concept of Relationship. These three observations lead to two further thoughts about how nations relate today. These do *not* supplant the concepts with which we have worked in the past. They transform those concepts by placing them in larger contexts. Analysts, practitioners, and scholars in a wide range of disciplines are already redefining familiar concepts and enlarging definitions of the tools used to bring about change. My aim is a conceptual framework that will enable us to begin integrating this rich collection of insights. If we do not, we will deprive ourselves of tools for guiding change peacefully and creatively.

First, I begin with the following thought: Focusing primarily on states amassing military and economic power to pursue objectively defined interests in competition with other states does not provide an adequate conception of relations among nations today. *Relations among nations today are increasingly a continuous political process of complex interaction among significant elements of whole bodies politic. That interaction includes but reaches beyond policymaking and policy-influencing communities on both sides of a relationship.* As civil societies develop and people increasingly influence and participate in cross-border relationships, change often takes place through that interaction on many levels at once rather than mainly through a linear series of government actions and responses. Looking beyond the power and policymaking of individual state governments acting on one another, we begin to

154

see the total pattern of interaction—the overall relationship—between whole bodies politic.

Shifting focus to that political process—the continuous multi-level interaction among significant elements of whole bodies politic—incorporates two important dimensions of experience into our thinking about foreign affairs. Initially, we pay more attention to the larger domestic political environments in which peoples reach fundamental value judgments about peace, war, negotiation, economic development, and trade. Next, when we turn to that political environment, we introduce ways of understanding how those judgments are influenced by external events and therefore how the course of change may be affected by political action rather than only by contests of force. If power is the ability to influence the course of events, then power today may emerge as much from the political ability to conduct that interactive process imaginatively as it does from wielding military or economic power or being an unyielding negotiator.

This statement may sound like a prescription for intervention in the internal political affairs of other nations, but the point is more complex. Relationships across borders today are facts of life. We cannot ignore them. If we look at these relationships in the context of changes in how nations interact, we may see not only the dangers of improper intervention; we may see that some cross-border interaction can offer opportunities for peaceful change with full respect for others. A sensible approach today might be neither to denounce this interaction nor to apply the principle of nonintervention in internal affairs in pure and rigid ways, but to build relationships in which mutual respect might keep that interaction within limits that define and protect the integrity of each party. Understanding the interaction more fully might even suggest imaginative approaches to common problems in an interdependent world.

To add a political dimension to defining national power—the ability to change the course of events—is to open the door to a range of political instruments alongside military and economic power. They are not coercive but persuasive and sometimes even cooperative. Political instruments form ideas and perspectives that have organizing and directing power—organizing power as they become widely accepted ways of understanding events and directing power because of the actions that flow from them.[1]

Politicians think this way because they understand the power of mental images to move people; theorists of international relations have not usually started from this perspective. Political acts that change the political environment, such as the Gorbachev-Reagan reconceptualization of the nuclear problem, Sadat's visit to Jerusalem,

Carter's invitation to Camp David, or the Arias peace plan in Central America originated with politicians, not with international relations analysts.

Second, my main point flows from this picture of relations among nations: *We need a concept for describing how nations relate that is large enough to encompass that continuous political process of complex interaction between significant elements of whole bodies politic. The totality of that interaction—the overall relationship between nations—is worthy of study in its own right.* Such a concept must include but go beyond analyzing the power, structures, decision-making, and formal positions of individual states and the instruments of state they have normally used to get what they want from one another. It must go beyond describing the international system only in the metaphor of strategy in a chess game.

To capture the totality of this dynamic interaction, I am suggesting the concept of relationship. At first hearing, *relationship* is such a commonplace word that we hardly notice it, but when we stop to think about relationships that sustain us as human beings, we begin to feel the power and depth of the concept. We also know that we think differently in a relationship from the way we think about "us and them" or "I and you." Thinking as "we" produces a recognizable shift in mental gears.

Relationship has the disadvantage of not translating well into other languages. Soviets suggest "interdependent relations" or "comprehensive pattern of relations." The Chinese have a strong concept of interpersonal relationships, but when they use that word in the phrase "international relations" it lacks the connotations suggested here. Even in English, specialists are not accustomed to applying to whole nations a word that normally refers to personal interdependence.

Commonplace words often acquire new meanings only when we imbue them with new ideas. Perhaps the problem in accepting any word is that we are still thinking of states and power politics; we are not yet looking through lenses that focus on the political, even human, process of continuous interaction between significant elements of whole bodies politic.

Some experts resist applying to international relationships a word normally reserved for interpersonal interaction. "States are different," they object. My response is that the world is changing; that the concept of state institutions acting rationally does not adequately explain how this world works; that the old tools of statecraft are not always effective in this world; and that we need a new vocabulary. After several years of searching for a word to capture the world's changing character, I decided to fall back on one we all understand and to use it in this new context, jarring as that may be for some. It does capture what needs to be said.

The very commonness of the concept may be the key to its usefulness. It is not a grand theory of international relations. It is an idea that human beings understand. It is a context in which human beings bring together, apply, and test in their intercourse with other human beings all the insights about life that help them understand and act. Those insights may have been learned from parents and teachers, from experience, from books, from the laboratory. Relationship is the context in which we humans integrate them. If we are increasingly in a world where people are more involved in the political process of interaction among whole bodies politic, then using a human word may provide a sounder basis for action in the real world than abstract theories about state institutions.

Three other points are important: (1) Relationships may be good and bad—conflictual or cooperative, immature or mature, destructive or constructive. There are different levels, kinds, or qualities of relationship. (2) Relationships are dynamic. They reflect kaleidoscopic shifts among external factors that affect them. They change character over time. They regress or mature and contract or enlarge their capacity to accomplish what needs to be done. A good relationship may sour, and a bad relationship may improve. (3) An overall relationship will involve many different interactions—or relationships—among subsets of people. That different use of the word may cause some confusion, but, as with many rich words, context will usually make the meaning clear.

I have been asked whether I consider *relationship* among nations as a condition or a creation.[2] Am I arguing for paying more attention to the process of interaction between nations? Or am I arguing for developing a particular kind of relationship especially conducive to close cooperation?

I am arguing both points, but I am especially highlighting the potential and the characteristics of creative, problem-solving relationships. Building such relationships depends on seeing interaction among nations as organic—not as mechanistic exchanges.

Relationship is a condition more often than we recognize. Israelis and Palestinians were developing a relationship long before a peace treaty between Egypt and Israel was even considered possible. To be sure, it was a relationship between occupier and occupied—in many ways a destructive rather than a constructive relationship. But by the end of the 1980s it was closer than that between Egypt and Israel more than a decade after a treaty of peace legally established

157

"normal" state-to-state relations. The Soviet Union and the U.S. have also had an intense relationship, and one can argue that not seeing it in all the complexities of relationship was partly responsible for the failure of efforts in the 1970s to sustain cooperation.

I also believe that developing problem-solving relationships to deal with problems that no one nation can deal with alone or to resolve conflict peacefully is both a goal and a creative human experience. Building relationships capable of generating peaceful and economical solutions to previously intractable problems should be an aspiration.[3]

My focus on changing relationships between nations and peoples is thus founded not only on experience in the Arab-Israeli peace process but on an effort to understand a wide range of relationships in our changing world. Anwar Sadat is not the only leader who decided that some issues are too complicated to negotiate without first changing the political environment; Gorbachev has repeatedly used unilateral acts to change the political landscape. In early 1990, the question was not whether the two Germanies would reunite; the productive questions would remain what their relationship has been, how they envision a creative relationship in European and global contexts over time, and by what steps they can realize such a relationship peacefully. Thinking about changing relationships—and all that they involve—is far more challenging and potentially more realistic and more gratifying than designing wars and negotiations, important as negotiation may remain.

Policymaking and Changing Relationships

If the Arab-Israeli peace process is a negotiating process embedded in a political process, leaders operating in the political arena must devise a policy that encompasses both processes. They must understand what can best be accomplished in each and select the instruments that are most effective in each. They must also sense how the two processes interact.

I raise this point now because the original version of this book may have contributed to confusion about the interaction between the political and the negotiating processes. I would like to speak now with more precision.

Part of the confusion may have begun because I wrote of the peace process and the negotiating process almost interchangeably. I should have been more precise in stating, as I do now, that the peace process is a political process that sometimes resorts to political instruments to reconcile conflicting parties and sometimes resorts to negotiation to define new relationships.

In 1985, just before this book was first published, I wrote an article cited in the Preface calling attention—as others have done—to the importance of the "pre-negotiating phases." I elaborated on the importance of getting the politics right before negotiation could begin or succeed. I spoke of the peace process as including a political period before negotiation—a period of analysis and precipitating a commitment to negotiate—followed by a period of arranging negotiation, negotiation itself, and implementation. But I was writing in retrospect about a political process that had produced five negotiated agreements. I was too quick to assume that negotiation automatically follows the political period.

Since that time, students of negotiation have produced some significant work on prenegotiation.[4] Most of this work also starts with negotiations that produced agreements, and then looks back into what led up to the negotiations. The consequence has been to designate as "prenegotiation" all that happens in the political arena before negotiation regardless of what instrument the policymaker eventually chooses for dealing with a problem.

The point is not an abstract one. I want to underscore and encourage attention to the importance of learning more about how to change the political environment by using political instruments apart from negotiation. I am not minimizing the importance of negotiation. But I do want leaders and their staffs to focus on what they can accomplish by political acts in the political arena when problems are too complicated to negotiate or when political resistance blocks negotiation. I even want leaders to think that they might resolve some problems without ever going to the negotiating table. I would like to see us all concentrate on what can be accomplished by thinking in new ways about politics—ways partly suggested in this book.[5] I do *not* want the policymaker to think of everything he or she does as a preparation for negotiation. I do not want the policymaker to lose the opportunity to resolve problems by political means since reconciliation may be a political and human act, not an outcome to be negotiated. I do want scholars and diplomats to devote more time to the politics of change—and not just to think of negotiation as the only peaceful instrument of change.

One reason we sometimes confuse the two processes is that they go on simultaneously and are intertwined. Although the focus may fall more heavily on one at a particular moment, policy thinking will apply to both at the same time. They need to be thought of separately because different instruments may be useful in each, but they are complementary—not mutually exclusive.[6]

Policymaking. The starting point for a leader in making policy is a situation that demands attention. Working in the political arena, he or she will ask three broad questions: (1) What is the situation, and must I do something about it? (2) What are alternatives, and what is the problem of moving to one of them? And (3) what direction must policy take to move to that preferable situation? Although the leader may talk with advisers and may even test public concerns, the focus is on her or his thinking through a situation and determining how to deal with it.

The policymaker's task is to build and conduct the relationships that are important to the nation's interests and goals. As each goes through her or his own policymaking, a leader will more specifically: (1) diagnose a situation to learn what is happening, what interests and relationships are involved, and whether interests are being hurt badly enough to warrant a change in policy; (2) if a change in course seems necessary, envision alternative situations, analyze obstacles to achieving them, and define the operational problem of overcoming those obstacles and moving toward a preferable alternative; and (3) set a policy direction for changing the situation, choose the effective instruments—war, negotiation, other political or economic actions— and then lay out a detailed scenario of actions and responses for moving from here to the desired destination.[7]

The point to be underscored here is that the focus is the leader's analysis of how to change a situation he or she judges to hurt the nation's interests. At one moment that task may involve political steps to change the political environment to support a preferable situation. At another, it may involve mediation or negotiation to capture the changes initiated in the political arena. The first question for the policymaker is how to deal with a troubling situation, keeping open the widest range of instruments. It is that perspective I want to protect and develop—the policymaker looking for ways of dealing with a situation imaginatively—and not only the perspective of the student of negotiation asking how negotiation begins or why it fails, important as those questions are.

In trying to move toward a preferable alternative, a leader will be conscious of operating in at least two contexts at the same time. Whatever instruments he or she may choose, the leader will need to work at getting the politics right for solving the problem. Very little attention is given in academic or bureaucratic study to this part of the process. In addition, if he or she has chosen, for instance, to try to negotiate a solution, specific tools of mediation and negotiation will be necessary in that process. That is where most academic and bureaucratic attention falls.

The Political and Negotiating Processes. Regardless of the instrument a policymaker chooses to change a situation, he or she will need to think about building a supportive political foundation for the chosen course of action. Using a particular instrument such as negotiation may help shape that environment, or it may not work until the political environment itself has been changed in some other way.

A political environment supporting negotiation is produced in the minds of people in the political arena, not first around the negotiating table. A strategy for reshaping a political environment differs from a strategy for constructing a negotiation. A central aim of this book has been to lay out those instruments in detail, particularly in Chapters 8 and 9.

Sometimes leaders can begin to change the relationship between nations even before agreeing explicitly to do so—or at least without negotiating a formal agreement. Watching Mikhail Gorbachev, we speak commonly now of a leader's option of taking a series of unilateral steps, each in response to another in the context of common knowledge about each other's concerns but without a detailed agreement. The judgment that "this may be too complicated to negotiate" does not mean that it is impossible to change the situation to both sides' mutual and recognized advantage.

The negotiating process may begin when two parties begin exploring, at least tacitly, how they might work together to change a situation by formal agreement. There may come a time when change in a relationship already begun in the political arena by political actions could be more precisely defined, crystallized, consolidated, and implemented. In preparation for an effort to define a new situation in a negotiated agreement, there may come a time when one party will want to explore whether such an agreement could be negotiated, and will communicate that intent to the other. Some of that stage-setting for negotiation and prenegotiation exploration may be part of a negotiating process, but that process really begins after a decision to try to move toward a solution by negotiation rather than by some other means. The learning and thinking that led to the decision—and even public actions before the decision—may in retrospect meld into the negotiating process, but that learning and thinking might just as well have led to actions other than negotiation. The decision to try to make negotiation happen imparts a new character and focus to the effort, and it is in that shift that one sees the beginnings of negotiation. But a leader will normally protect the option to pull back and use other instruments, either instead of or as a complement to negotiation to move a stalled negotiation forward.

The five stages of the peace process described in Chapter 2 were based on a situation in which Arabs and Israelis had already negotiated interim agreements and were trying to negotiate further agreements.[8] If I had been applying that thinking to a situation in which a leader did not yet know that negotiation would be possible, I would perhaps have drawn a sharper line between the political and negotiating processes. Normally, I would prefer to avoid drawing exclusive lines because the policymaker's world is not so neat as the academic's, but I recognize the need for some distinctions in academic study.

I prefer at this point to accept that the distinction between the political and the negotiating processes in the real world is blurred and to deal with the blurring by understanding differences between the two. The blurring is both understandable and legitimate so long as we keep two points in mind:

First, we need to temper the notion of phases in sequence, as in a political phase leading to prenegotiation followed by negotiation. It is true that leaders work primarily in the political arena before committing themselves to negotiate, but their explorations with the other side during that period on what agreement may be achievable may have some of the character of negotiation. They may exchange views in some detail on large issues determining the overall shape of a solution to determine whether they can solve a problem through negotiation. At the same time, they may decide something is too complicated to negotiate at that time and try to deal with the situation in some other way. Even when negotiation begins and the work is concentrated in the negotiating room, a mediator or negotiator may need to move back to the political arena to increase flexibility. We need to recognize the functions that are best performed in each arena so as to recognize where the greatest opportunity to overcome impasses lies.

Second, while avoiding too rigid a distinction between the processes, it *is* important to be clear about the context in which one is working at a given moment. Knowing whether one is preparing or conducting negotiation or is engaged in the larger business of changing the political environment makes a difference because the tools in one arena differ from those in the other. Failure to be clear about the distinction may obscure a leader's understanding of what her or his exact purposes and opportunities are at a particular moment. The danger in calling everything that happens before negotiation "prenegotiation" is that one will think mainly in terms of negotiation and will not give creative thought to the political instruments needed to change the political environment. The obvious example is one cited in this book—the shift from advanced stages of Egyptian-Israeli negotiation at the end of the 1970s back to the early stages of attempting Israeli-Palestinian reconciliation at a time when neither body politic was committed to peace and when their conflict was increasingly becoming an intercommunal conflict.

I do not want to fuel an academic debate over the definition of "prenegotiation," but I do want to return to my original purpose of encouraging attention to the politics of bringing about peaceful change. I do not want to discourage those working to refine the concept of prenegotiation, but I do not want them to obscure the fact that policymakers need help in solving problems by political means when negotiation does not seem possible. I consider this essential in a world that is changing so rapidly that negotiators cannot keep up. It may be more important now to help leaders envision new relationships and alternative situations and design scenarios of political actions for reaching those destinations than it is to help them learn the intricacies of prenegotiation.

The Book in a Larger Context

I have said that experience in the Arab-Israeli peace process provides some of the insights that may help shape a new paradigm for understanding our changing world and acting within it. As a step toward integrating these insights into a new conceptual framework for understanding relationships among nations, I want to conclude this introduction by stating how I perceive the approach to which this book contributes differing from much of the more familiar writing about international relations.

First, this approach suggests a larger context for seeing in a new light such traditional concepts as state, power, and interests and such instruments of statecraft as negotiation. It does so partly by opening the door to insights from a broader range of practical experience and academic study than is usually included in the analysis of international relations. In addition to the political scientist, the specialist in international relations and security, the historian, and the economist, it invites the perspectives of the practicing politician and diplomat; the psychoanalyst, psychiatrist, and psychologist; the physicist, biologist, and philosopher; the theologian and ethicist; the anthropologist and sociologist; and the student and practitioner of conflict management and resolution, mediation, and negotiation. It suggests that human beings as well as states are integral to studying how nations relate.

Second, in introducing a more human context, this approach focuses not just on the capabilities and policymaking of individual states acting on other states but also on the overall relationships among bodies politic. In considering relations among nations as a political process of continuous interaction between policymaking and policy-influencing communities on both sides of a relationship, it suggests that these relationships will not be understood unless we reach well beyond objectively defined state interests to determine what human beings are interested in—their hopes and fears—and how they interact. That process of interaction—the overall relationship—is an essential focus of study in its own right.

Third, this approach suggests that focusing on the relationships among bodies politic can expand their capacity for generating and guiding change peacefully. As nations face problems that no one nation can resolve by itself, we must widen our focus to include the relationships necessary for dealing with those problems. Sometimes, focusing on relationship causes the concept of a narrow national interest to give way partially to the broader interests of the relationship itself. Representatives of two nations expand their ability to change the course of events when they think together and act together. If power is the capacity to change the course of events, they expand their power in political ways.

Fourth, this approach challenges those studying and conducting international relationships to develop a conceptual framework that integrates rather than fragments understanding of those relationships. Thinkers and practitioners in many fields are well along in articulating different ways of knowing and thinking. Those fields range from quantum physics through the study and practice of community relations, from philosophy and religion through problem-solving, from individual pathology through the study of group behavior. The charge is not to scrap present ways of knowing and thinking; the charge is to build from them a broader human understanding. Isolating individual aspects of a problem for study in depth will continue to be useful in analysis, but integrating insights into a larger human picture is even more necessary. Leaders and citizens alike need a view of the world that permits them to act as whole human beings.[9]

The reflection on the politics of the Arab-Israeli peace process begun in this book has now become, in my life, a reflection on the politics of international relationships. When I wrote of the peace process, I felt that the experience of the 1970s compelled a broader approach than the traditional. Watching the dazzling changes in the world of late 1989, I felt more than ever the critical need for new lenses in bringing that world into focus so as not to waste the opportunities it offers. Putting ourselves in a position to seize those opportunities in the Arab-Israeli arena and now in other arenas of past and potential conflict and potential peacemaking is a matter of life and death. Contributing to thinking about how to do that remains the larger purpose of *The Other Walls*.

Notes

1. I am indebted to John D. Steinbruner, Director of the Foreign Policy Studies Program at The Brookings Institution, for this formulation.

2. I. William Zartman of Johns Hopkins University's Paul H. Nitze School of Advanced International Studies posed this perceptive question.

3. I first developed these observations on our changing world and the concept of relationship in two papers: "Beyond 'Us and Them'—Building Mature International Relationships," a draft monograph prepared in 1987–1988 under a grant from the United States Institute of Peace in collaboration with the Kettering Foundation; and an early version of that paper published as a work in progress, "Beyond 'We' and 'They'—Conducting International Relationships," in *Negotiation Journal: On the Process of Dispute Settlement*, vol. 3, no. 3 (July 1987), pp. 245–77. The observations were refined under a grant from the Carnegie Corporation of New York for "The Arab-Israeli Conflict in a Global Perspective," in John D. Steinbruner, ed., *Restructuring American Foreign Policy* (Washington, D.C.: The Brookings Institution, 1988), Chapter 8, where they are applied in detail to that conflict. A fuller presentation written with the support of the Ford and MacArthur Foundations appears as "An Historic Challenge to Rethink How Nations Relate," in Vamik D. Volkan, Demetrios Julius, and Joseph V. Montville, eds., *The Psychodynamics of International Relationships: Vol. 1: Concepts and Theories* (Lexington, Mass.: Lexington Books, 1990), Chapter 1. This approach is also applied to "The Soviet-U.S. Relationship and the Third World," in Robert Jervis and Seweryn Bialer, eds., *Soviet-American Relations after the Cold War* (Durham, N.C.: Duke University Press, 1991), Chapter 6. It is the starting point for my next book, tentatively entitled *When Walls Come Down: The Politics of International Relationships*. Others will follow. In each case, these observations and the concept of relationship are stated in more-or-less the same—often verbatim—form as the necessary starting point for analysis of a particular question. Each publisher has agreed to this practice.

4. Janice Gross Stein, ed., *Getting to the Table: The Processes of International Prenegotiation* (Baltimore: Johns Hopkins University Press, 1989). Jay Rothman has launched a program in prenegotiation at the Hebrew University in Jerusalem.

5. Some of the most creative thinking about "public politics" to which I am exposed is work on alternatives to "politics as usual" that appears in

165

unpublished working papers by President David Mathews and colleagues at the Kettering Foundation in Dayton, Ohio. As we think more about international relationships as political process, insights from new ways of thinking about politics—domestic or international—will need to inform the study and conduct of relationships among nations.

6. This discussion of the interaction between the political and negotiating processes is discussed more fully in a case study I co-authored with Cecilia Albin, *Sinai II: The Politics of International Mediation* (Washington, D.C.: Foreign Policy Institute, Paul H. Nitze School of Advanced International Studies, Johns Hopkins University, 1991).

7. Policymaking in the conduct of international relationships is discussed more fully in my "International Relationships—It's Time To Go Beyond 'We' and 'They'," *Negotiation Journal*, vol. 3, no. 3 (July, 1987), pp. 245–77, and "Mediation in the Arab-Israeli Conflict," in Edward E. Azar, Harold H. Saunders, and I. William Zartman, *Mediation in Middle East Conflicts*, Maxwell Summer Lecture Series (Syracuse, N.Y.: School of Citizenship and Public Affairs, Syracuse University, 1986), pp. 43–65.

8. See also I. William Zartman and Maureen R. Berman, *The Practical Negotiator* (New Haven: Yale University Press, 1982). The important point is not so much the specific delineation of the phases but the work that needs to be done before, during, and after negotiation.

9. This reflection of differences in approach is also stated in "An Historic Challenge to Rethink How Nations Relate" in Vamik D. Volkan et al., eds., *The Psychodynamics of International Relationships*.

Appendix I

United Nations Security Council Resolution 242,
November 22, 1967

The Security Council,

Expressing its continuing concern with the grave situation in the Middle East,

Emphasizing the inadmissibility of the acquisition of territory by war and the need to work for a just and lasting peace in which every State in the area can live in security,

Emphasizing further that all Member States in their acceptance of the Charter of the United Nations have undertaken a commitment to act in accordance with Article 2 of the Charter,

1. *Affirms* that the fulfillment of Charter principles requires the establishment of a just and lasting peace in the Middle East which should include the application of both the following principles:

   (i) Withdrawal of Israel armed forces from territories occupied in the recent conflict;

   (ii) Termination of all claims or states of belligerency and respect for and acknowledgement of the sovereignty, territorial integrity and political independence of every State in the area and their right to live in peace within secure and recognized boundaries free from threats or acts of force;

2. *Affirms further* the necessity

   (*a*) For guaranteeing freedom of navigation through international waterways in the area;

   (*b*) For achieving a just settlement of the refugee problem;

   (*c*) For guaranteeing the territorial inviolability and political independence of every State in the area, through measures including the establishment of demilitarized zones;

3. *Requests* the Secretary-General to designate a Special Representative to proceed to the Middle East to establish and maintain contacts

with the States concerned in order to promote agreement and assist efforts to achieve a peaceful and accepted settlement in accordance with the provisions and principles in this resolution;

4. *Requests* the Secretary-General to report to the Security Council on the progress of the efforts of the Special Representative as soon as possible.

Appendix II

Arab Summit Conference Communiqué, Excerpt, Khartoum, Sudan, September 1, 1967

3—The Arab heads of state have agreed to unite their political efforts on the international and diplomatic level to eliminate the effects of the aggression and to ensure the withdrawal of the aggressive Israeli forces from the Arab lands which have been occupied since the 5 June aggression. This will be done within the framework of the main principles to which the Arab states adhere, namely: no peace with Israel, no recognition of Israel, no negotiations with it, and adherence to the rights of the Palestinian people in their country.

Appendix III

King Hussein Ibn Talal of Jordan, Proposal for a United Arab Kingdom, Excerpts, March 15, 1972

We are happy to declare that the bases of the proposed formula for the new phase are as follows:

1. The Hashemite Kingdom of the Jordan shall become a United Arab Kingdom and shall bear this name.

2. The United Arab Kingdom shall consist of two regions:

a. The Palestine region which will consist of the West Bank and any other Palestinian territories which are liberated and whose inhabitants desire to join it.

b. The Jordan region which will consist of the East Bank.

3. Amman shall be the central capital of the kindgom as well as the capital of the Jordan region.

4. Jerusalem shall be the capital of the Palestine region.

5. The head of the state shall be the king, who will assume the central executive authority with the help of a central cabinet. The central legislative authority shall be vested in the king and an assembly to be known as the national assembly. Members of this assembly shall be elected by direct secret ballot. Both regions shall be equally represented in this assembly.

6. The central judicial authority shall be vested in a central supreme court.

7. The kingdom shall have unified armed forces whose supreme commander is the king.

8. The responsibilities of the central executive authority shall be confined to affairs connected with the kingdom as an international entity to guarantee the kingdom's safety, stability and prosperity.

9. The executive authority in each region shall be assumed by a governor general from among its sons and a regional cabinet from among its sons as well.

10. Legislative authority in each region shall be assumed by a council to be called the people's council. It shall be elected by direct secret voting. This council will elect the region's governor general.

11. The judicial authority in the region shall be in the hands of the region's courts, and no one will have power over them.

12. The executive authority in each region shall assume responsibility for all the affairs of the region except such affairs as the constitution defines as coming under the jurisdiction of the central executive authority.

Naturally the implementation of this formula and its bases should be according to the constitutional norms in force. It will be referred to the [Jordanian] National Assembly to adopt the necessary measures to prepare a new constitution for the country.

Appendix IV

United Nations Security Council Resolution 338, October 22, 1973

The Security Council

1. *Calls upon* all parties to the present fighting to cease all firing and terminate all military activity immediately, no later than 12 hours after the moment of the adoption of this decision, in the positions they now occupy;

2. *Calls upon* the parties concerned to start immediately after the cease-fire the implementation of Security Council resolution 242 (1967) in all of its parts;

3. *Decides* that, immediately and concurrently with the cease-fire, negotiations shall start between the parties concerned under appropriate auspices aimed at establishing a just and durable peace in the Middle East.

Appendix V

Arab League Summit Conference Communiqué, Rabat, Morocco, October 29, 1974

The Seventh Arab Summit Conference after exhaustive and detailed discussions conducted by their Majesties, Excellencies, and Highnesses, the Kings, Presidents and Amirs on the Arab situation in general and the Palestine problem in particular, within their national and international frameworks; and after hearing the statements submitted by His Majesty King Hussein, King of the Hashemite Kingdom of Jordan and His Excellency Brother Yasser Arafat, Chairman of the Palestine Liberation Organization, and after the statements of their Majesties and Excellencies the Kings and Presidents, in an atmosphere of candour and sincerity and full responsibility; and in view of the Arab leaders' appreciation of the joint national responsibility required of them at present for confronting aggression and performing duties of liberation, enjoined by the unity of the Arab cause and the unity of its struggle; and in view of the fact that all are aware of Zionist schemes still being made to eliminate the Palestinian existence and to obliterate the Palestinian national entity; and in view of the Arab leaders' belief in the necessity to frustrate these attempts and schemes and to counteract them by supporting and strengthening this Palestinian national entity, by providing all requirements to develop and increase its ability to ensure that the Palestinian people recover their rights in full; and by meeting responsibilities of close cooperation with its brothers within the framework of collective Arab commitment;

And in light of the victories achieved by Palestinian struggle in the confrontation with the Zionist enemy, at the Arab and international levels, at the United Nations, and of the obligation imposed thereby to continue joint Arab action to develop and increase the scope of these victories; and having received the views of all on all the above, and having succeeded in cooling the differences between brethren within the framework of consolidating Arab solidarity, the Seventh Arab Summit Conference resolves the following:

1. To affirm the right of the Palestinian people to self-determination and to return to their homeland;

2. To affirm the right of the Palestinian people to establish an independent national authority under the command of the Palestine Liberation Organization, the sole legitimate representative of the Palestinian people in any Palestinian territory that is liberated. This authority, once it is established, shall enjoy the support of the Arab states in all fields and at all levels;

3. To support the Palestine Liberation Organization in the exercise of its responsibility at the national and international levels within the framework of Arab commitment;

4. To call on the Hashemite Kingdom of Jordan, the Syrian Arab Republic, the Arab Republic of Egypt and the Palestine Liberation Organization to devise a formula for the regulation of relations between them in the light of these decisions so as to ensure their implementation;

5. That all the Arab states undertake to defend Palestinian national unity and not to interfere in the internal affairs of Palestinian action.

Appendix VI

President Anwar al-Sadat,
Statement before the Israeli Knesset, November 20, 1977

In the name of God, Mr. Speaker of the Knesset, ladies and gentlemen, allow me first to thank deeply the Speaker of the Knesset for affording me this opportunity to address you.

As I begin my address I wish to say, peace and the mercy of God

Almighty be upon you and may peace be with us all, God willing. Peace for us all, of the Arab lands and in Israel, as well as in every part of this big world, which is so beset by conflicts, perturbed by its deep contradictions, menaced now and then by destructive wars launched by man to annihilate his fellow men.

Finally, amidst the ruins of what man has built among the remains of the victims of mankind there emerges neither victor nor vanquished. The only vanquished remains always a man, God's most sublime creation. Man, whom God has created, as Gandhi, the apostle of peace puts it, to forge ahead, to mold the way of life and to worship God Almighty.

I come to you today on solid ground to shape a new life and to establish peace. We all love this land, the land of God, we all, Moslems, Christians and Jews, all worship God.

Under God, God's teachings and commandments are: love, sincerity, security and peace.

I do not blame all those who received my decision when I announced it to the entire world before the Egyptian People's Assembly. I do not blame all those who received my decision with surprise and even with amazement, some gripped even by violent surprise. Still others interpreted it as political, to camouflage my intentions of launching a new war.

I would go so far as to tell you that one of my aides at the presidential office contacted me at a late hour following my return home from the People's Assembly and sounded worried as he asked me: "Mr. President, what would be our reaction if Israel actually extended an invitation to you?"

I replied calmly: "I would accept it immediately. I have declared that I would go to the end of the earth. I would go to Israel, for I want to put before the people of Israel all the facts."

I can see the faces of all those who were astounded by my decision and had doubts as to the sincerity of the intentions behind the declaration of my decision. No one could have ever conceived that the president of the biggest Arab state, which bears the heaviest burden and the main responsibility pertaining to the cause of war and peace in the Middle East, should declare his readiness to go to the land of the adversary while we were still in a state of war.

We all still bear the consequences of four fierce wars waged within 30 years. All this at the time when the families of the 1973 October war are still mourning under the cruel pain of bereavement of father, son, husband and brother.

As I have already declared, I have not consulted as far as this decision is concerned with any of my colleagues or brothers, the Arab heads of state or the confrontation states.

172

Most of those who contacted me following the declaration of this decision expressed their objection because of the feeling of utter suspicion and absolute lack of confidence between the Arab states and the Palestine people on the one hand and Israel on the other that still surges in us all.

Many months in which peace could have been brought about have been wasted over differences and fruitless discussions on the procedure of convening the Geneva conference. All have shared suspicion and absolute lack of confidence.

But to be absolutely frank with you, I took this decision after long thought, knowing that it constitutes a great risk, for God Almighty has made it my fate to assume responsibility on behalf of the Egyptian people, to share in the responsibility of the Arab nation, the main duty of which, dictated by responsibility, is to exploit all and every means in a bid to save my Egyptian Arab people and the pan-Arab nation from the horrors of new suffering and destructive wars, the dimensions of which are foreseen only by God Himself.

After long thinking, I was convinced that the obligation of responsibility before God and before the people make it incumbent upon me that I should go to the far corners of the world—even to Jerusalem to address members of the Knesset and acquaint them with all the facts surging in me, then I would let you decide for yourselves.

Following this, may God Almighty determine our fate.

Ladies and gentlemen, there are moments in the lives of nations and peoples when it is incumbent upon those known for their wisdom and clarity of vision to survey the problem, with all its complexities and vain memories, in a bold drive towards new horizons.

Those who like us are shouldering the same responsibilities entrusted to us are the first who should have the courage to make determining decisions that are consonant with the magnitude of the circumstances. We must all rise above all forms of obsolete theories of superiority, and the most important thing is never to forget that infallibility is the prerogative of God alone.

If I said that I wanted to avert from all the Arab people the horrors of shocking and destructive wars I must sincerely declare before you that I have the same feelings and bear the same responsibility toward all and every man on earth, and certainly toward the Israeli people.

Any life that is lost in war is a human life, be it that of an Arab or an Israeli. A wife who becomes a widow is a human being entitled to a happy family life, whether she be an Arab or an Israeli.

Innocent children who are deprived of the care and compassion of their parents are ours. They are ours, be they living on Arab or Israeli land.

They command our full responsibility to afford them a comfortable life today and tomorrow.

For the sake of them all, for the sake of the lives of all our sons and brothers, for the sake of affording our communities the opportunity to work for the progress and happiness of man, feeling secure and with the right to a dignified life, for the generations to come, for a smile on the face of every child born in our land—for all that I have taken my decision to come to you, despite all the hazards, to deliver my address.

I have shouldered the prerequisites of the historic responsibility and therefore I declared on February 4, 1971, that I was willing to sign a peace agreement with Israel. This was the first declaration made by a responsible Arab official since the outbreak of the Arab-Israeli conflict. Motivated by all these factors dictated by the responsibilities of leadership, on October 16, 1973, before the Egyptian People's Assembly, I called for an international conference to establish permanent peace based on justice. I was not heard.

I was in the position of man pleading for peace or asking for a cease-fire, motivated by the duties of history and leadership, I signed the first disengagement agreement, followed by the second disengagement agreement in Sinai.

Then we proceeded, trying both open and closed doors in a bid to find a certain road leading to a durable and just peace.

We opened our heart to the peoples of the entire world to make them understand our motivations and objectives and actually to convince them of the fact that we are advocates of justice and peacemakers. Motivated by all these factors, I also decided to come to you with an open mind and an open heart and with a conscious determination so that we might establish permanent peace based on justice.

It is so fated that my trip to you, which is a journey of peace, coincided with the Islamic feast, the holy Feast of the Sacrifice when Abraham—peace be upon him—forefather of the Arabs and Jews, submitted to God. I say, when God Almighty ordered him, not out of weakness, but through a giant spiritual force and by free will to sacrifice his very own son, personified a firm and unshakeable belief in ideals that had for mankind a profound significance.

Ladies and gentlemen, let us be frank with each other. Using straightforward words and a clear conception with no ambiguity, let us be frank with each other today while the entire world, both East and West, follows these unparalleled moments, which could prove to be a radical turning point in the history of this part of the world if not in the history of the world as a whole.

Let us be frank with each other, let us be frank with each other as we answer this important question.

How can we achieve permanent peace based on justice? Well, I have come to you carrying my clear and frank answer to this big question, so that the people in Israel as well as the entire world may hear it. All those devoted prayers ring in my ears, pleading to God Almighty that this historic meeting may eventually lead to the result aspired to by millions.

Before I proclaim my answer, I wish to assure you that in my clear and frank answer I am availing myself of a number of facts which no one can deny.

The first fact is that no one can build his happiness at the expense of the misery of others.

The second fact: never have I spoken, nor will I ever speak, with two tongues; never have I adopted, nor will I ever adopt, two policies. I never deal with anyone except in one tongue, one policy and with one face.

The third fact: direct confrontation is the nearest and most successful method to reach a clear objective.

The fourth fact: the call for permanent and just peace based on respect for United Nations resolutions has now become the call of the entire world. It has become the expression of the will of the international community, whether in official capitals where policies are made and decisions taken, or at the level of world public opinion, which influences policymaking and decision-taking.

The fifth fact, and this is probably the clearest and most prominent, is that the Arab nation, in its drive for permanent peace based on justice, does not proceed from a position of weakness. On the contrary, it has the power and stability for a sincere will for peace.

The Arab declared intention stems from an awareness prompted by a heritage of civilization, that to avoid an inevitable disaster that will befall us, you and the whole world, there is no alternative to the establishment of permanent peace based on justice, peace that is not swayed by suspicion or jeopardized by ill intentions.

In the light of these facts which I meant to place before you the way I see them, I would also wish to warn you, in all sincerity I warn you, against some thoughts that could cross your minds.

Frankness makes it incumbent upon me to tell you the following: First, I have not come here for a separate agreement between Egypt and Israel. This is not part of the policy of Egypt. The problem is not that of Egypt and Israel.

An interim peace between Egypt and Israel, or between any Arab confrontation state and Israel, will not bring permanent peace based on justice in the entire region.

Rather, even if peace between all the confrontation states and Israel were achieved in the absence of a just solution of the Palestinian problem, never will there be that durable and just peace upon which the entire world insists.

Second, I have not come to you to seek a partial peace, namely to terminate the state of belligerency at this stage and put off the entire problem to a subsequent stage. This is not the radical solution that would steer us to permanent peace.

Equally, I have not come to you for a third disengagement agreement in Sinai or in Golan or the West Bank.

For this would mean that we are merely delaying the ignition of the fuse. It would also mean that we are lacking the courage to face peace, that we are too weak to shoulder the burdens and responsibilities of a durable peace based upon justice.

I have come to you so that together we should build a durable peace based on justice to avoid the shedding of one single drop of blood by both sides. It is for this reason that I have proclaimed my readiness to go to the farthest corner of the earth.

Here I would go back to the big question:

How can we achieve a durable peace based on justice? In my opinion, and I declare it to the whole world, from this forum, the answer is neither difficult nor is it impossible despite long years of feuds, blood, faction, strife, hatreds and deep-rooted animosity.

The answer is not difficult, nor is it impossible, if we sincerely and faithfully follow a straight line.

You want to live with us, in this part of the world.

In all sincerity I tell you we welcome you among us with full security and safety. This in itself is a tremendous turning point, one of the landmarks of a decisive historical change. We used to reject you. We had our reasons and our fears, yes.

We refused to meet with you, anywhere, yes.

We were together in international conferences and organizations and our representatives did not, and still do not, exchange greetings with you. Yes. This has happened and is still happening.

It is also true that we used to set as a precondition for any negotiations with you a mediator who would meet separately with each party.

Yes. Through this procedure, the talks of the first and second disengagement agreements took place.

Our delegates met in the first Geneva conference without exchanging a direct word, yes, this has happened.

Yet today I tell you, and I declare it to the whole world, that we accept to live with you in permanent peace based on justice. We do not want to encircle you or be encircled ourselves by destructive missiles ready for launching, nor by the shells of grudges and hatreds.

I have announced on more than one occasion that Israel has become a fait accompli, recognized by the world, and that the two superpowers have undertaken the responsibility for . . . its existence. As we really and truly seek peace we really and truly welcome you to live among us in peace and security.

176

There was a huge wall between us which you tried to build up over a quarter of a century, but it was destroyed in 1973. It was the wall of an implacable and escalating psychological warfare.

It was a wall of the fear of the force that could sweep the entire Arab nation. It was a wall of propaganda that we were a nation reduced to immobility. Some of you had gone as far as to say that even for 50 years to come, the Arabs would not regain their strength. It was a wall that always threatened with a long arm that could reach and strike anywhere. It was a wall that warned us of extermination and annihilation if we tried to use our legitimate rights to liberate the occupied territories.

Together we have to admit that that wall fell and collapsed in 1973. Yet, there remains another wall. This wall constitutes a psychological barrier between us, a barrier of suspicion, a barrier of rejection; a barrier of fear, of deception, a barrier of hallucination without any action, deed or decision.

A barrier of distorted and eroded interpretation of every event and statement. It is this psychological barrier which I described in official statements as constituting 70 percent of the whole problem.

Today, through my visit to you, I ask why don't we stretch out our hands with faith and sincerity so that together we might destroy this barrier? Why shouldn't our and your will meet with faith and sincerity so that together we might remove all suspicion of fear, betrayal and bad intentions?

Why don't we stand together with the courage of men and the boldness of heroes who dedicate themselves to a sublime aim? Why don't we stand together with the same courage and daring to erect a huge edifice of peace?

An edifice that builds and does not destroy. An edifice that serves as a beacon for generations to come with the human message for construction, development and the dignity of man.

Why should we bequeath to the coming generations the plight of bloodshed, yes, orphans, widowhood, family disintegration and the wailing of victims?

Why don't we believe in the wisdom of God conveyed to us by the wisdom of the proverbs of Solomon. [Sadat went on to quote extensively from the proverbs.]

Ladies and gentlemen, to tell you the truth, peace cannot be worth its name unless it is based on justice and not on the occupation of the land of others. It would not be right for you to demand for yourselves what you deny to others. With all frankness and in the spirit that has prompted me to come to you today, I tell you you have to give up once and for all the dreams of conquest and give up the belief that force is the best method for dealing with the Arabs.

You should clearly understand the lesson of confrontation between you and us. Expansion does not pay. To speak frankly, our land does not yield itself to bargaining, it is not even open to argument. To us, the nation's soil is equal to the holy valley where God Almighty spoke to Moses. Peace be upon him.

We cannot accept any attempt to take away or accept to seek one inch of it nor can we accept the principle of debating or bargaining over it.

I sincerely tell you also that before us today lies the appropriate chance for peace. If we are really serious in our endeavor for peace, it is a chance that that may never come again. It is a chance that if lost or wasted, the resulting slaughter would bear the curse of humanity and of history.

What is peace for Israel? It means that Israel lives in the region with her Arab neighbors in security and safety. Is that logical? I say yes. It means that Israel lives within its borders, secure against any aggression. Is that logical? And I say yes. It means that Israel obtains all kinds of guarantees that will ensure these two factors. To this demand, I say yes.

Beyond that we declare that we accept all the international guarantees you envisage and accept. We declare that we accept all the guarantees you want from the two superpowers or from either of them or from the Big Five or from some of them. Once again, I declare clearly and unequivocally that we agree to any guarantees you accept, because in return we shall receive the same guarantees.

In short then, when we ask what is peace for Israel, the answer would be that Israel lives within her borders, among her Arab neighbors in safety and security, within the framework of all the guarantees she accepts and that are offered to her.

But, how can this be achieved? How can we reach this conclusion that would lead us to permanent peace based on justice? There are facts that should be faced with courage and clarity. There are Arab territories that Israel has occupied and still occupies by force. We insist on complete withdrawal from these territories, including Arab Jerusalem.

I have come to Jerusalem, the city of peace, which will always remain as a living embodiment of coexistence among believers of the three religions. It is inadmissible that anyone should conceive the special status of the city of Jerusalem within the framework of annexation or expansionism. It should be a free and open city for all believers.

Above all, this city should not be severed form those who have made it their abode for centuries. Instead of reviving the precedent of the Crusades, we should revive the spirit of Omar Emil Khtab and Saladin, namely the spirit of tolerance and respect for right.

The holy shrines of Islam and Christianity are not only places of worship but a living testimony of our interrupted presence here. Politically, spiritually and intellectually, here let us make no mistake about the importance and reverence we Christians and Moslems attach to Jerusalem.

Let me tell you without the slightest hesitation that I have not come to you under this roof to make a request that your troops evacuate the occupied territories. Complete withdrawal from the Arab territories occupied after 1967 is a logical and undisputed fact. Nobody should plead for that. Any talk about permanent peace based on justice and any move to ensure our coexistence in peace and security in this part of the world would become meaningless while you occupy Arab territories by force of arms.

For there is no peace that could be built on the occupation of the land of others, otherwise it would not be a serious peace. Yet this is a foregone conclusion that is not open to the passion of debate if intentions are sincere or if endeavors to establish a just and durable peace for our and for generations to come are genuine.

As for the Palestine cause—nobody could deny that it is the crux of the entire problem. Nobody in the world could accept today slogans propagated here in Israel, ignoring the existence of a Palestinian people and questioning even their whereabouts. Because the Palestine people and their legitimate rights are no longer denied today by anybody; that is nobody who has the ability of judgment can deny or ignore it.

It is an acknowledged fact, perceived by the world community, both in the East and in the West, with support and recognition in international documents and official statements. It is of no use to anybody to turn deaf ears to its resounding voice, which is being heard day and night, or to overlook its historical reality.

Even the United States of America, your first ally, which is absolutely committed to safeguard Israel's security and existence and which offered and still offers Israel every moral, material and military support— I say, even the United States has opted to face up to reality and admit that the Palestinian people are entitled to legitimate rights and that the Palestine problem is the cause and essence of the conflict and that so long as it continues to be unresolved, the conflict will continue to aggravate, reaching new dimension.

In all sincerity I tell you that there can be no peace without the Palestinians. It is a grave error of unpredictable consequences to overlook or brush aside this cause.

I shall not indulge in past events such as the Balfour Declaration 60 years ago. You are well acquainted with the relevant text. If you have found the moral and legal justification to set up a national home on a land that did not all belong to you, it is incumbent upon you to show understanding of the insistence of the people of Palestine for establishment once again of a state on their land. When some extremists ask the

179

Palestinians to give up this sublime objective, this in fact means asking them to renounce their identity and every hope for the future.

I hail the Israeli voices that called for the recognition of the Palestinian people's right to achieve and safeguard peace.

Here I tell you, ladies and gentlemen, that it is no use to refrain from recognizing the Palestinian people and their right to statehood as their right of return. We, the Arabs, have faced this experience before, with you. And with the reality of the Israeli existence, the struggle which took us from war to war, from victims to more victims, until you and we have today reached the edge of a horrible abyss and a terrifying disaster unless, together, we seize this opportunity today of a durable peace based on justice.

You have to face reality bravely, as I have done. There can never be any solution to a problem by evading it or turning a deaf ear to it. Peace cannot last if attempts are made to impose fantasy concepts on which the world has turned its back and announced its unanimous call for the respect of rights and facts.

There is no need to enter a vicious circle as to Palestinian rights. It is useless to create obstacles, otherwise the march of peace will be impeded or peace will be blown up. As I have told you, there is no happiness [based on] the detriment of others.

Direct confrontation and straightforwardness are the shortcuts and the most successful way to reach a clear objective. Direct confrontation concerning the Palestinian problem and tackling it in one single language with a view to achieving a durable and just peace lie in the establishment of that peace. With all the guarantees you demand, there should be no fear of a newly born state that needs the assistance of all countries of the world.

When the bells of peace ring there will be no hands to beat the drums of war. Even if they existed, they would be stilled.

Conceive with me a peace agreement in Geneva that we would herald to a world thirsting for peace. A peace agreement based on the following points:

Ending the occupation of the Arab territories occupied in 1967.

Achievement of the fundamental rights of the Palestinian people and their right to self-determination, including their right to establish their own state.

The right of all states in the area to live in peace within their boundaries, their secure boundaries, which will be secured and guaranteed through procedures to be agreed upon, which will provide appropriate security to international boundaries in addition to appropriate international guarantees.

Commitment of all states in the region to administer the relations

180

among them in accordance with the objectives and principles of the United Nations Charter. Particularly the principles concerning the non-use of force and a solution of differences among them by peaceful means.

Ending the state of belligerence in the region.

Ladies and gentlemen, peace is not a mere endorsement of written lines. Rather it is a rewriting of history. Peace is not a game of calling for peace to defend certain whims or hide certain admissions. Peace in its essence is a dire struggle against all and every ambition and whim.

Perhaps the example taken and experienced, taken from ancient and modern history, teaches that missiles, warships and nuclear weapons cannot establish security. Instead they destroy what peace and security build.

For the sake of our peoples and for the sake of the civilization made by man, we have to defend man everywhere against rule by the force of arms so that we may endow the rule of humanity with all the power of the values and principles that further the sublime position of mankind.

Allow me to address my call from this rostrum to the people of Israel. I pledge myself with true and sincere words to every man, woman and child in Israel. I tell them, from the Egyptian people who bless this sacred mission of peace, I convey to you the message of peace of the Egyptian people, who do not harbor fanaticism and whose sons, Moslems, Christians and Jews, live together in a state of cordiality, love and tolerance.

This is Egypt, whose people have entrusted me with their sacred message. A message of security, safety and peace to every man, woman and child in Israel. I say, encourage your leadership to struggle for peace. Let all endeavors be channeled toward building a huge stronghold for peace instead of building destructive rockets.

Introduce to the entire world the image of the new man in this area so that he might set an example to the man of our age, the man of peace everywhere. Ring the bells for your sons. Tell them that those wars were the last of wars and the end of sorrows. Tell them that we are entering upon a new beginning, a new life, a life of love, prosperity, freedom and peace.

You, sorrowing mother, you, widowed wife, you, the son who lost a brother or a father, all the victims of wars, fill the air and space with recitals of peace, fill bosoms and hearts with the aspirations of peace. Make a reality that blossoms and lives. Make hope a code of conduct and endeavor.

The will of peoples is part of the will of God. Ladies and gentlemen, before I came to this place, with every beat of my heart and with every sentiment, I prayed to God Almighty. While performing the prayers at the Al Aksa mosque and while visiting the Holy Sepulcher I asked the

181

Almighty to give me strength and to confirm my belief that this visit may achieve the objective. I look forward to a happy present and a happier future.

I have chosen to set aside all precedents and tranditions known by warring countries. In spite of the fact that occupation of Arab territories is still there, the declaration of my readiness to proceed to Israel came as a great surprise that stirred many feelings and confounded many minds. Some of them even doubted its intent.

Despite all that, the decision was inspired by all the clarity and purity of belief and with all the true passions of my people's will and intentions and I have chosen this road, considered by many to be the most difficult road.

I have chosen to come to you with an open heart and an open mind. I have chosen to give this great impetus to all international efforts exerted for peace. I have chosen to present to you, in your home, the realities, devoid of any scheme or whim. Not to manuever, or win a round, but for us to win together, the most dangerous of rounds embattled in modern history, the battle of permanent peace based on justice.

It is not my battle alone. Nor is it the battle of the leadership in Israel alone. It is the battle of all and every citizen in all our territories, whose right it is to live in peace. It is the commitment of conscience and responsibility in the hearts of millions.

When I put forward this initiative, many asked what is it that I conceived as possible to achieve during this visit and what my expectations were. And as I answer the questions, I announce before you that I have not thought of carrying out this initiative from the precepts of what could be achieved during this visit. And I have come here to deliver a message. I have delivered the message and may God be my witness.

I repeat with Zachariah: Love, right and justice. From the holy Koran I quote the following verses: "We believe in God and in what has been revealed to us and what was revealed to Abraham, Ishmael, Isaac, Jacob and the 13 Jewish tribes. And in the books given to Moses and Jesus and the prophets from their Lord, who made no distinction between them." So we agree Salam Aleikum—peace be upon you.

Appendix VII

A Framework for Peace in the Middle East Agreed at Camp David, Signed September 17, 1978

Muhammad Anwar al-Sadat, President of the Arab Republic of Egypt, and Menachem Begin, Prime Minister of Israel, met with Jimmy Carter, President of the United States of America, at Camp David from September 5 to September 17, 1978, and have agreed on the following framework for peace in the Middle East. They invite other parties to the Arab-Israeli conflict to adhere to it.

Preamble

The search for peace in the Middle East must be guided by the following:

— The agreed basis for a peaceful settlement of the conflict between Israel and its neighbors is United Nations Security Council Resolution 242, in all its parts.*

— After four wars during thirty years, despite intensive human efforts, the Middle East, which is the cradle of civilization and the birthplace of three great religions, does not yet enjoy the blessings of peace. The people of the Middle East yearn for peace so that the vast human and natural resources of the region can be turned to the pursuits of peace and so that this area can become a model for coexistence and cooperation among nations.

— The historic initiative of President Sadat in visiting Jerusalem and the reception accorded to him by the Parliament, government and people of Israel, and the reciprocal visit of Prime Minister Begin to Ismailia, the peace proposals made by both leaders, as well as the warm reception of these missions by the peoples of both countries, have created an unprecedented opportunity for peace which must not be lost if this generation and future generations are to be spared the tragedies of war.

— The provisions of the Charter of the United Nations and the other accepted norms of international law and legitimacy now provide accepted standards for the conduct of relations among all states.

— To achieve a relationship of peace, in the spirit of Article 2 of the United Nations Charter, future negotiations between Israel and any neighbor prepared to negotiate peace and security with it, are necessary for the purpose of carrying out all the provisions and principles of Resolutions 242 and 338.

---

*The texts of Resolutions 242 and 338 are annexed to this document.

— Peace requires respect for the sovereignty, territorial integrity and political independence of every state in the area and their right to live in peace within secure and recognized boundaries free from threats or acts of force. Progress toward that goal can accelerate movement toward a new era of reconciliation in the Middle East marked by cooperation in promoting economic development, in maintaining stability, and in assuring security.

— Security is enhanced by a relationship of peace and by cooperation between nations which enjoy normal relations. In addition, under the terms of peace treaties, the parties can, on the basis of reciprocity, agree to special security arrangements such as demilitarized zones, limited armaments areas, early warning stations, the presence of international forces, liaison, agreed measures for monitoring, and other arrangements that they agree are useful.

Framework

Taking these factors into account, the parties are determined to reach a just, comprehensive, and durable settlement of the Middle East conflict through the conclusion of peace treaties based on Security Council Resolutions 242 and 338 in all their parts. Their purpose is to achieve peace and good neighborly relations. They recognize that, for peace to endure, it must involve all those who have been most deeply affected by the conflict. They therefore agree that this framework as appropriate is intended by them to constitute a basis for peace not only between Egypt and Israel, but also between Israel and each of its other neighbors which is prepared to negotiate peace with Israel on this basis. With that objective in mind, they have agreed to proceed as follows:

A. West Bank and Gaza

1. Egypt, Israel, Jordan and the representatives of the Palestinian people should participate in negotiations on the resolution of the Palestinian problem in all its aspects. To achieve that objective, negotiations relating to the West Bank and Gaza should proceed in three stages:

(a) Egypt and Israel agree that, in order to ensure a peaceful and orderly transfer of authority, and taking into account the security concerns of all the parties, there should be transitional arrangements for the West Bank and Gaza for a period not exceeding five years. In order to provide full autonomy to the inhabitants, under these arrangements the Israeli military government and its civilian administration will be withdrawn as soon as a self-governing authority has been freely elected by the inhabitants of these areas to replace the existing military government. To negotiate the details of a transitional arrangement, the Government of Jordan will be invited to join the negotiations on the basis of this framework. These new arrangements should give due consideration both to the principle of self-government by the inhabitants of these territories and to the legitimate security concerns of the parties involved.

(b) Egypt, Israel, and Jordan will agree on the modalities for establishing the elected self-governing authority in the West Bank and Gaza. The delegations of Egypt and Jordan may include Palestinians from the West Bank and Gaza or other Palestinians as mutually agreed. The parties will negotiate an agreement which will define the powers and responsibilities of the self-governing authority to be exercised in the West Bank and Gaza. A withdrawal of Israeli armed forces will take place and there will be a redeployment of the remaining Israeli forces into specified security locations. The agreement will also include arrangements for assuring internal and external security and public order. A strong local police force will be established, which may include Jordanian citizens. In addition, Israeli and Jordanian forces will participate in joint patrols and in the manning of control posts to assure the security of the borders.

(c) When the self-governing authority (administrative council) in the West Bank and Gaza is established and inaugurated, the transitional period of five years will begin. As soon as possible, but not later than the third year after the beginning of the transitional period, negotiations will take place to determine the final status of the West Bank and Gaza and its relationship with its neighbors, and to conclude a peace treaty between Israel and Jordan by the end of the transitional period. These negotiations will be conducted among Egypt, Israel, Jordan, and the elected representatives of the inhabitants of the West Bank and Gaza. Two separate but related committees will be convened, one committee, consisting of representatives of the four parties which will negotiate and agree on the final status of the West Bank and Gaza, and its relationship with its neighbors, and the second committee, consisting of representatives of Israel and representatives of Jordan to be joined by the elected representatives of the inhabitants of the West Bank and Gaza, to negotiate the peace treaty between Israel and Jordan, taking into account the agreement reached on the final status of the West Bank and Gaza. The negotiations shall be based on all the provisions and principles of UN Security Council Resolution 242. The negotiations will resolve, among other matters, the location of the boundaries and the nature of the security arrangements. The solution from the negotiations must also recognize the legitimate rights of the Palestinian people and their just requirements. In this way, the Palestinians will participate in the determination of their own future through:

185

1) The negotiations among Egypt, Israel, Jordan and the representatives of the inhabitants of the West Bank and Gaza to agree on the final status of the West Bank and Gaza and other outstanding issues by the end of the transitional period.

2) Submitting their agreement to a vote by the elected representatives of the inhabitants of the West Bank and Gaza.

3) Providing for the elected representatives of the inhabitants of the West Bank and Gaza to decide how they shall govern themselves consistent with the provisions of their agreement.

4) Participating as stated above in the work of the committee negotiating the peace treaty between Israel and Jordan.

2. All necessary measures will be taken and provisions made to assure the security of Israel and its neighbors during the transitional period and beyond. To assist in providing such security, a strong local police force will be constituted by the self-governing authority. It will be composed of inhabitants of the West Bank and Gaza. The police will maintain continuing liaison on internal security matters with the designated Israeli, Jordanian, and Egyptian officers.

3. During the transitional period, representatives of Egypt, Israel, Jordan, and the self-governing authority will constitute a continuing committee to decide by agreement on the modalities of admission of persons displaced from the West Bank and Gaza in 1967, together with necessary measures to prevent disruption and disorder. Other matters of common concern may also be dealt with by this committee.

4. Egypt and Israel will work with each other and with other interested parties to establish agreed procedures for a prompt, just and permanent implementation of the resolution of the refugee problem.

B. Egypt-Israel

1. Egypt and Israel undertake not to resort to the threat or the use of force to settle disputes. Any disputes shall be settled by peaceful means in accordance with the provisions of Article 33 of the Charter of the United Nations.

2. In order to achieve peace between them, the parties agree to negotiate in good faith with a goal of concluding within three months from the signing of this Framework a peace treaty between them, while inviting the other parties to the conflict to proceed simultaneously to negotiate and conclude similar peace treaties with a view to achieving a comprehensive peace in the area. The Framework for the Conclusion of a Peace Treaty between Egypt and Israel will govern the peace negotiations between them. The parties will agree on the modalities and the timetable for the implementation of their obligations under the treaty.

C. Associated Principles

1. Egypt and Israel state that the principles and provisions described below should apply to peace treaties between Israel and each of its neighbors—Egypt, Jordan, Syria and Lebanon.

2. Signatories shall establish among themselves relationships normal to states at peace with one another. To this end, they should undertake to abide by all the provisions of the Charter of the United Nations. Steps to be taken in this respect include:

    (a) full recognition;

    (b) abolishing economic boycotts;

    (c) guaranteeing that under their jurisdiction the citizens of the other parties shall enjoy the protection of the due process of law.

3. Signatories should explore possibilities for economic development in the context of final peace treaties, with the objective of contributing to the atmosphere of peace, cooperation and friendship which is their common goal.

4. Claims Commissions may be established for the mutual settlement of all financial claims.

5. The United States shall be invited to participate in the talks on matters related to the modalities of the implementation of the agreements and working out the timetable for the carrying out of the obligations of the parties.

6. The United Nations Security Council shall be requested to endorse the peace treaties and ensure that their provisions shall not be violated. The permanent members of the Security Council shall be requested to underwrite the peace treaties and ensure respect for their provisions. They shall also be requested to conform their policies and actions with the undertakings contained in this Framework.

For the Government
of the Arab
Republic of Egypt:

    A. SADAT

For the Government
of Israel:

    M. BEGIN

Witnessed by:

JIMMY CARTER

Jimmy Carter, President
of the United States of America

Appendix VIII

President Reagan, "United States Policy for Peace in the Middle East," Address to the Nation, September 1, 1982

My fellow Americans:

Today has been a day that should make us proud. It marked the end of the successful evacuation of PLO from Beirut, Lebanon. This peaceful step could never have been taken without the good offices of the United States and especially the truly heroic work of a great American diplomat, Ambassador Philip Habib.

Thanks to his efforts, I'm happy to announce that the U.S. Marine contingent helping to supervise the evacuation has accomplished its mission. Our young men should be out of Lebanon within 2 weeks. They, too, have served the cause of peace with distinction, and we can all be very proud of them.

But the situation in Lebanon is only part of the overall problem of conflict in the Middle East. So, over the past 2 weeks, while events in Beirut dominated the front page, America was engaged in a quiet, be-hind-the-scenes effort to lay the groundwork for a broader peace in the region. For once there were no premature leaks as U.S. diplomatic mis-sions traveled to Mideast capitals, and I met here at home with a wide range of experts to map out an American peace initiative for the long-suffering peoples of the Middle East—Arab and Israeli alike.

It seemed to me that with the agreement in Lebanon we had an opportunity for a more far-reaching peace effort in the region, and I was determined to seize that moment. In the words of the scripture, the time had come to "follow after the things which make for peace." Tonight I want to report to you the steps we've taken and the prospects they can open up for a just and lasting peace in the Middle East.

America has long been committed to bringing peace to this troubled region. For more than a generation, successive United States administra-tions have endeavored to develop a fair and workable process that could lead to a true and lasting Arab-Israeli peace.

Our involvement in the search for Mideast peace is not a matter of preference; it's a moral imperative. The strategic importance of the region to the United States is well known, but our policy is motivated by more than strategic interests. We also have an irreversible commitment to the survival and territorial integrity of friendly states. Nor can we ignore the fact that the well-being of much of the world's economy is tied to stability in the strife-torn Middle East. Finally, our traditional humanitarian con-cerns dictated a continuing effort to peacefully resolve conflicts.

When our administration assumed office in January of 1981, I decided that the general framework for our Middle East policy should follow the broad guidelines laid down by my predecessors. There were two basic issues we had to address. First, there was the strategic threat to the region posed by the Soviet Union and its surrogates, best demonstrated by the brutal war in Afghanistan, and, second, the peace process between Israel and its Arab neighbors.

With regard to the Soviet threat, we have strengthened our efforts to develop with our friends and allies a joint policy to deter the Soviets and their surrogates from further expansion in the region and, if necessary, to defend against it.

With respect to the Arab-Israeli conflict, we've embraced the Camp David framework as the only way to proceed. We have also recognized, however, solving the Arab-Israeli conflict in and of itself cannot assure peace throughout a region as vast and troubled as the Middle East.

Our first objective under the Camp David process was to ensure the successful fulfillment of the Egyptian-Israeli peace treaty. This was achieved with the peaceful return of the Sinai to Egypt in April 1982. To accomplish this, we worked hard with our Egyptian and Israeli friends and, eventually, with other friendly countries to create the multinational force which now operates in the Sinai. Throughout this period of difficult and time-consuming negotiations, we never lost sight of the next step of Camp David—autonomy talks to pave the way for permitting the Palestinian people to exercise their legitimate rights. However, owing to the tragic assassination of President Sadat and other crises in the area, it was not until January 1982 that we were able to make a major effort to renew these talks.

Secretary of State Haig and Ambassador Fairbanks made three visits to Israel and Egypt early this year to pursue the autonomy talks. Considerable progress was made in developing the basic outline of an American approach which was to be presented to Egypt and Israel after April.

The successful completion of Israel's withdrawal from Sinai and the courage shown on this occasion by Prime Minister Begin and President Mubarak in living up to their agreements convinced me the time had come for a new American policy to try to bridge the remaining differences between Egypt and Israel on the autonomy process. So, in May, I called for specific measures and a timetable for consultations with the Governments of Egypt and Israel on the next steps in the peace process. However, before this effort could be launched, the conflict in Lebanon preempted our efforts.

The autonomy talks were basically put on hold while we sought to untangle the parties in Lebanon and still the guns of war. The Lebanon war, tragic as it was, has left us with a new opportunity for Middle East peace. We must seize it now and bring peace to this troubled area so vital to world stability while there is still time. It was with this strong conviction that over a month ago, before the present negotiations in Beirut had been completed, I directed Secretary of State Shultz to again review our policy and to consult a wide range of outstanding Americans on the best ways to strengthen chances for peace in the Middle East.

We have consulted with many of the officials who were historically involved in the process, with Members of the Congress, and with individuals from the private sector. And I have held extensive consultations with my own advisors on the principles that I will outline to you tonight.

The evacuation of the PLO from Beirut is now complete, and we can now help the Lebanese to rebuild their war-torn country. We owe it to ourselves and to posterity to move quickly to build upon this achievement. A stable and revived Lebanon is essential to all our hopes for peace in the region. The people of Lebanon deserve the best efforts of the international community to turn the nightmares of the past several years into a new dawn of hope. But the opportunities for peace in the Middle East do not begin and end in Lebanon. As we help Lebanon rebuild, we must also move to resolve the root causes of conflict between Arabs and Israelis.

The war in Lebanon has demonstrated many things, but two consequences are key to the peace process. First, the military losses of the PLO have not diminished the yearning of the Palestinian people for a just solution of their claims; and, second, while Israel's military successes in Lebanon have demonstrated that its armed forces are second to none in the region, they alone cannot bring just and lasting peace to Israel and her neighbors.

The question now is how to reconcile Israel's legitimate security concerns with the legitimate rights of the Palestinians. And that answer can only come at the negotiating table. Each party must recognize that the outcome must be acceptable to all and that true peace will require compromises by all.

So, tonight I'm calling for a fresh start. This is the moment for all those directly concerned to get involved—or lend their support—to a workable basis for peace. The Camp David agreement remains the foundation of our policy. Its language provides all parties with the leeway they need for successful negotiations.

I call on Israel to make clear that the security for which she yearns can only be achieved through genuine peace, a peace requiring magnanimity, vision, and courage.

I call on the Palestinian people to recognize that their own political aspirations are inextricably bound to recognition of Israel's right to a secure future.

And I call on the Arab States to accept the reality of Israel—and the reality that peace and justice are to be gained only through hard, fair, direct negotiation.

In making these calls upon others, I recognize that the United States has a special responsibility. No other nation is in a position to deal with the key parties to the conflict on the basis of trust and reliability.

The time has come for a new realism on the part of all the peoples of the Middle East. The State of Israel is an accomplished fact; it deserves unchallenged legitimacy within the community of nations. But Israel's legitimacy has thus far been recognized by too few countries and has been denied by every Arab State except Egypt. Israel exists; it has a right to exist in peace behind secure and defensible borders; and it has a right to demand of its neighbors that they recognize those facts.

I have personally followed and supported Israel's heroic struggle for survival, ever since the founding of the State of Israel 34 years ago. In the pre-1967 borders Israel was barely 10 miles wide at its narrowest point. The bulk of Israel's population lived within artillery range of hostile Arab armies. I am not about to ask Israel to live that way again.

The war in Lebanon has demonstrated another reality in the region. The departure of the Palestinians from Beirut dramatizes more than ever the homelessness of the Palestinian people. Palestinians feel strongly that their cause is more than a question of refugees. I agree. The Camp David agreement recognized that fact when it spoke of the legitimate rights of the Palestinian people and their just requirements.

For peace to endure it must involve all those who have been most deeply affected by the conflict. Only through broader participation in the peace process, most immediately by Jordan and by the Palestinians, will Israel be able to rest confident in the knowledge that its security and integrity will be respected by its neighbors. Only through the process of negotiation can all the nations of the Middle East achieve a secure peace.

These, then, are our general goals. What are the specific new American positions, and why are we taking them? In the Camp David talks thus far, both Israel and Egypt have felt free to express openly their views as to what the outcome should be. Understandably their views have differed on many points. The United States has thus far sought to play the role of mediator. We have avoided public comment on the key issues. We have always recognized and continue to recognize that only the voluntary agreement of those parties most directly involved in the conflict can provide an enduring solution. But it's become evident to me that some clearer sense of America's position on the key issues is necessary to encourage wider support for the peace process.

First, as outlined in the Camp David accords, there must be a period of time during which the Palestinian inhabitants of the West Bank and

Gaza will have full autonomy over their own affairs. Due consideration must be given to the principle of self-government by the inhabitants of the territories and to the legitimate security concerns of the parties involved. The purpose of the 5-year period of transition which would begin after free elections for a self-governing Palestinian authority is to prove to the Palestinians that they can run their own affairs and that such Palestinian autonomy poses no threat to Israel's security.

The United States will not support the use of any additional land for the purpose of settlements during the transitional period. Indeed, the immediate adoption of a settlement freeze by Israel, more than any other action, could create the confidence needed for wider participation in these talks. Further settlement activity is in no way necessary for the security of Israel and only diminishes the confidence of the Arabs that a final outcome can be freely and fairly negotiated.

I want to make the American position well understood. The purpose of this transitional period is the peaceful and orderly transfer of authority from Israel to the Palestinian inhabitants of the West Bank and Gaza. At the same time, such a transfer must not interfere with Israel's security requirements.

Beyond the transition period, as we look to the future of the West Bank and Gaza, it is clear to me that peace cannot be achieved by the formation of an independent Palestinian state in those territories, nor is it achievable on the basis of Israeli sovereignty or permanent control over the West Bank and Gaza. So, the United States will not support the establishment of an independent Palestinian state in the West Bank and Gaza, and we will not support annexation or permanent control by Israel.

There is, however, another way to peace. The final status of these lands must, of course, be reached through the give and take of negotiations. But it is the firm view of the United States that self-government by the Palestinians of the West Bank and Gaza in association with Jordan offers the best chance for a durable, just, and lasting peace. We base our approach squarely on the principle that the Arab-Israeli conflict should be resolved through negotiations involving an exchange of territory for peace.

This exchange is enshrined in United Nations Security Council Resolution 242, which is, in turn, incorporated in all its parts in the Camp David agreements. U.N. Resolution 242 remains wholly valid as the foundation stone of America's Middle East peace effort. It is the United States position that, in return for peace, the withdrawal provision of Resolution 242 applies to all fronts, including the West Bank and Gaza. When the border is negotiated between Jordan and Israel, our view on the extent to which Israel should be asked to give up territory will be heavily affected by the extent of true peace and normalization, and the security arrangements offered in return.

Finally, we remain convinced that Jerusalem must remain undivided, but its final status should be decided through negotiation.

In the course of the negotiations to come, the United States will support positions that seem to us fair and reasonable compromises and likely to promote a sound agreement. We will also put forward our own detailed proposals when we believe they can be helpful. And, make no mistake, the United States will oppose any proposal from any party and at any point in the negotiating process that threatens the security of Israel. America's commitment to the security of Israel is ironclad, and, I might add, so is mine.

During the past few days, our Ambassadors in Israel, Egypt, Jordan, and Saudi Arabia have presented to their host governments the proposals, in full detail, that I have outlined here today. Now I'm convinced that these proposals can bring justice, bring security, and bring durability to an Arab-Israeli peace. The United States will stand by these principles with total dedication. They are fully consistent with Israel's security requirements and the aspirations of the Palestinians.

We will work hard to broaden participation at the peace table as envisaged by the Camp David accords. And I fervently hope that the Palestinians and Jordan, with the support of their Arab colleagues, will accept this opportunity.

Tragic turmoil in the Middle East runs back to the dawn of history. In our modern day, conflict after conflict has taken its brutal toll there. In an age of nuclear challenge and economic interdependence, such conflicts are a threat to all the people of the world, not just the Middle East itself. It's time for us all—in the Middle East and around the world—to call a halt to conflict, hatred, and prejudice. It's time for us all to launch a common effort for reconstruction, peace, and progress.

It has often been said—and, regrettably, too often been true—that the story of the search for peace and justice in the Middle East is a tragedy of opportunities missed. In the aftermath of the settlement in Lebanon, we now face an opportunity for a broader peace. This time we must not let it slip from our grasp. We must look beyond the difficulties and obstacles of the present and move with a fairness and resolve toward a brighter future. We owe it to ourselves—and to posterity—to do no less. For if we miss this chance to make a fresh start, we may look back on this moment from some later vantage point and realize how much that failure cost us all.

These, then, are the principles upon which American policy toward the Arab-Israeli conflict will be based. I have made a personal commitment to see that they endure and, God willing, that they will come to be seen by all reasonable, compassionate people as fair, achievable, and in the interests of all who wish to see peace in the Middle East.

Tonight, on the eve of what can be a dawning of new hope for the people of the troubled Middle East—and for all the world's people who dream of a just and peaceful future—I ask you, my fellow Americans, for your support and your prayers in this great undertaking.

Thank you, and God bless you.

Appendix IX

Arab League Summit Conference Declaration, Fez, Morocco, September 9, 1982

The 12th Arab Summit was held in Fez on the 27th Moharrem 1402, corresponding to the 25th November 1981.

After suspending its work, it resumed from the 17th to the 20th Doualkiada 1402, corresponding to the 6th to 9th September 1982, under the chairmanship of His Majesty King Hassan II, King of the Kingdom of Morocco. All Arab countries took part in the work of the summit with the exception of the Libyan Arab Jamahirya.

In view of the grave and delicate circumstances through which the Arab nation is passing and of the feeling of historic national responsibility, their majesties and their excellencies, the kings, presidents and emirs of the Arabs, examined the important questions submitted to the summit and took the following decisions:

I. The Israeli-Arab Conflict. The summit paid homage to the resistance of the forces of the Palestine revolution, the Lebanese and Palestinian peoples and the Syrian Arab armed forces, and reaffirmed its support to the Palestinian people in the struggle to recover its inalienable national rights.

The summit, convinced of the power of the Arab nation to achieve its legitimate objectives and put an end to the aggression on the basis of the fundamental principles laid down by the Arab summits and in view of the desire of the Arab countries to pursue action by every means for the achievement of a just peace in the Middle East, taking account of the plan of His Excellency President Habib Bourguiba which considers international legality to be the basis for the solution of the Palestinian question, and of the plan of His Majesty King Fahd Ibn Abdelaziz concerning peace in the Middle East, and in the light of discussions and observations made by their majesties, excellencies and highnesses, the kings, presidents and emirs, the summit adopted the following principles:

[1] The withdrawal of Israel from all Arab territories occupied in 1967 including Arab Al Qods.

[2] The dismantling of settlements established by Israel on the Arab territories after 1967.

[3] The guarantee of freedom of worship and practice of religious rites for all religions in the holy shrines.

[4] The reaffirmation of the Palestinian people's right to self-determination and the exercise of its imprescriptible and inalienable national rights under the leadership of the Palestine Liberation Organization, its sole and legitimate representative, and the indemnification of all those who do not desire to return.

[5] Placing the West Bank and Gaza Strip under the control of the United Nations for a transitory period not exceeding a few months.

[6] The establishment of an independent Palestinian state with Al Qods as its capital.

[7] The Security Council guarantees peace among all states of the region including the independent Palestinian state.

[8] The Security Council guarantees the respect of these principles.

II. The Israeli Agression Against Lebanon.

[1] The summit strongly condemns the Israeli aggression against Lebanon and the Palestinian and Lebanese peoples, and draws the attention of the international public opinion to the seriousness and the consequences of this aggression on the stability of the region.

[2] The summit decides to support Lebanon in everything allowing the implementation of the Security Council resolutions and particularly Resolutions 508 and 509 concerning the withdrawal of Israel from the Lebanese territory back to the internationally recognized frontiers.

[3] The summit reaffirms the solidarity of Arab countries with Lebanon in its tragedy and its readiness to grant all assistance that it would demand to solve its problems.

The summit was informed of the Lebanese Government's decision to put an end to the mission of the Arab deterrent forces in Lebanon. To this effect, the Lebanese and Syrian Governments will start negotiations on measures to be taken in the light of the Israeli withdrawal from Lebanon.

III. Arab Stance on the Gulf War. The summit has studied the situation in the gulf war and has noted with great affliction and regret the continuation of the Iraq-Iran war despite repeated attempts to reach a cease-fire and despite offers of mediation and good offices on the part of international organizations while lauding the positive initiative of Iraq to withdraw its forces back to international frontiers.

Taking into account the principle of solidarity and the unity of Arab ranks and out of the conference's concern to see an atmosphere of clarity, understanding and good neighborhood prevail between Arab countries and their neighbors, the summit has decided to reaffirm its commitment to defend all Arab territories and to consider any aggression against an Arab country as being an aggression against all Arab countries, and to call upon the two involved parties to fully comply with the resolutions 479 of the year 1982 and 514 of the year 1982 of the Security Council and to implement them.

The summit asks all countries to abstain from taking any measure likely to encourage directly or indirectly the continuation of war.

IV. The Horn of Africa. The summit has taken note of what has been exposed by the Democratic Republic of Somalia regarding the incursion of Ethiopia in the Somalian territory and decided the following:

[1] To support the Democratic Republic of Somalia to face the requirements of the safeguard of its sovereignty over its territories and to drive out the Ethiopian forces from Somali territory.

[2] The mutual respect by the countries, Ethiopia and the Democratic Republic of Somalia, of the sovereignty and independence of each state after the withdrawal of Ethiopia from the Somali territories.

[3] Support of the summit to the peaceful steps for solving, on this ground, the bilateral problems.

The summit has decided to set up a committee entrusted with undertaking contacts with the permanent members of the United Nations Security Council to follow up the summit's resolutions on the Arab-Israeli conflict and to get informed on these countries' stance and to get informed on the stance the United States of America has made public in the past few days concerning the Arab-Israeli conflict. This committee will regularly report on the results of its contacts and endeavors to the kings and heads of state.

Appendix X

Jordanian-Palestinian Agreement between King Hussein and Chairman Arafat, February 11, 1985

Proceeding from the spirit of the Fes summit resolutions approved by the Arabs and from UN resolutions on the Palestine question, in accordance with international legitimacy, and proceeding from a joint understanding toward building a distinguished relationship between the Jordanian and Palestinian peoples, the Government of the Hashemite Kingdom of Jordan and the PLO have agreed to march together toward a just, peaceful settlement of the Middle East issue and toward the termination of the Israeli occupation of the Arab territories, including Jerusalem, in accordance with the following bases and principles:

1. Land in exchange for peace as cited in the UN resolutions, including the Security Council resolutions.

2. The Palestinian people's right to self-determination. The Palestinians should exercise their inalienable right to self-determination when the Jordanians and Palestinians manage to achieve this within the framework of an Arab confederation that is intended to be established between the two states of Jordan and Palestine.

3. Solving the Palestinian refugees problem in accordance with the UN resolutions.

4. Solving all aspects of the Palestine question.

5. Based on this, peace negotiations should be held within the framework of an international conference to be attended by the five UN Security Council permanent member-states and all parties to the conflict, including the PLO, which is the Palestinian people's sole legitimate representative, within a joint delegation—a joint Jordanian-Palestinian delegation.

Appendix XI

King Hussein Ibn Talal of Jordan, Speech Discontinuing Jordan's Legal and Administrative Links with the West Bank, July 31, 1988

In the name of God, the merciful, the compassionate, and peace be upon his faithful Arab messenger. Brother citizens: I send you greetings and am pleased to address you in your cities and villages, in your camps and dwellings, in your factories, institutions, offices, and establishments. I would like to address your hearts and minds in all parts of our beloved Jordanian land.

This is all the more important at this juncture, when we have initiated—after seeking God's help and after thorough and extensive study—a series of measures to enhance Palestinian national orientation and highlight Palestinian identity; our goal is the benefit of the Palestinian cause and the Arab Palestinian people. Our decision, as you know, comes after 38 years of the unity of the two banks and 14 years after the Rabat summit resolution designating the PLO as the sole legitimate representative of the Palestinian people. It also comes 6 years after the Fes summit resolution that agreed unanimously on the establishment of an independent Palestinian state in the occupied West Bank and the Gaza Strip as one of the bases and results of the peaceful settlement.

We are certain our decision to initiate these measures does not come as a surprise. Many of you have anticipated it, and some of you have been calling for it for some time. As for its contents, it has been a topic of discussion and consideration for everyone since the Rabat summit. Nevertheless, some may wonder: Why now? Why today and not after the Rabat or Fes summits, for instance? To answer this question, we need to recall certain facts that preceded the Rabat resolution. We also need to recall considerations that led to the debate over the slogan-objective which the PLO raised and worked to gain Arab and international support for, namely, the establishment of an independent Palestinian state. This meant, in addition to the PLO's ambition to embody the Palestinian identity on Palestinian national soil, the separation of the West Bank from the Hashemite Kingdom of Jordan.

I reviewed the facts preceding the Rabat resolution, as you recall, before the Arab leaders in the Algiers extraordinary summit last June. It may be important to recall that one of the main points I emphasized was the text of the unity resolution of the two banks of April 1950. This resolution affirms the preservation of all Arab rights in Palestine and the defense of such rights by all legitimate means without prejudicing the final settlement of the just cause of the Palestinian people—within the scope of the people's aspirations and of Arab cooperation and international justice.

Among these facts there was our 1972 proposal regarding our concept of alternatives, on which the relationship between Jordan on one hand and the West Bank and Gaza on the other may be based after their liberation. Among these alternatives was the establish-

198

ment of a relationship of brotherhood and cooperation between the Hashemite Kingdom of Jordan and the independent Palestinian state in case the Palestinian people opt for that. Simply, this means that we declared our clear-cut position regarding our adherence to the Palestinian people's right to self-determination on their national soil, including their right to establish their own independent state, more than 2 years before the Rabat summit resolution. This will be our position until the Palestinian people achieve their complete national goals, God willing.

The relationship of the West Bank with the Hashemite Kingdom of Jordan in light of the PLO's call for the establishment of an independent Palestinian state, can be confined to two considerations. First, the principled consideration pertaining to the issue of Arab unity as a pan-Arab aim, to which the hearts of the Arab peoples aspire and which they want to achieve. Second, the political consideration pertaining to the extent of the Palestinian struggle's gain from the continuation of the legal relationship of the Kingdom's two banks. Our answer to the question now stems from these two considerations and the background of the clear-cut and firm Jordanian position toward the Palestine question, as we have shown.

Regarding the principled consideration, Arab unity between any two or more countries is an option of any Arab people. This is what we believe. Accordingly, we responded to the wish of the Palestinian people's representatives for unity with Jordan in 1950. From this premise, we respect the wish of the PLO, the sole and legitimate representative of the Palestinian people, to secede from us as an independent Palestinian state. We say that while we fully understand the situation. Despite this, Jordan will continue to take pride in carrying the message of the Great Arab Revolt, adhering to its principles, believing in the one Arab destiny, and abiding by the joint Arab action.

Regarding the political consideration, since the June 1967 aggression we have believed that our action and efforts should be directed at liberating the land and the sanctities from Israeli occupation. Therefore, we have concentrated all our efforts, over the past 21 years of occupation, on that goal. We did not imagine that maintaining the legal and administrative relationship between the two banks could constitute an obstacle to liberating the occupied Palestinian land. Hence, in the past and before we took measures, we did not find anything requiring such measures, especially since our support for the Palestinian people's right to self-determination was clear.

Of late, it has become clear that there is a general Palestinian and Arab orientation which believes in the need to highlight the Palestinian identity in full in all efforts and activities that are related to the

Palestine question and its developments. It has also become obvious that there is a general conviction that maintaining the legal and administrative relationship with the West Bank—and the consequent special Jordanian treatment of the brother Palestinians living under occupation through Jordanian institutions in the occupied territories—goes against this orientation. It would be an obstacle to the Palestinian struggle which seeks to win international support for the Palestine question, considering that it is a just national issue of a people struggling against foreign occupation.

In view of this orientation, which was bound to stem from a purely Palestinian desire and an unflinching Arab determination to support the Palestine question, we have a duty to favorably respond to its requirements. First and last, we are part of our nation and we are eager to support its causes, foremost among which is the Palestine question. Since there is unanimous conviction that the struggle for liberating the occupied Palestinian territory can be bolstered by disengaging the legal and administrative relationship between the two banks, then we must perform our duty and do what is required of us.

As we favorably responded to the appeals made to us by Arab leaders at the Rabat summit of 1974 which asked us to continue to deal with the occupied West Bank through Jordanian institutions to support the steadfastness of brethren there, we today favorably respond to the desire of the PLO, the sole legitimate representative of the Palestinian people, and also to the Arab orientation regarding consecrating the purely Palestinian identity in all of its elements in terms of form and content. We beseech God to make this step of ours a qualitative addition to the growing struggle being waged by the Palestinian people for the sake of attaining liberation and independence.

Brother citizens, these are the reasons, the considerations, and the convictions that prompted us to respond favorably to the PLO's desire and to the general Arab orientation which is in harmony with this desire, as we cannot continue to maintain this undecided situation which serves neither Jordan nor the Palestine question. We had to go out of the tunnel of fears and doubts to the atmosphere of tranquillity and clarity where mutual confidence flourishes and blossoms into understanding, cooperation, and affection in favor of the Palestine question and also in favor of Arab unity—which will remain a cherished objective sought and demanded by all Arab peoples.

However, it should be clear that our measures regarding the West Bank are connected only with the Palestinian territory and its people, and not the Jordanian citizens of Palestinian origin in the

Hashemite Kingdom of Jordan. All of them have citizenship rights and commitments just like any other citizen regardless of his origin.

They are an integral part of the Jordanian state to which they belong, on whose soil they live, and in whose life and various activities they participate. Jordan is not Palestine and the independent Palestinian state will be established on the occupied Palestinian territory after its liberation, God willing. On this territory the Palestinian identity will be embodied and the Palestinian struggle will blossom as confirmed by the blessed uprising of the Palestinian people under occupation.

If national unity in any country is dear and precious, it is for us in Jordan more than that. It is the basis of our stability and the cause of our development and prosperity as well as the foundation of our national security and the source of our faith in the future. It is also a living embodiment of the principles of the Great Arab Revolt which we inherited and whose banner we are proudly carrying. It is also a living example of constructive plurality and a sound nucleus for any formula of a more comprehensive Arab unity. Based on this, safeguarding national unity is a sacred matter that will not be compromised. Any attempt to tamper with it under any slogan will only help the enemy carry out its expansionist policy at the expense of Palestine and Jordan alike. Consequently, true nationalism and genuine pan-Arabism lie in bolstering and strengthening national unity. Moreover, the responsibility to safeguard it falls on every one of you. There should be no room among us for a slanderer or a traitor. With God's help, we shall always be one cohesive family whose members are joined by bonds of brotherhood, affection, awareness, and the common national and pan-Arab objectives.

Perhaps the most important thing to remember as we stress the need to preserve national unity is that the stable, productive communities are those in which order and discipline prevail. Discipline is the solid fabric that binds all people in a solid, harmonious structure that blocks all avenues before the enemies and opens the horizons of hope for the coming generations.

The constructive plurality which Jordan has been practicing since its establishment and through which it is witnessing progress and prosperity in all aspects of life, does not only increase our belief in the sacredness of national unity, but also in the importance of Jordan's pan-Arab role by presenting itself as a living example of the merger of various Arab groups on its soil within the framework of a good citizenship and one Jordanian people. This example, which we are experiencing on our soil, is the one which gives us confidence in the inevitability of attaining Arab unity, God willing.

If we closely examine the spirit of the age, we will see that self-assertion does not conflict with the achievement of institutional unity formulas that include all Arabs. There are living and existing examples in foreign countries. Perhaps the clearest example is the EC, which now seeks to achieve political European unity after it has succeeded in achieving economic integration among its members. As is known, the ties, relations, and basic elements that connect the Arabs are much greater than those connecting the European peoples.

O citizens, brother Palestinians in the occupied Palestinian territory, in order to eliminate any doubts that would be cast on our measures, we would like to stress to you that these measures do not mean the relinquishment of our pan-Arab duty toward the Arab-Israeli conflict or the Palestine question. These measures also do not mean a relinquishment of our belief in Arab unity. We have basically taken these measures, as I said, in response to the wish of the PLO, the sole and legitimate representative of the Palestinian people, and in response to the prevailing Arab conviction that such measures would contribute to supporting the Palestinian people's struggle and their blessed uprising.

Jordan will continue to support the Palestinian people's steadfastness and their valiant uprising in the occupied Palestinian territory with the limits of its capabilities. I will not forget to say that when we decided to cancel the Jordanian development plan in the occupied territories, at the same time we managed to contact the various friendly governments and the international institutions that expressed their desire to contribute to the plan. We urged them to continue to finance development projects in the occupied Palestinian territory through the concerned Palestinian circles.

Brothers, Jordan has not relinquished and will not relinquish its support for the Palestinian people until they achieve their national objectives, God willing. No one outside Palestine has ever had or will ever have connection with Palestine or with its cause that is stronger than the connection of Jordan or my family with it. This is on the one hand. On the other hand, Jordan is a confrontation state, and its border with Israel is longer than that of any other Arab state.

In fact, Jordan's border with Israel is longer than the borders of the West Bank and the Gaza Strip together with it. Jordan also will not relinquish its commitment to participation in the peace process. We contributed to the efforts to achieve an international unanimity on holding an international conference for peace in the Middle East to reach a just and comprehensive peaceful settlement to the Arab-Israeli conflict, and to reach a settlement of all aspects of the Palestine question. We have defined our stands in this regard, as everyone knows, through the six principles that we previously announced to the public. Jordan, brethren, is a basic party to the Arab-Israeli conflict and the peace process. It shoulders its national and pan-Arab responsibilities accordingly.

I thank you and I repeat my heartfelt wishes to you, beseeching Almighty God to help us, guide us, make us please Him, and to grant our Palestinian brothers victory and success. He is the best of helpers.

Appendix XII

Palestine National Council, The Declaration of Independence, Algiers, November 15, 1988

[*Reading of independence document by Yasser Arafat to PNC session in Algiers at the Palais de Nations on November 15*]

In the name of God, the compassionate, the merciful,
The Declaration of Independence:
On the land of the heavenly messages to mankind, on the land of Palestine, the Palestinian Arab people were born. This people grew up, became developed, and introduced creativity into their human and national existence through an unbreakable and continuous organic relationship between the people and the land and history. And by their epic steadfastness through time, the people of Palestine molded their national identity to a miraculous level.

Despite the ambitions, greed, and invasions which were the outcome of the charm of this old land and its vital position along the borders of engagement among the powers and civilizations—the ambitions, greed, and invasions which used to lead to depriving the people of realizing political independence—the everlasting adherence of the people to the land granted the land its identity and breathed into the people the spirit of the homeland, fortified by the dynasties of civilizations and the multiplicity of cultures, inspired by their spiritual and historic heritage.

The Palestinian Arab people throughout history continued to develop itself by total unity between the land and man. Following in the continuous footsteps of the prophets on this blessed land, they raised their voices from every minaret with prayers of thanks to the

Creator and rang the bell of every church and temple and sang hymns of mercy and peace. From one generation to another, the Palestinian Arab people never stopped their valiant defense of their homeland. The successive revolutions of our people were a heroic embodiment of the will of national independence.

At a time when the modern world was formulating a new value system, the local and international balances of power were leaving aside the Palestinian fate from the general fate. It became clear yet again that justice alone does not turn the wheels of history. Thus the great Palestinian wound was ripped open to witness a wounding difference—the people who were deprived of independence and whose homeland was subjected to a new type of occupation have been subjected to an attempt to publicize the lie which says that Palestine is a land without people.

Despite this historic falsification, the international community, in Article 22 of the Charter of the League of Nations of 1919 and in the Lausanne Treaty of 1923, recognized that the Palestinian Arab people—like the rest of the Arab people which cut their relations with the Ottoman state—are a free and independent people. Despite the historical injustice which was inflicted on the Palestinian Arab people by making them homeless and by depriving them of their right to self-determination following the resolution passed by the UN General Assembly, No. 181 of 1947, which partitioned Palestine into states—an Arab state and a Jewish state—this resolution still provides conditions for international legitimacy to guarantee the right of the Palestinian Arab people to sovereignty and national independence.

The Israeli forces' occupation of Palestinian territory and parts of Arab territory, the uprooting of the majority of the Palestinians and scattering them away from their homeland by organized terrorism, the subjection of the rest of them to occupation and oppression, and the operations to destroy the characteristics of their national life are flagrant violations of the principles of legitimacy and of the United Nations Charter and its resolutions which recognize the national rights of the Arab Palestinian people, including the right to return and the right to self-determination, independence, and sovereignty on the land of their homeland.

Neither in the heart of the homeland nor at its boundaries nor near or far have the Arab Palestinian people lost their firm faith in the right to return nor their solid conviction in the right to independence. The occupation, massacres, and dispersal could not expel the Palestinian from his awareness or deprive him of his identity. He continued his epic struggle and pursued the crystallization of his na-

204

tional personality through the growing accumulation of militancy. The national will defined its political framework in the Palestinian Liberation Organization as the sole and legitimate representative of the Palestinian people with the recognition of the international community represented by the United Nations and its institutions and other regional and international organizations.

On the basis of faith in inalienable rights, on the basis of pan-Arab unanimity, and on the basis of international legitimacy, the Palestinian Liberation Organization led the battles of its great people who are fused in their ideal national unity and their legendary steadfastness in the face of massacres and sieges in the homeland and outside it. The epic of the national Palestinian resistance manifested itself in Arab awareness and international awareness of it as one of the most prominent national liberation movements in this era. The great and escalating popular uprising in the occupied land, along with legendary steadfastness in the camps inside and outside the homeland, has raised human awareness of the Palestinian truth and Palestinian national rights to a higher level of absorption and maturity. It has drawn the final curtain on a complete stage of falsification and a languid conscience; it has encircled the official Israeli mentality, which became addicted to myth and terror in denying Palestinian existence.

With the uprising and the revolutionary and militant accumulation of all the revolutionary positions, the Palestinian time has reached one of the important historic turning points so the Palestinian Arab people may once again affirm their inalienable rights as well as their right to exercise them over its Palestinian soil.

On the basis of the natural, historic, and legal right of the Palestinian Arab people to its homeland, Palestine, and the sacrifices of its successive generations in defense of the freedom and independence of their homeland and proceeding from the resolutions of the Arab summits and from the strength of international legality, embodied in UN resolutions since 1947, and in exercising the right to self-determination and political independence and sovereignty over their soil by the Palestinian Arab people, the PNC declares in the name of God and in the name of the Palestinian Arab people the establishment [qiyam] of the State of Palestine over our Palestinian soil—over our Palestinian soil—and its capital holy Jerusalem. . . the PNC declares in the name of God and in the name of the Palestinian Arab people, the emergence of the State of Palestine over our Palestinian soil and its capital holy Jerusalem.

The State of Palestine belongs to Palestinians wherever they may be. And in it they develop their national and cultural identity and enjoy complete equality of rights and religious and political beliefs

205

and human dignity are safeguarded in the shadow of a democratic parliamentary system based on the freedom of opinion and the freedom of forming parties, on the majority taking care of the rights of the minority, on the respect of the minority for the decisions of the majority, and on social justice and equality and nondiscrimination on the basis of race, religion, color, or sex, in the shadow of a constitution which ensures the rule of law and independence of the judiciary . . . in the shadow of a constitution which ensures the rule of law and the independence of the judiciary and on the basis of complete loyalty to the spiritual and contemporary heritage of Palestine—tolerance and tolerant coexistence of religions throughout the centuries.

The State of Palestine is an Arab state. It is an indivisible part of the Arab nation—from its heritage and civilization and from its present aspiration for the realization of its aims of liberation, development, democracy, and unity. While it stresses its commitment to the Arab League Charter and its insistence to consolidate joint Arab action, it appeals to the sons of its nation to assist it to complete its practical birth by mobilizing energies and concentrating efforts to end the Israeli occupation.

The State of Palestine declares its commitment to the principles and objectives of the United Nations and to the international declaration of human rights, as well as its commitment to the principles of nonalignment and the latter's policy.

The State of Palestine, while declaring it is a peace-loving state, committed to the principles of peaceful coexistence, will work with all states and peoples for the realization of a permanent peace based on justice and respect for rights. Under the auspices of this peace the energies of mankind will be opened up to construction and under the auspices of this peace there will be competition for the beautification of life without fear from what tomorrow might bring, as tomorrow does not hold but security for those who are just or lean toward justice.

In the course of its struggle for the establishment of peace on the land of love and peace, the State of Palestine calls on the United Nations—which shoulders a special responsibility toward the Palestinian Arab people and its homeland—and calls on the peoples of the world and their peace and freedom–loving states to assist it to realize its aims and put an end to the tragedy of its people by providing it with security and by working to end the Israeli occupation of the Palestinian lands.

It also declares in this respect that it believes in the settlement of international and regional problems by peaceful means according to the UN Charter and its resolutions, and that it rejects threats to use force, violence, or terrorism or to use these against its territorial integrity and its political independence or the territorial integrity of any other state, without infringing its own natural right to defend its own territories and independence.

On this immortal day—15 November 1988—while standing on the threshold of a new era, we solemnly bow out of respect before the spirits of our martyrs and the martyrs of the Arab nation, who with their pure blood lit the torch of this stubborn dawn and were martyred so the homeland could live, and raise our hearts on our palms to fill them with the light coming from the blessed intifada and from the epic of those standing their ground in the camps, in diaspora, and in exile and those carrying the standard of freedom—our children, our old people, and our youth, as well as our people who have been taken prisoner, our detainees, and our wounded who are living on the sacred soil in every camp, in every village, and in every town, and the brave Palestinian woman—the guardian of our existence and our life and the guardian of our eternal fire.

We vow to our heroic martyrs and the masses of our Palestinian Arab people, our Arab nation, and all the upright free men in the world to continue the struggle for the removal of occupation and entrenching sovereignty and independence.

We call on our great people to rally around their Palestinian flag—to rally around their Palestinian flag and to take pride in it and defend it so it will remain forever a symbol of our freedom and our dignity in a homeland that will always remain a free homeland of a nation of free men.

In the name of God the merciful, the compassionate. Say: O God! Lord of power. Thou givest power to whom thou pleasest and thou strippest power from whom thou pleasest; thou embuest with honor whom thou pleasest and thou bringest low whom thou pleasest. In thy hand is all good; verily over all things thou hast power.

Appendix XIII

Palestine National Council, Political Statement, Algiers, November 15, 1988

In the name of God, the merciful, the compassionate.

On heroic Algerian territory, and with the hospitality of its people and President Chadli Benjedid, the PNC held its extraordinary 19th session. This was the session of the uprising and national independence, the session of the heroic martyr Abu Jihad [Khalil al-Wazir], that lasted from 12 to 15 November 1988. It was crowned by the declaration of the establishment of the Palestinian state on our Palestinian territory. This is the natural coronation of a popular, daring, and stubborn struggle which has continued for more than 70 years and is characterized by great sacrifices of our people in the homeland, on its borders, and in all the camps and areas of the diaspora. The session was characterized by its planning for the great national Palestinian uprising—the most prominent militant event in the contemporary history of the Palestinian people's revolution, alongside the epic and mythical steadfastness of our people in their camps inside and outside our occupied territory.

Ever since the first days of the uprising and during the 12 months of its continuation, the basic outlines of our people's great uprising were clarified. It is a comprehensive popular revolution manifesting the unanimity of the nation—men and women, children and elderly, camps, villages, and cities—to reject the occupation and to struggle to overthrow and end it.

This great uprising unveiled the deeply entrenched national unity of our people and their total rallying round the PLO, the sole legitimate representative of our people—all our people—in all their places of concentration inside and outside the homeland. This has been manifested in the participation of the Palestinian masses—all the national, professional, student, workers, women, peasant, businessmen, landlord, vocational, academic union, and institutional sectors—in the uprising through the United Leadership of the Uprising and the popular committees which have been formed in all city districts, villages, and camps. . . . In light of all this, in order to consolidate the steadfastness of our people and their blessed uprising, in response to the will of our masses in the occupied homeland and abroad, and in faithfulness to the martyrs, wounded, and detainees, the PNC decides:

I. In the field of the continuation and escalation of the uprising:
   A. To secure all means and capabilities to step up the uprising of our people on all levels and by all means to guarantee its continuation and escalation.
   B. To support mass institutions and organizations in the occupied Palestinian territories.
   C. To consolidate and promote the popular committees and mass and specialized trade organizations in order to increase their effectiveness and role, including the strike forces and the popular army.

D. To affirm the national unity, which consecrated and manifested itself splendidly during the uprising.

E. To intensify work on the international scene to release the detainees, repatriate the deportees, and end the acts of organized and institutionalized oppression and terrorism against our children, women, men, and institutions.

F. To call on the United Nations to place the occupied Palestinian territories under international supervision to protect our masses and to end the Israeli occupation.

G. To call on the Palestinian masses outside the homeland to increase their support and consecrate the feeling of family solidarity.

H. To call on the Arab nation—its masses, forces, institutions, and governments—to increase their political, material, and media support for the uprising.

I. To call on all honorable and free men in the entire world to support our masses, revolution, and uprising to confront the Israeli occupation, its means of oppression, and its Fascist formal organized military terrorism, perpetrated by the occupation army, armed men, and fanatic settlers against our masses, universities, schools, institutions, national economy, and Islamic and Christian holy places.

II. In the political field, and in light of all the aforementioned, the PNC—from a position of responsibility toward our Palestinian people, their national rights, and their desire for peace; based on the declaration of independence issued on 15 November 1988; and in response to the human will that seeks to consolidate international detente, eliminate nuclear arms, and settle regional conflicts by peaceful means—stresses the determination of the PLO to reach a comprehensive political settlement to the Arab-Israeli conflict and its crux—the Palestinian question—within the framework of the UN Charter, the provisions and principles of international legitimacy, the rules of international law, and the UN resolutions, including UN Security Council Resolutions Nos. 605, 607, and 608, and the Arab summit resolutions. The PNC stresses its determination in a manner that guarantees the Palestinian Arab people's right to repatriation, self-determination, and the establishment of their independent national state on their national soil, and in a manner that will ensure security and peace arrangements for all the countries in the region. To attain this, the PNC stresses the following:

1. The need to convene an effective international conference on the Middle East, with the Palestinian issue as the prime

topic. The conference should be convened under UN supervision with the participation of the UN Security Council permanent members, and all the parties to the conflict in the region, including the PLO—the Palestinian people's sole and legitimate representative—on an equal footing. The premise on which the international conference is convened is the basis of Security Council Resolutions 242 and 338 and guaranteeing the legitimate national rights of the Palestinian people, foremost being the right to self-determination in accordance with the principles and provisions of the UN Charter on the peoples' right to self-determination, the impermissibility of seizing the lands of others by force or by armed invasion, and accordance with the UN resolution on the Palestinian cause.

2. Israel's withdrawal from all the Palestinian and Arab territories it has occupied since 1967, including Arab Jerusalem.

3. Cancellation of all the attachment [ilhaq] and annexation measures, the removal of settlements Israel has set up on Palestinian and Arab territories occupied since 1967.

4. Endeavoring to place the occupied Palestinian territories, including Arab Jerusalem, under UN supervision for a specific period of time to protect our people and to create a suitable atmosphere which would render the international conference a success, lead to a comprehensive political settlement, and achieve peace and security for everyone through mutual agreement and consent to enable the Palestinian state to exercise its real authority over these territories.

5. Resolution of the issue of the Palestinian refugees in accordance with the UN resolutions in this respect.

6. Securing freedom of worship and of the performance of religious rites in the holy places in Palestine for the followers of all the religions.

7. The UN Security Council shall enact and guarantee security and peace arrangements among all the countries concerned in the region, including the Palestinian state.

The PNC reaffirms its previous resolutions on the unique relationship between the two fraternal people, the Jordanian and Palestinian people. The future relationship between the states of Jordan and Palestine will be established on confederal bases and also on the basis of a free and voluntary choice by the two fraternal people to entrench the historical bonds and the vital interests that they commonly share.

The PNC reiterates its abidance by the UN resolutions that acknowledge the peoples' right to resist foreign occupation, colonialism, and racial discrimination, as well as their right to struggle for their independence. The PNC also reiterates its rejection of terrorism in all its forms, including institutionalized terrorism, stressing its commitment to its previous resolutions in this respect, to the resolution of the Arab summit in Algeria in 1988, UN Resolution 159/42 of the 1967, Resolution 40/61 of 1985, and the contents of the Cairo Declaration issued on 7 November 1985 in this respect.

III. In both the Arab and international fields, the PNC affirms the importance of the unity of the land, people, and institutions of Lebanon and of standing firmly against attempts to partition the territory and scatter the fraternal Lebanese people. It also affirms the importance of joint Arab efforts to resolve the Lebanese crisis which contribute toward crystallizing and implementing solutions that preserve its unity. The PNC also affirms the importance of entrenching the right of the Palestinian citizens in Lebanon to practice their political and media activities, to enjoy security and protection, to work toward eliminating all forms of conspiracy and aggression that target them, to give them the right to work, live, provide them with all the conditions that ensure that they can defend themselves, and provide for their security and protection.

The PNC also affirms its solidarity with the Lebanese nationalist Islamic forces in their struggle against the Israeli occupation and its agents in southern Lebanon. It also expresses its pride in the solidarity struggle between the Lebanese and Palestinian people in confronting the aggression and ending the Israeli occupation of parts of the south. It affirms the importance of strengthening this solidarity between our masses and the struggling fraternal Lebanese masses.

On this occasion, the PNC sends greetings of appreciation to the steadfast in Lebanon's camps and in the south against aggression, murder, starvation, massacres, destruction, air raids, shelling, and siege, which the Israeli Forces, Air Force, and Navy are practicing against the Palestinian camps and Lebanese villages, where they are helped in that by the agent forces in the region. The PNC rejects the resettlement policy because the Palestinian homeland is in Palestine.

The PNC also affirms the importance of the ceasefire resolution between Iran and Iraq to establish a permanent peace between the two countries in the Gulf region. It calls for strengthening the exerted efforts so that the peace negotiations will succeed and become established on stable and firm bases. On this occasion, the PNC affirms the Palestinian Arab people's and all the Arab nations' pride in fraternal Iraq's steadfastness and victories while defending the eastern gate of the Arab nation. The PNC also expresses its deep pride in the

211

support by the masses of our Arab nation for our Palestinian Arab people's struggle, the PLO, and our people's uprising in the occupied territories.

It affirms the importance of strengthening the militant relations between the forces, parties, and organizations of the liberation movements in the Arab world in defense of the rights of the Arab nation and its masses, development, democracy, and unity, and to take all measures to ensure the unity of the struggle among parties of the Arab liberation movements. The council, while addressing its greetings and thanks to the Arab countries for their support to our people's struggle, appeals to them to fulfill their commitments decided at the Algiers summit: to support the struggle of the Palestinian people and their blessed uprising.

As the council directs this appeal, it expresses its great confidence that the leaders of the Arab nation shall remain, as we know them, supportive of Palestine and its people. The PNC reiterates its appeal to the PLO toward using Arab unity as a framework which will order the efforts of the Arab nation and its countries to confront Israeli aggression and U.S. support of this aggression, and to strengthen the Arab position and required role to influence international policies for the benefit of Arab rights and issues.

The PNC directs its deep thanks to all international countries, powers, and organizations that support the Palestinian national rights and affirms its concern to strengthen the bonds of friendship and cooperation with the friendly Soviet Union, the friendly PRC, the socialist countries, nonaligned countries, Islamic countries, African countries, Latin American countries, and other friendly nations.

The PNC notes with satisfaction aspects of the positive development in the positions of some West European countries and Japan on unique support for the Palestinian people's rights. The PNC greets this development and calls for reinforcing efforts to deepen it.

The PNC reiterates the fraternal solidarity of the Palestinian people and the PLO with the struggle of the peoples in Asia, Africa, and Latin America to achieve their liberation and reinforce their independence. The PNC denounces all U.S. attempts to threaten the independence of Central American countries and to interfere in their affairs.

The PNC expresses the PLO's support for the national liberation movements in Southern Africa and Namibia under the leadership of SWAPO. A special greeting is addressed to Brother Struggler Nelson Mandela against the racist Pretoria regime. The PNC calls for allowing the peoples of both countries to achieve their freedom and independence.

The PNC also expresses support for the African confrontation states and its condemnation of the aggressions of the South African racist regime against them.

While the PNC is monitoring with concern the expansion of the Zionist fascist and extremist forces and the escalation of their open call for implementing the policy of annihilation and the individual and collective expulsion of our people from their homeland, the PNC calls for intensifying the work and efforts in all arenas to confront this fascist danger.

At the same time, the PNC expresses its appreciation for the role and courage of the Israeli peace forces in confronting and exposing the forces of fascism, racism, and aggression and for their support for our people's uprising and their brave uprising, and for their support for our people's right to self-determination and the establishment of their independent state. The PNC reiterates its previous resolutions on reinforcing and developing the relationship with these democratic forces.

The PNC also appeals to various quarters of the American people to work to stop the U.S. Administration's policy that disavows the Palestinian people's national rights, including their sacred right to self-determination. The PNC appeals to all sectors of the American people to work to adopt policies that are identical with the legitimacy of human rights and the international charters and resolutions to serve the efforts to achieve peace in the Middle East and to provide security for all peoples, including the Palestinian people.

The council empowers the Executive Committee to complete the measures to form the committee for commemorating the symbol martyr Abu Jihad [Khalil al-Wazir] so that the committee will begin its work immediately after the conclusion of the PNC's work.

The council extends special greetings to the UN Committee for the Palestinian People's Exercise of Their Inalienable Rights, international institutions and organizations, fraternal and friendly nongovernmental organizations, media people, and all the media that backed our people's uprising and struggle.

The PNC, while expressing its profound pain over the continued detention of hundreds of strugglers from among the sons of our people in several Arab countries and strongly denouncing their continued detention, calls on these countries to put an end to these anomalous conditions and to release these strugglers so they can play their role in the struggle.

Finally, the PNC expresses its full confidence that the justice of the Palestinian cause and the demands for which the Palestinian people are struggling will continue to gain the support of free and honorable people in the whole world. It also affirms its full confidence in complete victory on the path to Jerusalem, the capital of our independent Palestinian state. . . .

Appendix XIV

PLO Chairman Yasser Arafat, Speech to the UN General Assembly, Geneva, December 13, 1988

Mr. Chairman and Members: It never occurred to me that my second meeting since 1974 with this esteemed assembly would take place in the hospitable city of Geneva.

I believed that the position and the new political stands which our Palestinian people had adopted during the PNC meeting in Algiers, all of which were announced amid great international appreciation and welcome, would have behooved me to go to the UN Headquarters in New York to acquaint you with our resolutions and views regarding the cause of peace in our homeland as formulated by our PNC, which is the highest legislative authority in the Palestinian political body.

Therefore, my meeting with you in Geneva today after an unjust U.S. decision which prevented me from going to you there is a cause of my pride and joy. My pride stems from the fact that I am with you and among you because you are the main platform for all issues of right and justice in the world.

My joy derives from the fact that I am present in Geneva where justice and neutrality are words on all tongues and are a constitution in a world in which the arrogance of the strong make them lose their neutrality and sense of justice.

Consequently, the resolution issued by your esteemed assembly, with the concurrence of 154 states to hold this meeting, was not a victory over the U.S. decision but a victory for the international unanimity in upholding right and the cause of peace in an unparalleled referendum. It is also evident that our people's just cause has taken root in the fabric of the human conscience.

Our Palestinian people will not forget this noble stand by your esteemed assembly and those friendly states in support of right and justice to safeguard the values and principles for which the United Nations was established. This stand will be translated into feelings of

214

confidence and reassurance by all peoples who suffer injustice, co-ercion, and occupation, and who are, like our Palestinian people, struggling for freedom, dignity, and life.

On this occasion, I express the deepest thanks to all the countries, forces, international organizations, and world personalities that have supported our people and backed their national rights, particularly the friends in the Soviet Union, the PRC, the socialist countries, the nonaligned countries, the Islamic countries, the African countries, the Asian countries, the Latin American countries, and all the other friendly countries.

I also thank the countries of Western Europe and Japan for their recent stands toward our people. I call on them to take more steps on the course of positive development of these decisions in order to open the vistas for peace and the just solution in our region, the Middle East region.

I also underline our solidarity with and backing for the liberation movements in Namibia and South Africa in their struggle, and also our support for the African confrontation states against the aggressions of the racist South African regime.

I take this opportunity too to express my thanks and gratitude to the friendly countries that have supported us and backed our PNC resolutions, and also recognized the State of Palestine.

I also thank His Excellency UN Secretary General Javier Perez de Cuellar and his assistants for their constant efforts to achieve the international detente sought by humanity and solutions for world problems, particularly those concerning the Palestinian issue.

I also express my thanks and appreciation to the chairman and members of the committee on the Palestinian peoples' exercise of their inalienable rights for their efforts toward our peoples' cause. I also greet and thank the nine-member committee of the nonaligned countries on the Palestinian issue for all its constructive work for our peoples' cause.

To you, Mr. Chairman, I express the warmest greetings on the occasion of your election as chairman of this assembly. I am fully confident of your wisdom and knowledge. I also greet your predecessor for his noble chairmanship of the former session.

Last, I express my greetings and deep thanks to the Swiss Government and people for the great help, facilities, and efforts they have extended for this session.

Mr. Chairman, members, on 13 November 1974—14 years ago— I received with gratitude an invitation from you to present the cause of our Palestinian people before this esteemed Assembly. Now I return to you here after all these years, which were fraught with grave events, to see that new peoples have taken their places among you, thus crowning their victories in the battles of freedom and independence.

To the representatives of these peoples I extend the warm congratulations of our people and to everyone I announce that I return to you with a louder voice, stronger determination, and greater confidence to emphasize that our struggle must bear fruit and that the State of Palestine, which we proclaimed in our National Council, must take its place among you, so it could take part with you in consolidating the charter of this organization and the human rights convention, in putting an end to the tragedies to which humanity is being subjected, and in laying down the bases of right, justice, peace, and freedom for all, for all, for all.

Fourteen years ago, when you said to us in the General Assembly hall yes to Palestine and the Palestinian people; yes to the PLO; and yes to the firm national rights of the Palestinian people, some thought your decisions would have hardly any effect. They failed to realize these decisions were among the most important springs that have watered the olive branch that I carried on that day. This branch, after we had it watered with blood, sweat, and tears, has become a tree whose root is in the ground and its branches in the sky, promising the yields of victory over repression, injustice, and occupation.

You have given us hope for the victory of freedom and justice and we have given you a generation from the sons of our people that have devoted their lifetime to achieving this dream. It is the generation of the blessed uprising which today is carrying the stones of the homeland to defend the honor of this homeland, so it can be worthy of belonging to a people that yearn for freedom and independence. Greetings to all of you from the sons of our hero people—men and women—and from the masses of our blessed uprising, which enters its 2d year with huge momentum, meticulously planned tactics, and a democratic civilized method in confronting the occupation, oppression, injustice, and the bestial crimes which the Israeli occupiers are committing against them daily.

Greetings to you from our male and female youths in occupation prisons and mass detention camps. Greetings to you from the stone-throwing children, who are challenging the occupation and its aircraft, tanks, and weaponry, reminiscent of the new image of the defenseless Palestinian David versus the heavily-armed Israeli Goliath.

At the conclusion of my speech during our first meeting I said that as chairman of the PLO and leader of the Palestinian revolution, we emphasize our desire not to see a drop of Jewish or Arab blood spilled. We also do not want to continue the fighting for 1 more minute. At that time I appealed to you to end all this suffering and pain and to hasten to draw up the basis for the just peace based on the guarantee of our peoples' rights, aspirations, and hopes and the right of all peoples.

At that time I appealed to you to support the struggle of our people to exercise their right to self-determination to enable our people to return from their compulsory exile to which they had been pushed under bayonets of rifles and to help us end this injustice which generations of our people have been suffering for several decades so they could live free and sovereign in their homeland and country while enjoying all their national and human rights.

The last thing I said from this platform is that war erupts from Palestine and that peace starts in Palestine. Our dream then was to set up the democratic state of Palestine, in which Muslims, Christians, and Jews would live on an equal footing, in terms of rights and duties, under a single, unified society, similar to other peoples on this earth and in our contemporary world.

We were greatly astonished when we saw Israeli officials interpreting this Palestinian dream—which is inspired by the legacy of the heavenly messages that have illuminated the skies of Palestine and by the civilized and humane values that call for coexistence in a free and democratic society—as a scheme that aims to destroy and annihilate their entity.

It is our duty, Mr. Chairman, to learn a lesson from this difficult situation and to note the distance between this situation and the dream. We, in the PLO, began searching for the realistic alternative formulas, which are applicable, to find a solution to the question based on the possible and not absolute justice which would guarantee our peoples' rights to freedom, sovereignty, and independence; guarantee peace, security, and stability to all; and avoid the Palestine and Middle East wars and battles which have, regrettably, been going on for 40 years.

Mr. Chairman, did we not adopt the UN Charter and its resolutions, the human rights declaration, and international legitimacy as a basis for solving the Arab-Israeli conflict? Did we not welcome the 1977 Vance-Gromyko declaration as an initiative which could serve as a basis for a plan to solve this conflict?

Did we not agree to participate in the Geneva conference in accordance with the 1977 Egyptian-U.S. statement to advance the process of peace and solution in our region? Did we not adopt the 1982 Fes Arab peace plan and later the call for an international peace conference under the auspices of the United Nations and according to its resolutions?

Did we not support Brezhnev's peace plan for the Middle East? Did we not welcome and support the statement issued by the EC countries in Venice concerning the establishment of just peace in the region?

Did we not welcome and support the initiative of Presidents Gorbachev and Mitterrand concerning the preparatory committee for an international conference?

Did we not welcome scores of political statements and initiatives put forward by African, Muslim, nonaligned, socialist, European, and other nations with the aim of finding a peaceful settlement, in accordance with the principles of international law and with the goal of establishing peace and resolving the conflict?

What was Israel's reaction to all that? Please note that all these peace initiatives, plans, and statements to which I have referred were evenhanded. None of these initiatives ignored the demands and interests of any of the parties involved in the Arab-Israeli conflict.

Israel reacted to all that by building more settlements, by escalating its expansionist policies, and by exacerbating the conflict. Israel engaged in a policy of destruction and bloodshed and widened the front of hostility to include brotherly Lebanon.

The occupation armies of Israel swept over Lebanon in 1982. The invasion of Lebanon was accompanied by the slaughter and massacre of the Lebanese and Palestinian people, including the Sabra and Shatila massacres. Israel is still at this moment occupying a part of the Lebanese south. Lebanon is daily coming under Israeli land, air, and sea attacks and raids against its towns and villages, a fate shared by our camps in the south of that country.

It is painful and regrettable that the U.S. Government alone should continue to back and support these Israeli expansionist and aggressive plans; support Israel's continuing occupation of Palestinian and Arab territory; and support its crimes and iron-fist policy against our children and women.

It also is sad and painful that the U.S. Government should continue to refuse to recognize the right of 6 million Palestinians to self-determination. This is a sacred right to the American people themselves and all the peoples of earth.

I remind them of President Wilson's stand, the architect of the two universal principles in international relations; namely, the inadmissibility of the occupation of the territories of others by force and the right of peoples to self-determination.

When the Palestinian people were consulted in 1919 by the King-Crane Commission, they chose the United States of America as the mandate country. But circumstances prevented this and Britain took its place.

I ask the American people; I ask the American people: Is it right, is it right that what President Wilson had decreed should not be applied to the Palestinian people? The subsequent U.S. Administrations know that the only birth certificate for the establishment of the State of Israel is international Resolution 181, which was issued by the UN General Assembly on 29 November 1947.

At that time, the United States and the Soviet Union approved this resolution. It stipulates the establishment of two states in Palestine—a Palestinian Arab state and a Jewish state.

How could the U.S. Government explain its stand, which acknowledges and recognizes the same resolution which pertains to Israel, while it simultaneously rejects the other half of this resolution which pertains to the Palestinian state?

How could the U.S. Government explain its noncommitment to implementing a resolution which it had repeatedly sponsored at your esteemed Assembly, Resolution 194, which provides for the Palestinians' right to return to their homeland and property from which they were expelled or to compensate those who do not wish to return.

The U.S. Government is aware that it is neither its right nor the right of others to divide international legitimacy and disintegrate the provisions of international laws.

Mr. Chairman and members of the Assembly, the continuing struggle of our people for the sake of their rights dates back scores of years, during which our people have presented hundreds of thousands of martyrs and wounded and suffered all kinds of tragic tortures. But these people have not relented and their determination has not faltered. But, rather, it has consolidated their determination to cling to their Palestinian homeland and to their national identity.

Israel's leaders, who were taken by deceptive intoxication, believed that, after our departure from Beirut, the sea would swallow the PLO. They did not expect that the departure into oblivion would turn into a road leading back to the homeland, the real arena of the struggle, and to occupied Palestine. The valiant popular uprising inside our occupied land broke out and will continue until our goals of freedom and national independence are realized.

I have the honor, Mr. Chairman, of being one of the sons of these people who record with the blood of their children, women, and men the most splendid epics of national resistance and who create daily miracles of which legends are made so that their uprising will continue and so this uprising will develop and grow stronger until they impose their willpower and until they prove that right can defeat might.

I extend greetings of admiration to the masses of our people who are now making this unique revolutionary and democratic experiment. Their faith has not been shaken by all of Israel's war machine, has not been terrorized by all kinds of bullets, and has not been affected by people being buried alive or having their bones broken, or by causing pregnant women to abort, or by the seizure of water sources.

The masses' resolution has not been weakened by detention, imprisonment, deportation, and expulsion outside the homeland. The collective punishment and demolition of houses, the closing of universities, schools, trade unions, societies and establishments, the suspension of newspapers, and the besieging of camps, villages, and cities have only established this faith more firmly. The revolution has spread to every house and taken root in every inch of the homeland's soil.

A people with such conduct and history cannot be defeated. All forces of repression and terrorism cannot dissuade the people from their firm belief in their right to their homeland and in the values of justice, peace, love, and tolerant coexistence.

The rebel's rifle has protected us and precluded our liquidation and the destruction of our national identity in the fields of hot confrontation. We are fully confident of our ability to protect the biggest olive branch in the fields of political confrontation.

That the world is rallying around our just cause to achieve just peace brilliantly indicates that the world realizes in no vague terms who is the executioner and who is the victim, who is the aggressor and who is aggressed upon, and who is the struggler for freedom and peace and who is the terrorist.

The daily practices of the occupation army's forces and fanatic armed settlers' gangs against our people, children, and women expose the ugly face and aggressive nature of the Israeli occupation.

This growing world awareness has affected the Jewish societies themselves inside and outside Israel. It has opened these societies' eyes to the reality of the problem and essence of the conflict, particularly to the inhuman daily Israeli practices which destroy the very spirit of the tolerant Jewish religion itself.

It has become difficult and almost impossible for a Jew to declare his rejection of racial oppression and his adherence to freedom and human rights while remaining silent over Israel's crimes and violations of the rights of the Palestinian man, the Palestinian people, and

220

the Palestinian homeland, particularly over the abominable daily practices of the occupiers and gangs of armed settlers.

Mr. Chairman: We differentiate between the Jewish citizen whose awareness of his conscience have been subject to the Israeli ruling circles' continual efforts to obliterate and falsify and between the practices of Israel's leaders.

Furthermore, we realize that both inside and outside Israel there are honorable and courageous Jews who do not agree with the Government of Israel over the policy of repression, massacres, expansion, settlement, and deportation and who admit the equal rights of our people for life, freedom, and independence. In the name of the Palestinian people, I thank them, thank them, thank them for this courageous and frank position.

Our people do not want any right to which they are not entitled and which is not compatible with international legality and laws. They are not seeking any freedom that encroaches upon the freedom of others or any destiny that cancels the destiny of another people.

Our people refuse to be more privileged than others, or for others to be more privileged than they are. Our people want equality with all other peoples, having the same rights and obligations.

Today I address this appeal to all the people of the world, particularly those who have suffered from the Nazi occupation and who have believed it to be their duty to turn the page of repression and injustice by any people against another and to extend help to all the victims of terrorism, fascism, and Nazism, so that they could clearly see the responsibilities dictated by history upon them toward our suffering people, who want a place under the sun for their children in their homeland, in which they could live like the rest of the children of the world.

They want a place under the sun for their children in their homeland in which they can live like the rest of the children of the world, free on their liberated land.

Mr. Chairman, members, it is a cause for optimism that our march of struggle has climaxed into the ongoing uprising at a time when the international climate is one of earnest detente and prosperity.

We have been following with great satisfaction the successes of the United Nations and the UN secretary general in bringing about solutions to many problems and in many areas of tension in the world in this new atmosphere of international detente.

The improvement in the international atmosphere cannot be consolidated without attention being paid to regional problems and areas of tension. We need to forge a human conscience that is more

221

sensitive and responsible in assessing the efforts of man and the policies of nations and more capable of carrying us into the next century.

We have new challenges and responsibilities to face away from, away from wars and destruction, and for more, for more freedom, prosperity, peace, and progress for all mankind.

Mr. Chairman, it is indisputable that the Palestinian issue is the most complicated problem of our time. It is the earliest problem on UN records, the most intricate issue, and the most menacing to international peace and security.

Therefore, the Palestinian issue, more than any other international problem, should be a reason of concern to the two superpowers and other world nations. Efforts should be made to find a solution to this issue. A just solution of the Palestinian problem would be the best guarantee for peace in the Middle East.

The PLO leadership, as it is responsible for the Palestinian people and its future, faithful to the struggle of the Palestinian people, loyal to the memory of the martyrs, responsive to the atmosphere of detente, aware of the need to engage in peaceful political efforts, and desirous of a political solution ending the course of war and fighting and opening the door to a peaceful existence governed by the norms of international law, had called the PNC for an extraordinary session in Algiers from 12 to 15 November of this year.

The goal was to define and clarify our position as a major party to the Arab-Israeli conflict; a party without the participation and endorsement of which a solution to this conflict cannot be achieved.

I am pleased to tell you with full pride that our National Council, through full democratic practice and under complete freedom, has once again proven its ability to shoulder its supreme national responsibilities and has made serious, constructive, and responsible decisions that have paved the way for deepening and showing our desire and our contribution toward finding a peaceful settlement that guarantees the national and political rights of our people and that ensures security and peace for everyone.

Mr. Chairman, the first and decisive resolution taken by our National Council was the declaration of the establishment of the Palestinian state with holy Jerusalem as its capital on the basis of the natural, historic, and legal right of the Palestinian Arab people to their homeland and the sacrifices of successive generations in defense of their homeland's freedom and independence.

It also stems from the resolutions of the Arab summits and from the strength of international legitimacy which is embodied by the UN resolutions since 1947. It is the Palestinian Arab people's exercise of their right to self-determination, political independence, and sovereignty over their land in accordance with your successive resolutions.

I would like to reiterate before the international community that this historic resolution—now that it has become an official UN document—is irreversible and that we will not stop to work until the occupation ends and our people exercise their sovereignty in their own state—the State of Palestine for all Palestinians wherever they are.

In this state they can develop their national and cultural identity, enjoy full equality of rights, and have their religious and political beliefs and their human dignity upheld in a democratic parliamentary system, established on the basis of freedom of opinion, the formation of parties, due regard by the majority for the rights of the minority, respect by the minority for the decisions of the majority, social justice and equality, and nondiscrimination on the basis of race, religion, or color or between man and woman under a constitution that imposes legal supremacy—legal supremacy—and an independent judiciary and on the basis of full loyalty to Palestine's spiritual and cultural heritage of tolerance and generous coexistence among religions throughout the centuries.

The State of Palestine is an Arab state and its people constitute a part of their Arab nation in terms of heritage, culture, and hopes regarding social development, unity, and liberation. This state abides by the Arab League Charter, UN principles, the International Declaration of Human Rights, and principles of nonalignment.

It is a peaceloving state committed to the principles of peaceful coexistence and to working alongside all countries and peoples to establish a just, lasting peace based on justice and a respect of rights.

It is a state which believes in the settlement of international and regional problems through peaceful means in accordance with the UN Charter and resolutions.

It rejects threats of violence, force, or terrorism against its territorial integrity and political independence and the territorial integrity of any other state, as well as any encroachment on its natural rights to defend its territories and independence.

It is a state which believes that the future will only bring security to those who acted justly and even those who renounced justice. This, Mr. Chairman, is the State of Palestine, which we had proclaimed and which we will consolidate so it will assume its position among world countries and participate and excel in forming a free world in which justice will prevail and in which peace will be enjoyed.

Our state will have its own provisional government at the nearest possible opportunity, God willing.

The PNC has entrusted the PLO Executive Committee with the obligation of assuming the tasks of this provisional government until it is formed. To implement this decision, the PNC adopted several important decisions which emphasize our determination to seriously forge ahead in the just, peaceful settlement process and to exert utmost efforts to render it a success.

Our National Council stressed the need to convene an international conference on the Middle East problem, whose core is the issue of Palestine, under UN auspices and with the participation of the states which are permanent members of the Security Council and all parties to the conflict in the region including the PLO, the sole legitimate representative of the Palestinian people, on an equal footing since the international conference will convene in accordance with Security Council Resolutions 242 and 338 and on the basis of the guarantee of the national, political, legitimate rights of the Palestinian people, foremost being their right to self-determination.

Our National Council also has emphasized that Israel must withdraw from all Palestinian and Arab territories which it has occupied since 1967, including Arab Jerusalem—including Arab Jerusalem; that the Palestinian state must be set up; that all the annexation decisions must be cancelled; and that the settlements which Israel has established in the Palestinian and Arab territories since 1967 must be removed. The Arab summits, particularly the Fes and Algiers summits, have endorsed this.

Our National Council has asserted that endeavors must be launched to place the occupied Palestinian territories, including Arab Jerusalem, under the supervision of the United Nations for a limited period to defend our people and to create the appropriate atmosphere to ensure the success of the activities of an international conference, to achieve a comprehensive political settlement, and to establish peace and security for all the peoples and states in the Middle East with their mutual consent to enable the State of Palestine to exercise its actual powers in these territories. This also has been emphasized by the resolutions adopted at Arab summits.

Our council also has emphasized the need to settle the issue of the Palestinian refugees in accordance with UN resolutions. It also has emphasized that freedom of worship and performance of religious rites in holy places in Palestine will be guaranteed to the followers of all religions.

The National Council has reaffirmed its previous decisions regarding the distinguished and special relationship between the two fraternal Jordanian and Palestinian peoples.

It affirmed the future relationship between the State of Palestine and the Hashemite Kingdom of Jordan will be established on a con-federal basis and on the basis of a voluntary and free choice of the two fraternal peoples to strengthen the historical bonds and vital interests between them.

The council reasserted the need for the Security Council to lay down and guarantee the security and peace arrangements among all the states concerned with the conflict in the region.

I would like to point out here, Mr. Chairman, that these decisions reflect—as is clear from their contents and phraseology—our firm conviction with regard to peace and freedom and with regard to our deep understanding and appreciation of the climate of the international rapprochement and detente and of the eagerness of the world community to achieve balanced solutions responding to the basic interests and demands of the parties to the conflict.

These decisions also reflect the seriousness of the Palestinian stand toward the issue of peace, its eagerness for it, and the need to guarantee and ensure it through the Security Council and under the supervision of the United Nations.

These decisions carry the clear-cut and decisive answer to all the excuses, preconditions, and pretexts which some countries have used with respect to the positions and policy of the PLO.

At a time when our people have been voting for peace through their uprising and their representatives in the PNC and at a time when our PNC has been voting for peace, stressing its response to the prevailing trend which is being strengthened by the era of new detente in international relations to resolve world conflicts through peaceful means, the Israeli Government is nourishing aggressive and expansionist tendencies and religious fanaticism to stress its adherence to the option of aggression and of ignoring our peoples' right.

The Palestinian side, for its part, has formulated clear-cut and responsible political stands that are in line with the will of the international community, in a bid to help convene an international peace conference and to ensure its success.

The courageous international support, as demonstrated by the recognition of the State of Palestine, which we appreciate, constitutes irrefutable evidence of the soundness of our course, the credibility of our decisions, and their compatibility with the international peace-loving will.

Despite our great appreciation for the free U.S. voices which have hastened to explain and support our positions and decisions, the U.S. Administration, however, still has no unified criterion to apply toward the parties to the conflict, requiring us alone to adopt positions that cannot be decided [la yumkin hasmaha] before negotiations and dialogue start within the framework of an international conference.

I would like to state that acknowledging the equality and rights of the two parties to the conflict, on a mutual basis, is the sole prelude toward answering the clarifications requested by any quarter. If the policies and deeds are any indication of intentions, the Palestinian party has a better reason to worry and demand clarifications and assurances about its destiny and future with regard to the State of Israel, which is armed with the most modern weapons, including nuclear weapons.

Mr. Chairman, members, our PNC has reiterated its adherence to UN resolutions endorsing the right of nations to resist foreign occupation, imperialism, and racial discrimination, as well as the right of nations to struggle for freedom.

The PNC reiterated its rejection of terrorism; it reiterated its rejection of terrorism of all kinds—of terrorism of all kinds, including state terrorism—including state terrorism.

In this respect, the PNC underscored its commitment to its own previous resolutions, to the resolutions of the Arab summit in Algiers in 1988, to UN Resolutions 159/42 for 1987 and 40/61 for 1985, and to the Cairo Declaration issued on 7 November 1985 in this regard.

Our position, Mr. Chairman, is clear and unambiguous. However, I, in my capacity as chairman of the PLO, declare from here once more—declare from here once more:

I condemn terrorism in all its forms, but, I, at the same time, salute all those before me in this hall who have been accused by their executioners and colonialists of being terrorists during the battles for the liberation of their land from the yoke of colonialism. They are today the faithful leaders of their people and sincerely devoted to the principles and values of justice and freedom.

I reverently salute the martyrs who have fallen at the hand of terrorism and terrorists, chief among those being my lifelong comrade, my deputy, Khalil al-Wazir, alias Abu Jihad, and the martyrs of the massacres which were inflicted on our people in many areas, towns, villages, and camps in the West Bank, Gaza Strip, and in south Lebanon.

Mr. Chairman, members, the situation in our Palestinian homeland can no longer be tolerated. The masses of our people, our heroes, are leading the way and holding high the torches of freedom. They die everyday so the occupiers will leave and so peace will be established in their free and independent homeland and in the entire region.

Therefore, the PNC has based its resolutions on a realistic understanding of the conditions of both the Palestinians and the Israelis. The goal of these resolutions is to establish an atmosphere of tolerance between the Palestinians and the Israelis.

The United Nations has a historic and singular obligation toward our people, their cause, and their rights. Over 40 years ago, the United Nations issued Resolution 181 setting up two states in Palestine, as I have mentioned—one to be an Arab Palestinian state and the other a Jewish state.

Today, despite the historic injustice that has been committed against our people, we still see that this resolution continues to provide international legitimacy to the right of the Arab Palestinian people to sovereignty and national independence.

Therefore, the acceleration of the peace process in the region requires additional efforts by all the parties concerned and by international powers, particularly the United States and the Soviet Union, both of which have a great responsibility toward the issue of peace in our region.

The United Nations, the permanent members of the UN Security Council, and all international groups and organizations have a vital and essential role to play at the current stage.

I hereby present the following Palestinian peace initiative in my capacity as the chairman of the PLO Executive Committee, which assumes the tasks of the provisional government of the State of Palestine:

1. Serious work should be undertaken to convene the preparatory committee of an international conference for peace in the Middle East under the auspices of the UN secretary general in accordance with the Gorbachev-Mitterrand initiative, which has been supported by many countries and which President Mitterrand thankfully presented to your Assembly at the end of last September, preparatory to convening an international conference, which is being supported by all the world countries with the exception of the Government of Israel;

2. Proceeding from our faith in the UN's vital role and international legitimacy, we believe the United Nations should assume temporary supervision of our Palestinian land; UN forces should be deployed to protect our people, and, at the same time, the UN forces should supervise the withdrawal of the Israeli forces from our country; and

3. The PLO will work to reach a comprehensive peaceful settlement between the sides involved in the Arab-Israeli struggle, including the State of Palestine and Israel, as well as the other neighboring states, within the framework of an international conference for peace

in the Middle East to realize equality and a balance of interests, particularly the right of our people to freedom and national independence, and the respect of the right to live, and the right of peace and security to everyone; namely, all the sides involved in the struggle in the area in accordance with Resolutions 242 and 338.

In the event these bases are recognized within the framework of such a conference, we would have made a principal stride toward a just solution, which would pave the way toward reaching an agreement over all the security and peace arrangements.

Mr. Chairman, I hope it is clear that to the extent they are eager to attain their legitimate national rights to self-determination and their return and to secure the termination of the occupation of the Palestinian land of their homeland, our Palestinian people also are eager to safeguard the peaceful process so as to achieve these goals within the framework of an international conference under UN auspices and in accordance with its charter and resolutions.

I stress that we are a people who yearn for peace like all the peoples on earth and, perhaps, more enthusiastically, because of our long endurance over the years; because of the harsh life that confronts our people and children; and because of their deprivation of an enjoyable, normal life without wars, tragedies, agonies, displacements, and harsh sufferings in their daily life.

Let the voices be raised in support of the olive branch, the policy of peaceful coexistence, and the climate of international relaxation. Let the hands unite in defense of an historical opportunity, which might not be repeated, to put an end to a long tragedy which has claimed the sacrifices of thousands of souls and resulted in the destruction of hundreds of cities and villages.

When we extend our hand with an olive branch and the peace branch, we do so because this branch stems from the tree of the homeland and freedom planted in our hearts.

Mr. Chairman, members, I have come to you in the name of our people to extend my hand so we may establish the real, just peace.

It is from this premise that I call on the leaders of Israel to come here, to come here, under UN auspices to create this peace. I also tell them that our people want dignity, freedom, and peace. They want peace for their state the same as they want it for all the countries and parties to the Arab-Israeli conflict.

I hereby address greetings to all factions, forces, and sects of the Israelis led by the forces of democracy and peace.

I tell them: Move away from fear and intimidation so we can make peace, make peace, make peace; move away from the specter of the wars of this conflict, which have been raging for 40 years, and away from the flare-up of coming wars, whose fuel would only be their children and our children.

Come, let us make peace. Come let us create peace—the peace of the brave—and move away from the arrogance of the strong and the weapons of destruction, and away from occupation, coercion, humiliation, killing, and torture.

Say: O people of the book, come to common terms to establish peace on the land of peace—the land of Palestine. Glory be to God in the heavens, peace on earth, and joy to the people. God, you are peace, peace is from you, and peace returns to you. Make us live in peace, O Lord, and admit us to paradise, the house of peace [Koranic verses and biblical quote as heard].

Finally, I tell our people: The dawn is coming and victory is coming. I see the homeland represented in your sacred stones.

I see the flag of our independent Palestinian state flying over the hills of the dear homeland. Thanks and God's peace and blessing be with you.

Appendix XV

PLO Chairman Yasser Arafat, Press Conference Statement, Geneva, December 14, 1988

Allow me to explain my viewpoints before you. Our desire for peace is strategic and not a temporary tactic. We work for peace regardless of whatever may happen, whatever may happen.

Our state provides salvation for the Palestinians and peace for both the Palestinians and Israelis. The right to self-determination means the existence of the Palestinians and our existence does not destroy the existence of the Israelis, as their rulers claim.

In my speech yesterday, I referred to UN Resolution No. 181 as a basis for Palestinian independence. I also referred to our acceptance of Resolution 242 and 338 as a basis for negotiations with Israel within the framework of the international conference.

Our PNC accepted these three resolutions at the Algiers session. Also in my speech yesterday, it was clear that we mean our people's rights to freedom and national independence in accordance with Resolution No. 181 as well as the right of all parties concerned with the Middle East conflict to exist in peace and security, including—as I said—the State of Palestine, Israel, and other neighbors in accordance with Resolutions 242 and 338.

Regarding terrorism, yesterday I announced beyond doubt—and nevertheless I repeat for the sake of recording stands, I repeat for the sake of recording stands—that we totally and categorically reject all forms of terrorism, including individual, group, and state terrorism.

We explained our stand in Geneva and Algiers. Any talk to the effect that the Palestinians must offer more—do you remember this slogan—or that what was offered is insufficient or that the Palestinians are playing propaganda games or public relations maneuvers will be harmful and unfruitful. That is enough.

All outstanding issues should be discussed on the table and at the international conference. Let it be perfectly clear that neither Arafat nor anyone else can stop the uprising.

The uprising will stop only when practical and tangible steps are taken toward the attainment of its national goals and establishment of its Palestinian state.

Within this framework, I expect the EEC states to play a more effective role in consolidating peace in our region. They assume a political and moral responsibility and they can deal with this.

Finally, I announce before you and ask you to convey these words on my behalf. We want peace, we want peace, we are committed to peace, we are committed to peace, and we want to live in our Palestinian state and let others live. Thank you.

Appendix XVI

U.S. Secretary of State George Shultz, News Conference Response to Chairman Arafat's Statements, Washington, D.C., December 14, 1988

Opening Statement

The Palestine Liberation Organization today issued a statement in which it accepted UN Security Council Resolutions 242 and 338, recognized Israel's right to exist in peace and security, and renounced terrorism. As a result, the United States is prepared for a substantive dialogue with PLO representatives.

I am designating our Ambassador to Tunisia as the only authorized channel for that dialogue. The objective of the United States remains as always, a comprehensive peace in the Middle East. In that light, I view this development as one more step toward the beginning of direct negotiations between the parties which alone can lead to such a peace.

Nothing here may be taken to imply an acceptance or recognition by the United States of an independent Palestinian state. The position of the U.S. is that the status of the West Bank and Gaza cannot be determined by unilateral acts of either side, but only through a process of negotiations. The United States does not recognize the declaration of an independent Palestinian state.

It is also important to emphasize that the United States commitment to the security of Israel remains unflinching.

Questions and Answers

Q. Mr. Secretary, what was it today that changed your mind?

A. I didn't change my mind, they changed their—they made their statement clear so that it doesn't have the ambiguities in it that earlier statements had, which tended to allow various people to give different interpretations of what was meant.

Q. What was different about it today?

A. It was clear. It was not encumbered.

Q. Mr. Secretary, what about the PLO's record which only two weeks—you decided the terrorism record—you called Arafat an accomplice or accessory to terrorism. You denied him a visa. Are you expunging the PLO record and saying let bygones be bygones?

A. No, when we have our dialogue you can be sure that the first item of business on our agenda in that dialogue will be the subject of terrorism. And we'll make it clear that our position about the importance of the renunciation of terrorism is central.

Q. What can the dialogue do about people who are already dead and what does your statement have—how does your statement bear on the promise Kissinger made the Israelis?

A. The promise that Kissinger made the Israelis, which had to do with 242 and 338 and with the recognition of Israel's right to exist—since that time we have added our insistence on a renunciation of terrorism. Those conditions have been U.S. conditions for a dialogue with the PLO going back to 1975. Our position has not changed. We have stayed with that position consistently. And now today we have an acceptance of those conditions in a clear-cut way.

231

Q. Mr. Secretary, have you told the State of Israel of your intentions, and can you tell us what their response was?

A. Everybody has been put on notice repeatedly for—since 1975, in effect, that if the PLO meets our conditions, then we're prepared for a substantive dialogue. That is well known. Of course we have had communications with Israel, as we have had with other states, and we have been engaged in the last hour or so of trying to call people to tell them explicitly what we are prepared to do now that there is this statement. But I don't want to try to speak for others. I'm only speaking for the United States.

Q. Do you have reason to believe that the Israelis would be willing to sit down with the PLO?

A. No, I don't have any reason to believe that. But all I'm telling you is what the U.S. policies are, and this policy has been in place for—since 1975. And it has been consistently adhered to. And now that we see a change in the posture of the PLO, all we're doing is following through on that policy. Our policy remains unchanged.

Q. Mr. Secretary, do you see this as a symbol meeting—at the beginning of a process in which a series of meetings and aimed at what result? Is it going to be a series of meetings, or where do you want it to go?

A. The meetings are not an end in themselves. Our object is a comprehensive peace, and so our object in any dialogue that we have with the PLO will emphasize our desire for that, and our views of what it takes to get there. I made a speech last September on behalf of the United States and set out our views as a supplement to the views contained in the initiative that we worked on earlier this year. So our object is not a dialogue. Our object is peace. And we will be talking to the PLO, as to others, in an effort to move things along to that objective.

Q. Mr. Secretary, Secretary Kissinger was at the White House this morning. Was that why he was there?

A. No, it wasn't. However, I did talk to Secretary Kissinger since we got the, got word of this development.

Q. Mr. Secretary, your statement at the American Colony was addressed specifically to Palestinians resident in the West Bank and Gaza and not, specifically not to the PLO. Does this dialogue with the PLO now mean that the United States is prepared to address that sort of statement to the PLO leadership as well as to other Palestinians?

A. That was a statement to Palestinians that I made in Jerusalem last spring, as I remember. Do you have the date of it in mind? I forget. It's been some while ago.

Anyway, I sought a meeting with Palestinians and I went to their turf, so to speak. And they would not meet. And of course the word we got was that they were afraid to meet because they were afraid they would be killed if they did. So I went and I made a statement that you referred to, saying here is what I would have told you if you had come. And we issued that statement as a statement of our efforts toward peace and of our recognition which has been consistent. And it's obviously so that if you're going to get to a peaceful settlement in the Middle East you have to include Palestinians in the process from the beginning and at the end. That is clear enough and that was basically what I said.

Q. As a result of this Mr. Secretary, are you going to be willing to talk with Mr. Arafat before you leave office?

A. What I am doing is authorizing our Ambassador in Tunisia to make himself available for a direct dialogue. And we are making it clear that this is the only authorized channel of communication. So anybody else who is representing themselves as a channel, is not a channel. This is the authoritative channel representing the United States Government.

Now what may evolve from this remains to be seen. But I think that when it comes to any genuine substantive discussion, we are in a transition phase and it is basically for the next Administration to decide what they do.

Q. When will the first meeting be held?

A. I don't, we have seen this PLO statement. I'm making this response on behalf of the President. I might say the President, the Vice President agree with this and I'm authorizing now the Ambassador in Tunis to undertake this dialogue. But when there will be a meeting, I don't know.

Q. Mr. Secretary, now that the United States has recognized the PLO as a legitimate partner for negotiations, do you feel that there's any reason for Israel not to negotiate with the PLO?

A. What we are doing as a result of the PLO's meeting our conditions is establishing a substantive dialogue with them. We hope that that dialogue may help bring about direct negotiations that will lead to peace. How those negotiations are structured, who is there to speak on behalf of the Palestinians, is a subject that's a difficult one; we've worked on it a long time, and I imagine it will continue to be difficult. But at any rate, we'll have a dialogue with the PLO and that dialogue will be designed to find answers to those questions.

Q. Now that the PLO has recognized Israel's right to exist and the UN resolutions, and renounced terrorism, do you feel there is any reason that Israel should not now talk to the PLO?

A. Israel has its own views and own policies, and Israel has always made it clear that these conditions that are U.S. conditions are not necessarily theirs. So I am not in any way speaking for Israel; it's totally for Israel to make its own decisions about what it wants to do and there's nothing to be inferred judgmentally about what they should do. I'm only saying that for the period since 1975, the U.S. has had a position in effect that if the PLO meets these conditions we will have a substantive dialogue, and since they have met the conditions, we are carrying through on our policy. And that's the sum and substance of it.

Q. Mr. Secretary, would the incumbent Administration, since they are (unintelligible) transition state, and would you be able to tell us what's their stand on this.

A. The President and the Vice President both have followed these developments very closely, and they have reviewed each of them—this most recent development—and they both agree that under these circumstances, the conditions for a substantive dialogue, which we have had in place since 1975, have been met, and so we should state that we are ready to undertake that dialogue. Now, as far as what will be the efforts of the Administration of President-elect Bush, that is for them to determine, and that remains to be seen.

Q. Thank you Mr. Secretary.

Index

Abdullah (king of Jordan), 73
Abu Jihad (Khalil al-Wazir), 208, 213, 226
Amnesty International, 150
Arab-Israeli conflict: changing definition of, 7–10; comprehensive settlement of, 11, 33, 97–98, 100–101; suggestions for resolving, xxvi–xxvii, 142–47, 163–65
Arab-Israeli peace process: definition of, 3–5, 158–60; and normalization of relations, 37; obstacles to, 22, 37–38; and policymaking, 160–61; and political process, 159, 161–63; role of third parties in, 106–9
—stages in negotiations: arranging a negotiation, 32–35, 118, 130–41, 159; definition of the problem, 23–24, 117, 118–26, 159; developing a commitment to negotiate, 24–32, 116, 117–18, 126–30, 153, 159, 161–63; implementing an agreement, 36–37, 159; reaching an agreement, 35–36, 159
Arab-Israeli relations since 1985, xxviii
Arab League summits: in Algeria (1988), 211, 212, 224, 226; in Fez (1982), 16, 35, 62, 127, 130, 137, 194–96, 198, 224; in Khartoum (1967), 16, 168; in Rabat (1974), 70, 74, 75, 76, 170–71, 198
Arab nationalism, 56
Arafat, Yasser: barred from UN in New York, 214; Israeli distrust of, 48; and Jordanian-Palestinian federation, xxii–xxiii, xxix, 17, 21, 34, 55, 62, 65, 75, 77, 93, 99, 103, 127, 134, 140, 197; and Palestinian independence, 203–7; and Palestinian role in peace process, xxx, 56; Palestinian support for, 29–30, 55, 127; and PLO's acceptance of UN resolutions in peace process, xxv; press conference statement by (1988), 229–30

Assad, Hafez al- (president of Syria), 84, 86–93, 122

Baker, James A., III, xxv
Balfour Declaration, 41, 144, 179
Begin, Menachem: and Camp David accords, 95, 106, 107, 133, 143; and Egyptian-Israeli peace, 15, 86, 189; and Israeli control of occupied territories, 41, 44, 46, 123; negotiations with Palestinians, 31, 76; Sadat's disappointment with, 128
Benjedid, Chadli, 207
Bourguiba, Habib, 194
Brezhnev, Leonid, 218
British Palestine Mandate, 41, 108, 218
Brzezinski, Zbigniew, 7, 111
Bush, George, xxv–xxvi, xxxii, 234

Cairo Declaration, 211, 226
Camp David accords, 17; and Egyptian commitment to peace process, xxxiii, 3; failure to follow up on, 14, 21, 37; and Israeli withdrawal from occupied territories, 17, 28, 44; Palestinian objections to, 64; and Palestinian self-determination, xxiii, xxix, 28, 34, 44, 98, 99; and partition of Palestine, 27; signing of, 95–96; and status of occupied territories, 32; Syrian objections to, 92; text of, 183–87; and U.S. commitment to peace process, 4
Carter, Jimmy: and Camp David accords, 95, 111, 156; and Palestinian self-determination in Jordan, xxiii, xxix; and U.S. commitment to peace process, 3, 4, 15, 21, 32, 33, 92, 131; use of diplomats by, 7; visit to Egypt and Israel (1979), 3, 4
China, 151, 152

Dayan, Moshe, 41, 128, 136
diplomacy: importance of in peace process, xxxiii; and politics, 5–7, 119

Eastern Europe, 151
Egypt: and ambassador to Israel, 15, 90; commitment to peace process, xxxiii, 1, 2, 16, 66, 96–97; isolation of, 135–36; and Palestinian autonomy in occupied territories, 55; relations with Jordan, 80; relations with Soviets, 3, 12, 97, 113; relations with U.S., 3, 12, 98, 104–5; support for PLO in, 103
Egyptian-Israeli disengagement agreement (1974), 3, 111, 128, 174
Egyptian-Israeli interim agreement (1975), 3, 84, 91, 128
Egyptian-Israeli peace treaty (1979), xxix, xxxiii, 3, 4, 5, 14, 15, 21, 70, 80, 84, 90, 92, 96, 98, 99, 104, 115, 130, 136, 157, 189
Eretz Israel, 41
Ethiopia, 196

Fahd Ibn Abdelaziz (king of Saudi Arabia), 194
Fahd Plan (1981), 21
Fairbanks, Richard, 189
Fatah, 77, 127
Fez Declaration (1982), 16, 17, 21, 62, 85, 90, 127, 134, 194–96, 217
Ford, Gerald, 9
"Framework for Peace in the Middle East Agreed at Camp David, A." See Camp David accords

Gaza: intifada in, xxiv, xxix; Israeli control of, xxviii, 56, 60, 120, 130; Palestinian autonomy in, 4, 15, 30, 34, 41, 55, 98, 99, 101, 103, 132–33, 136–37, 184–86, 191–92; popular resistance in, 151; and Shamir's proposal for Palestinian elections, xxvi, xxxii
global thinking (since 1985), xxii, xxxviii–xxxix, 148–54
Golan Heights, 86, 87, 88, 89, 91
Gorbachev, Mikhail: and Arab-Israeli peace process, 218, 227; and human rights concerns, xxxi; and political

change, 148, 158, 161; and U.S.-Soviet relationship since 1985, xxxvii–xxxviii
Great Arab Revolt, 199
Gromyko, Andrei, 217

Habbash, George, 58
Habib, Philip, 188
Haig, Alexander, 189
Hassan bin Talal (crown prince of Jordan), 71, 141
Hassan II (king of Morocco), 194
Helsinki accords, 150
Hussein-Arafat agreement. See Hussein ibn Talal (king of Jordan), and Jordanian-Palestinian federation
Hussein ibn Talal (king of Jordan): ability to implement any negotiated peace agreement, 47–48; and barriers to peace, 2; discontinuation of "Jordanian crutch" for PLO, xxiv; and four-stage peace process, xxiii, 32–33; interest in Palestinian self-determination, xxx, 65, 74–75, 82, 122; and Israeli withdrawal from occupied territories, 47; and Jordanian-Palestinian federation, xxii–xxiii, xxix, 17, 21, 34, 55, 62, 65, 75, 77, 93, 99, 103, 127, 134, 140, 197; and Palestinian acceptance of UN Resolutions 242 and 338, 35, 62; rejection of Camp David accords, 48; relations with U.S., 31, 77; support for Arafat, 103; U.S. support for, 140–41

international justice, 109
intifada: outbreak of, xxiv, xxix–xxx; psychological impact of, xxxi–xxxii; support for, 208, 212
Iran, 45
Iran-Iraq war, xxix, 13, 80, 211
Iraq: invasion of Kuwait, xix, 154; Israeli bombing of nuclear reactor in, 15; Jordanian support for, 80, 86; military force of, 13; Palestinian support for, 211–12; relations with Egypt, 104
Islamic fundamentalism, 14, 45, 67, 72, 97, 152
Israel: Arab opposition to at heart of conflict, 9; creation of (1948), 8, 109; identity of, 142–43; increasing political fragmentation of, xxxi–xxxii, 14, 30,

102, 133; military buildup in, 49–50, 58, 145, 190; and military control over Palestinian occupied territories, xxxi, xxxiii, 8; nuclear weapons of, 51, 145; refusal to negotiate with PLO, xxvi, xxxi, xxxiv, 28, 34, 65, 74, 122–23, 137; refusal to withdraw from occupied territories, xxvi, xxxi, xxxiii, 2, 10, 16, 17, 27, 28, 30–31, 41, 43, 44–45, 46, 57, 62, 65, 75, 85, 88–91, 179; relations with Soviets, xxxvii, 31, 33, 110–12, 113; security concerns of, xxxi, xxxiii, xxxiv, 39, 40, 42, 49–50, 108, 128, 178, 190; Soviet Jewish immigration to, xxxi; U.S. support for, 52, 87, 108, 113, 125–26, 139–40, 179, 218. *See also* Lebanon, Israeli invasion of; Palestine, UN partition of
Israeli-Syrian disengagement agreement (1974), 3, 21, 74, 86, 89, 91
Israel-Lebanon agreement (1983), 21

Jarring, Gunnar, 10, 11
Jarring Mission, 10–11
Jerusalem: freedom of worship in, 17, 178–79, 210; joint occupation of, 2, 17, 48, 137, 193
Johnson, Lyndon B., 2, 10
Jordan: as base for Palestinian support, 13–14, 66, 70–73, 225; expulsion of PLO (1970), 47, 74; negotiations with Israel, 16, 70, 76, 77, 78–79; Palestinian population of, 13, 41, 55, 64, 72; and Palestinian self-determination, xxiii, xxviii, xxx, 30, 46, 56–57, 63, 65, 73–75, 77–78, 82–83, 210; relationship with the West Bank, xxx, 73–75, 197–203; relations with Egypt, 80, 103–4; relations with Saudi Arabia, 80; relations with Soviets, 113; relations with U.S., 140–41; U.S. arms supplies to, xxiii

Kahane, Meir, 46
Khomeini (ayatollah of Iran), 72, 152
King-Crane Commission, 218
Kissinger, Henry: consulted at White House, 232; as diplomat, 7; and Jordan control of West Bank, 74; and Middle East Peace Conference, 135; and negotiations with Egypt, 12, 81, 84, 96;

promise to Israelis made by, 231; and shuttle diplomacy, 33, 35, 81, 111, 130–31; and step-by-step diplomacy, 36; and U.S. commitment to peace process, 3, 9, 10
Kuwait: Iraqi invasion of, xix, 154

Labor party, Israeli: loss of support for in late 1980s, xxxi; in national unity government, 31; and Palestinian self-determination in Jordan, xxiii, xxix, 41, 75; and withdrawal from occupied territories, 45, 47, 102–3
Laussane Treaty (1923), 204
League of Nations, 108, 204
Lebanon: civil war in, 14; expulsion of PLO from, 62, 65, 188; Israeli invasion of (1982), xxxii, 14, 15, 37, 42, 50, 51, 65, 66, 67, 99, 100, 102, 121, 195, 218; negotiations with Israel, 16; Palestinian refugee camps in, 59, 211; Palestinian support for, 211; Syrian intervention in, xxxiii, 13, 84, 87, 88, 92; U.S. hostages in, 84; U.S. support for, 190
Lebanon War (1982), 19
Libya, 113, 194
Likud: and Israeli control of occupied territories, 90–91, 123, 139; prime minister appointed from, 45; and shift to the right in Israeli politics, xxxi

Mandela, Nelson, 212
Middle East Peace Conference (Geneva, 1973), 4, 12, 31, 32, 33, 92, 108, 131, 135, 173, 176, 180
Mitterand, François, 218, 227
Mubarak, H., 15, 99, 103, 104, 189
multipolar world, xxi–xxii, 149–50, 154–58
Murphy, Richard, xxiii

Namibia, 212, 215
Nasser, Gamal Abdel, 11, 136
nation-states, as political paradigm, xxi, 149–50
1973 War, xxx, 4, 11–12, 15, 19, 31, 97, 131, 138, 172
1967 War. *See* Six Day War
Nixon, Richard M., 6, 10–11

occupied territories, xxvi, xxxii; recognition of Camp David accords, 31

Sharon, Gen. Ariel, 46, 76, 86

Shatila refugee camp, xxxii, 50

Shultz, George: and Arab-Israeli peace process, 190; and Jordanian suggestion for four-stage peace process, xxiii; and U.S. dialogue with PLO, xxv, 230–34

Sinai, Israeli occupation of and withdrawal from, 22, 86, 95, 101, 102, 128, 174, 176, 189

Six Day War (June 5–10, 1967), 8, 10, 27, 56, 58, 73, 76

Somalia, 196

South Africa, 212–13, 215

South Yemen, 113

Soviet Union: in Afghanistan, 151, 189; anti-Semitism in, xxxviii; arms to Middle East from, 107, 125; commitment to peace process, 12, 31, 136; Jewish emigration to Israel from, xxxi; relationship with U.S. since 1985, xxxvii–xxxviii; relations with Israel, xxxvii; and superpower role in the Middle East, xxxvii–xxxviii, 109–14, 176, 189, 219

Strait of Tiran, 11

Suez Canal, 11

superpowers. *See* Soviet Union; United States

Syria: as difficult to engage in peace process, xxxiii–xxxiv, 30, 33, 80, 85; and intervention in Lebanon, xxxiii, 13; isolation of, 84–86, 87, 92–93, 135; Israeli opposition to, 86; and Israeli pre-1967 borders, 52; Jordanian negotiations with, 80, 82; military buildup in, xxv, 13, 50, 88, 92, 145; negotiations with Israel, 16, 32, 70, 79, 84–86, 92; opposition to PLO in, 103; relations with Soviets, 13, 83, 91, 92, 93, 113; relations with U.S., 84–85, 91–92, 93–94; Saudi financial support for, 86; support for PLO in, 54, 65, 66, 72, 73, 79; terrorist activities of, 92

Taba, Israeli withdrawal from, 99

terrorism: Palestinian rejection of, xxv, xxxiv, 66–67, 211, 223, 226, 230, 231; PLO use of, 66, 231; Syrian, 92

Touhami, Hassan, 136

United Arab Kingdom, 65, 74, 78, 168–69

United Nations: and human rights issues, 150; and partition of Palestine (1947), xxiv, 8, 27, 62, 144, 204, 219, 227; and supervision of Israeli withdrawal from occupied territories, 17, 27, 210, 227

United Nations Charter, 109, 112, 209

United Nations Committee for the Palestinian People's Exercise of Their Inalienable Rights, 213, 215

United Nations General Assembly: Arafat's appearance before, xxv, 214–29; Resolution 40/61, 211, 226; Resolution 159/42, 211, 226; Resolution 181, xxiv, 204, 219, 227, 229; Resolution 194, 219

United Nations Security Council: Resolution 242, xxiii, xxiv, xxv, xxxiv, 10, 12, 17, 27, 28, 34, 35, 44, 47, 62, 74, 79, 89, 94, 97, 134, 138, 167–68, 183, 184, 185, 192, 210, 224, 228, 229, 230; Resolution 338, xxiv, xxv, xxxiv, 11–12, 17, 34, 35, 62, 89, 90, 94, 134, 170, 183, 184, 210, 224, 228, 229, 230; Resolution 479, 196; Resolution 514, 196; Resolutions 605, 607, and 608, 209; Resolutions 508 and 509, 195

United States: and arms supplies to Jordan, xxiii; attempt to implement Israeli proposals for peace process, xxxii; commitment to peace process, 12–18, 31, 35, 188; relationship with Soviets since 1985, xxxvii–xxxviii; relations with PLO, xxx–xxxi, xxxvii, 112; and superpower role in the Middle East, xxxvii–xxxviii, 109–14, 126, 139–41, 176, 219; support for Israel from, 52, 87, 108, 113, 125–26, 139–40, 179, 218; as third party in Arab-Israeli peace process, 106–7, 146–47; in Vietnam, 151

U.S. House Foreign Affairs Committee, Middle East Subcommittee, 9

Vance, Cyrus, 111, 217

Weizman, Ezer, 41, 128

West Bank: freedom of worship in, 17; intifada in, xxiv, xxix; Israeli control of, xxviii, 48, 56, 60, 120, 121, 130; Israeli withdrawal from, 31, 43; Jordanian

239

Harold H. Saunders, a Visiting Fellow at the Brookings Institution, participated in the mediation of five Arab-Israeli agreements at the height of the Arab-Israeli peace process, from 1973 through 1979. He flew on the Kissinger shuttles and worked with President Carter and Secretary of State Cyrus Vance at Camp David and in negotiating the Egyptian-Israeli peace treaty. From 1961 to 1981, he served on the National Security Council staff and then in the State Department as Deputy Assistant Secretary, Director of Intelligence and Research, and Assistant Secretary for Near Eastern and South Asian Affairs.